No greater love than this hath no man
than to give up his life for his friends.

In memory of
Cpl. Joseph Moffo, S-2 Scout 509
The Fighting Moffos

Pvt. Kenneth Edney, S-2 Scout 509
British Paratrooper

"I am not a writer. It is a story that just had to be written."

Staff Sergeant Richard D. Fisco stood in the open doorway of the C-47 military aircraft and secured his parachute. He looked beyond the tops of the clouds below for land, but waiting beneath him was the hostile Mediterranean Sea.

Head down, arms folded—he jumped.

Steering his chute through the clouds, Richard panicked, realizing he was over water and screamed out for God's help. Immediately, the warm Sirocco wind guided him over the sea for a safe landing on the steps of a French villa—one of the countless phenomena that would save his life.

Recounting his daring childhood during the Depression, his exhilarating war adventures in the 509th Parachute Infantry Battalion, shoot-outs at the Battle of the Bulge and his training with the New York City Fire Department, Richard Fisco's autobiography is a true American tale of courage, triumph and many miracles.

Life is not devoid of struggle, but if you allow it to, it can be beautiful.

Your Lives Will Be Beautiful

The Depression
The 509 Parachute Infantry Bn., WWII
God Almighty

The Autobiography of
Richard D. Fisco

(Lead S-2 Scout, 509 Parachute Infantry Bn., WWII)

Second Edition

Arbor Books, Inc.

Edited by Melinda Conner

Book design by Arbor Books, Inc.
www.arborbooks.com

Printed in the United States of America

Your Lives Will Be Beautiful
Richard D. Fisco

1. Title 2. Author 3. Autobiography

Library of Congress Control Number: 2008931204

ISBN-10: 0-9818658-0-1
ISBN-13: 978-0-9818658-0-5

Dedicated to
All married couples,
the 509 Parachute Infantry Bn. WWII,
the new 509 Parachute Infantry Regiment,
Sgt. James W. Nunn Buddy S-2 Scout,
Pvt. Murphy Trahan, Deacon, S-2 Scout and
Cpt. Miller's seventeen-man planeload
that drowned on the jump in Southern France.

Gratitude to
Melinda Conner (Jim's Daughter)—editor
Penelope Warren—computer work
Christine from "Before & After Photo" (207-725-9499)—the best
in the business
Michelle Sirois—computer work
Henri & Maryse Cecchetti—family in France
George & Liliane Feligioni—Louise's cousins in France
Richard J. Fisco—son
Sgt. Nicholas DeGaeta—509
Cpt. Ernest "Bud" Siegel—509
Christiane Abdelnour, MD—interpreter, close friend from Lebanon
Sgt. Harvey S. Sutherland of the 509—flight manifests
Gen. Yarborough—flight manifests
Paul DeGaeta—of the 509 & historian; pray for Paul's wife, Joyce, who
has terminal cancer
Joe Hoben—age 95; 509 medic; see Joe if you want to remember anything
509 Parachute Infantry Association
The Blessed Mother Mary (The Immaculate Conception)
François Coppola—Deputy Mayor, St. Tropez
Charles Giraud—French paratrooper, former director of Roblot;
will personally handle burying me with Louise in France
John Devanie—Former Pres. of 509 Retirement Association
Susan Conroy—Another Mother Theresa
Charlie Doyle—Pres. of 509 Association
Barry Simpson—Current Pres. of 509
The *Staten Island Advance*, for sending me photos of William T. Davis
and of me in my teenage years
Rev. James L. Nadeau Stl., on suffering
Rev. Frank J. Murray SM, pastor, on suffering

"I write my story in forgiveness for all I have done wrong.
And God has forgiven me."

Your Lives
Will Be Beautiful

Married on December 8, 1944—the date of the Immaculate Conception—at L'eglise Notre Dame, Nice, France.

Louise's first communion, Notre Dame, Nice.

My first communion, Guardian Angel Church, Coney Island.

We were married just before the Battle of the Bulge.

Louise, age seventeen. She sent me this picture and signed it, "To my little Richard, whom I adore." I trimmed the top of the photo so it fit the inside pocket of my IKE jacket.

Mom and Pop—Mary and Joseph Fisco.

Rich, in Vietnam, gives a bath to the Montagnards with the soap he asked us to mail to him.

Photo taken by Johnny McDonald

Me, age eighty-six, in Dayton, Ohio. Note the drooping eyelids as a result of myasthenia gravis. This condition affects one in six million.

Table of Contents

Chapter 1

The Neighborhood

I was born on April 7, 1920, to A. (for Americo) Joseph Fisco and Mary Charlotte (born Paganini) at 108 Chester Avenue in Brooklyn, New York. My father was a native New Yorker—born on the lower East Side and lived on Mott Street; my mother was born in Genoa, Italy. My family lived at the time in one of a row of one-story attached wood frame dwellings with cellars and front porches. My father later told me that when I was born the doctor thought I was dead and had put me aside while he worked on saving my mother. Suddenly I started to move. Years later, my sister, Theresa, told me that my mother had a vision of the Blessed Mother when I was born.

It was all very long ago, but some memories of that house are still clear. My dad used the cellar to make his wine. A stray cat attached itself to us and would sometimes come in through the back window bringing a chicken it had killed. The young man who lived next door made a small replica of a milk wagon for me. Our large front room had a flat-topped coal-burning stove. On cold nights, it was the center of the family circle. Dad would rock me in the big chair that sat in front of the stove. Once, while he was rocking me, I fell off his lap and split my chin on the stove. I still have the scar.

My brother Marian was a year and a half older than I. He became the famous one in the family. A talented musician, he taught himself to play the violin and played first fiddle in the high school orchestra. When he was seventeen, Marian moved to San Francisco to live with some of my mother's relatives. He played violin in a San Francisco orchestra. He changed his name to Marty Fiscoe and became an actor (he played the guard in *The China Syndrome*). In later years he became an art and antique dealer; he even auctioned million-dollar paintings. Marian was successful in everything he did.

One magical Christmas the two of us received tricycles and boxing gloves. We tried on the boxing gloves, and Marian promptly gave me a bloody nose.

When I was about seven we moved to an apartment on the second floor of a two-family brick dwelling. I still remember the beautiful craftex walls in that house. We arrived there just in time for the holidays. A week before Thanksgiving, my parents purchased a live turkey, which we fed in the kitchen. Thanksgiving Day was its day of reckoning. The "dirty deed" was a family affair: Marian held its neck and I held the legs while my father swung the cleaver. He missed. There was an immediate uproar, with loud screams and blood all over the kitchen. The neighbors called the police.

There must have been a huge snowstorm that winter. I remember our parents calling to us because it was time to go somewhere, but we had tunneled under the snow and couldn't hear them. We moved from this apartment soon afterward—most likely because my father didn't have a cellar to make his wine. Or maybe the Thanksgiving Day massacre had damaged our reputation.

Our new home was on the first floor of a two-family attached brick dwelling a short distance from Ocean Parkway on Avenue Y. I remember helping my father make the red wine. Open fields backed our row of houses. To the right there were backyards belonging to single-family homes. After that, there were creeks that ran all the way to Coney Island. On summer evenings, an old man would sit on his back porch at the edge of the creeks and play "Ramona" on his accordion, and the mellow sounds would float over the marshlands. A private patch of bamboo back there was surrounded by a tall fence about two hundred feet long. Near the elevated tracks there was a tomato farm where we stole tomatoes and ate them on the spot.

This was a real neighborhood. The residents included cops, court attendants, Danny the iceman (with big biceps), gangsters, and a Red Sox player who used to play with us sometimes in the field where we flew our kites. Attached brick dwellings across the street from where we lived were built on a foundation dug by horse and plow. In the winter, the sharp odor of construction materials mixed with the snow.

My mother was not well at the time, and a neighbor, Mrs. Spiegel, enrolled me in Mrs. O'Leary's kindergarten class. She gave my name as Richard D. (for Dominick), dropping "Anthony" from my given names. School wasn't so bad those first few years. My third-grade teacher, Mrs. Kaplan, would take me out in the hall and hug me when I misbehaved.

My sister, Theresa, was seven years younger than I, and my younger brother, Joey, was two years younger than Theresa. We have never been sure, but we think Joey was briefly kidnapped. He was found in Sheepshead Bay, about two miles away from our house, and would have had to cross Ocean Parkway to get there. He was less than a year old at the time and could hardly walk. I remember he was wearing red shorts and a white top with a red bow. My father had seen a body being stuffed in the trunk of a car. Perhaps they were warning us.

Our neighborhood was a great place to be a kid. No one had much money, so we made our own toys. We would tie creosoted logs together and pole our way behind Dewitt Clinton High School and the Guardian Angel Catholic Church where Marian and I made our first communion and confirmation. Some days we poled our way almost to Coney Island with our friends the Corbett's—Frank, David and Jack. They had a sister. We used to stay out in the marshland at night until the mosquitoes chased us inside. When we got hungry we would build a fire and bake "mickeys" in a can. Our "baking pan" was a can with a perforated bottom and a wire handle attached. We would build a fire, remove some of the embers and place them in the bottom of the can, then put in the potato and swing the can around until the heat had charred the potato. They were delicious. I wonder if anyone makes them that way today.

We made slingshots by cutting a half-inch crotch from a hedge, tying it together in the shape of a U and baking it so that it would hold its shape. The rubber bands came from inner tubes; the slings were from shoe tongue leather. I was a good shot even then; I could knock a chippy off a high wire. I didn't know it then, but my right eye was weaker than my left, and I learned to "square the target," that is, to shoot for the center of a large square. We always ate the chippies we killed, first skinning them and then roasting them over a fire.

We had other games, too. Sometimes we played caddy—a kind of cross between baseball and golf. We used two sticks cut from a broom handle, one about two and a half feet long and the other about five inches long and tapered to a blunt point. We would place this smaller peg on the pavement, tap it up to about waist high, and then smack it out and run to first base. The older boys played touch tackle on the street that crossed Avenue Y.

On weekends, the Corbett's would sometimes take Marian and me to Bear Mountain with them in their Essex. Mrs. Corbett would invite us to sleep overnight with the boys, but she always made us take a bath first. I think it was because we always had dirty feet. She supplied the pajamas.

In the evenings, the men played an Italian card game called "brisc" (briscola) in the cellar where my father made his wine. They sat at a round table: Jack Corbett, a motorcycle cop who had been gassed in World War I; next to him an elderly man with a shoulder holster, a police detective, I think; Mr. Cassale, a court attendant; and my father, the pressman, who ran Kelly presses.

One night when they were playing, shots rang out in the street; Mr. Corbett looked at the man with the shoulder holster, who nodded. Mr. Corbett said, "There's someone on duty that will cover it." They all kept right on playing. Within an hour we heard, "Extra! Extra! Read all about it." A gangster had been shot at his front door just off the corner.

On Saturdays, my dad would come home from a half day's work at Garfield Press, first stopping for butter, eggs, and cheese at Hearn's. He always brought me Muenster cheese, which I liked melted on toast made in the oven.

My father was not a religious man, but when he drank his wine he would say, "He who eats my bread and drinks my blood has life everlasting." Anyway, all of us were baptized. We made our first communion and confirmation at Guardian Angel Catholic Church on Ocean Parkway near Coney Island. Our parents always made us go to Sunday mass, at a church nearby under the elevated elevator train, for which I am eternally grateful. They always bought us wool tweed suits for Easter.

We had to move again. At the time I didn't realize that it was to a less expensive apartment. Kids roll with the punches. We moved diagonally across the street to the second floor of a frame building.

My father bought an Emerson radio and was carrying it up the stairs to plug it in to listen to a Jack Dempsey—Gene Tunney fight when a ball of lightning the size of an indoor baseball flashed up the stairs between his legs.

We moved again soon after that, this time away from Avenue Y to a tenement section. Times were really bad. I remember that I used to ask for stale bread at Pechter's, downstairs next door. The Spiegel's were our neighbors. Mrs. Spiegel loved my mother's "spisgetti." The Spiegel's and my parents had earmarked me for Ruthy, their daughter, but it didn't work out.

We still had fun, of course, even in those bad times. In the evenings we sometimes watched movies that were projected on the walls between the buildings.

I finished my last grade of grammar school at Dongan Hills on Staten Island, where my mother's aunt and uncle, Lalla and Barbera Paganini, had invited us to stay with them during the depression. They had brought my mother to this country from Genoa when she was fourteen. My mother was supposed to receive some money when Uncle Barbera died, but she never did. She had taken care of their daughter when she had tuberculosis.

Chapter 2

Staten Island

The Paganini's were rich. Uncle Barbera owned a restaurant in the Wall Street area, and he and Aunt Lalla lived in a beautiful corner house on Cromwell Avenue in Dongan Hills with their little dog, Buster. The garage housed a brand-new Buick sports car. Aunt Lalla, who went to mass every day, was a wonderful cook. She would bake four apple pies at a time, and they never lasted very long.

While we lived there I attended Curtis High in Saint George, but we didn't stay long. My parents soon rented a house at 411 Amherst Avenue in Oakwood Heights, which was about seven miles from Saint George. Whenever we visited Uncle Barbera after that, he would give us kid's five dollars each.

Our new house wasn't insulated, and the only source of heat was a kerosene heater. We had a metal icebox outside the kitchen window to keep food cool. Times were still tough. People who wanted meat and eggs had to raise their own. We kept chickens and a rooster. Once in a while, our relatives from Brooklyn would come to visit in a large hearse. (The men were all undertakers.) There were about a dozen children, and the only thing that kept them in line was that rooster. Whenever he saw them coming he would charge them from inside his pen. They were terrified of him.

Then my dad started working again. This was in the late 1930s, and America was finally coming out of the Depression. Dad had been working in the WPA. It is difficult to overstate the hardships breadwinners faced during the depression. Work was scarce, and keeping a family fed and clothed was next to impossible. My older brother and I tried to help. I cleaned windows for five cents a window and Marian worked in a bank for fifteen dollars a week.

Dad used to smoke Di Nobili cigars, and it was my job to buy them for him. He didn't like them too dark or too light. We called them "Guinea stinkers." One time we found Joey smoking the short ends behind a chair in a corner of the front porch.

Marian and I slept in the same bed upstairs. He would practice his music until early morning. Now and then, he would wake me up and ask me to comment on his bowing or the tone of his new violin.

On winter days after a good snowfall, Marian and I would go to Todt Hill to bum a sleigh ride. We trudged through the snow, the soles of our shoes flapping, and up to Todt Hill, in the middle of Staten Island. We could always find a sleigh owner willing to let us have a go. The big ride was probably two miles long when the roads were icy. We would start at the top of Todt Hill, descend the steep hill, cross Richmond Road—where someone would have stopped traffic—and continue down to the railroad tracks in Dongan Hills.

There was an ice-skating pond alongside Hylan Boulevard. We couldn't afford ice skates, so I would improvise. I would bring two empty carnation milk cans, stomp them into the instep of my shoes, and skate among the fortunate skaters with real ice skates. I would not be alone.

I hitchhiked the seven miles back and forth to Curtis High, stopping along the way at a bakery to get cream doughnuts for two cents each. I would also stop in Saint George at the Staten Island Institute of Arts and Sciences, a small museum where I joined a study group in natural history under Hans Stecher, an Austrian. I heard he went back to Austria just before World War II broke out. I met Peter Crowe, who would become my best friend, at the museum. He and his two younger sisters lived in Oakwood Heights in a beautiful home up near the railroad station.

I specialized in entomology. William T. Davis, the world-renowned historian and naturalist, was president emeritus of the museum. He was eighty-two years old at the time, and his collections of insects took up the entire top floor of the museum. I took care of the collections, and he paid me the princely sum of three dollars and fifty cents a week. I would check each box for dermestid beetles and their larvae, the bane of insect collectors, and would apply naphthalene flakes—or dichlorobenzene for serious infestations. Dermestids can completely destroy a collection if left untreated. Mr. Davis named many species of singing cicadas (some people incorrectly call them locusts, but locusts are grasshoppers). I would accompany him to the monthly meetings of the Brooklyn Entomological Society at the Brooklyn Museum of Art, and he would buy me dates to eat on the way. On one trip, I saw two neatly dressed army soldiers eating chocolate bars. That picture stayed in the back of my mind.

There were monthly bird walks. Although we were supposed to be looking at birds, Mr. Davis would carry a butterfly net folded up in one of the deep pockets of his black coat in case something interesting fluttered by. He had a mustache, and he wore a white straw hat on these outings. Hans always carried his Leika camera.

I met my first girlfriend, a young Swedish girl named Dottie Johnson on these bird walks. Dottie had blonde hair and big, beautiful blue eyes. Her parents were wonderful people. Her father installed refrigeration on steamships, and her mother was a schoolteacher. Best of all, they used to invite me over for steak dinners. Sometimes when I would go to visit, Dottie would be taking a shower in the basement and I would have to throw the towel over the top to her. Our relationship was completely platonic, though, as it was with most young people in those days. Kissing never entered our minds. They came several times to watch me compete in cross-country races.

Peter's uncle would drive us to Lakehurst, New Jersey, for naturalist field trips. Peter collected field mice, which he turned into study skins, and I collected insects. We weren't narrow-minded, though; we each appreciated the other's work. Peter especially liked the Cicindelidae, a family of half-inch-long beetles that are a beautiful metallic usually blue-green. We sometimes stirred them up as we were walking. They would fly about six feet and land on a sunny spot just ahead.

We didn't go to Lakehurst during the hunting season; it was too dangerous. When we went after the season was over there would be blood all through the pines. I loved those pine forests. I thought they were beautiful, especially the dark cedar forests, whose cool darkness fascinated me. There was always the smell of charcoal burning in the woods.

One hot, sunny day as we were returning to the empty hunters' cabin, in which we stayed, a young man joined us. We were thirsty, and I mentioned to Peter that I couldn't wait to drink some of the "blood" that we had back in the cabin, meaning tomato juice. The young man perked up his ears and quickened his pace to keep up. As we arrived at the cabin and went for the can of tomato juice on the shelf, the young man burst into laughter. He was from a nearby Alcoholics Anonymous camp and insisted on inviting us over that night to meet all of the other AA members to tell them about the joke we had played on him. He had thought that the blood I referred to was wine.

While we were running Peter's trap lines early one evening, we saw the *Hindenburg* burst into flames. We ran to the gate to help, but they wouldn't let us in.

After a short time at Curtis High I transferred to New Dorp High School, a brand-new school only a half-mile away from home. I didn't do well in school. It was not that I was stupid; I just never studied. In English class, for instance, the teacher had asked us to write a one-page story about a real experience. I couldn't think of one good enough to write about, so I made one up. When she read my story to the class, they all cried. I was interested only in entomology, and no one tried to convince me of the importance of the other subjects. A few of the teachers were chummy with some of the other students, but the poorer students didn't get much attention. Once, I even got expelled. I got poison ivy on my privates while collecting in the woods, and I didn't attend school for about ten days because I couldn't sit down. I was bashful and refused to give a reason for my absence, so Mr. Barlowe expelled me.

If I lacked enthusiasm for academics, I made up for it in sports. I started the New Dorp High School track team with others and started running the mile. Distance running was my specialty, and I started running cross-country with the Staten Island Harriers. Our coach, Mike Doyle, ran the Boston fifty miler. I came in second in an eight-mile Harlem race. It wasn't easy. The local spectators would push out at the corners when I came along and pull back for my competitor. I slowly pulled away from him on purpose and beat him to the finish line where he collapsed foaming at the mouth. George Currey, another Harrier, was first all the way. I earned my letter in track and got a beautiful white wool sweater with the letters ND in green and gold. I was really upset when someone stole it from my locker at Van Cortland Park.

My friend Larry Lueckoff from Huguenot also ran for the Staten Island Harriers. We trained together at Clove Lakes during the week and competed on Saturdays. I won the Staten Island borough championship in the six-mile Tapen Post race in 1938, beating the Manhattan College five-mile champion by about a hundred yards. I won because I was totally relaxed, thinking I didn't have a chance against the best runners in the race—and maybe also because my mother had fed me pasta, although in those days we didn't know that carbohydrates give extra energy.

One of the worst days of my life started in the normal way with Larry and me running our usual two three-mile laps around Clove Lakes. When we began, I had noticed a man following a woman, and when we finished running I saw that he was still following her from a distance. We had changed back from our running gear into our street clothing, and I told Larry that I would go up and warn the woman. I passed the man, came up to the woman, and told her that she was being followed. She sat down and we started talking, and the next thing I knew the man came up and put handcuffs on me. In fact, he twisted them tight. It had been a trap, and I had fallen right into it. Someone had been exposing himself to women in the area, and the police were trying to find him.

I was taken to the jail and kept overnight until court the next day. I called my father, and he and Mr. Martin, a neighbor, got involved. The court wanted to know if I had a witness to back up my story, and I said no because I didn't want Larry to be brought into court. The hearing was held, the woman told the truth, and I was acquitted, but the whole case should have been dismissed.

The small article about it that was printed in the newspaper took up only about one inch of a column, but I didn't assume that no one would read it. I had been working at the Barrett Park Zoo under the National Youth Administration, and right away I told Mr. Carroll Stryker, the director, what had happened. I was sure he believed me. I had been accompanying his wife, Midge, on overnight trips with the children, and he knew that I was trustworthy. I also had been babysitting for Mr. Martin's two children. He stopped asking me to baby-sit after that.

I used to run away once in a while, as many boys did back then. Mostly, I was looking for adventure, but one of the reasons I did it was to get my mother accustomed to not having me around. I was growing up, and I knew that someday I would leave home for good. On one trip, my friend Andy Thompson and I hitch-hiked a day's drive away. We planned to sleep in the woods, but I dreamed that the leaves were as tall as people and were chasing us home. I woke Andy and said, "Let's go back."

Larry Lueckoff and I each chipped in ten dollars and bought a used Old Town canoe. We kept it at my house because I was closer to the beach. We paddled around Staten Island two or three times. We would stop for hamburgers in Richmond, then paddle past the ferry slips at Saint George, where we had the right of way. You can imagine the frustration of the ferry pilots, especially when we had to paddle against the tide.

On one trip, we portaged through the Delaware and Raritan Canal, down the storm-filled Delaware to Philadelphia. We turned our canoe over on the beach and crawled beneath it to sleep. I had another strange dream. This time I dreamed the water was lapping all around me. The dream was real; the tide was coming in. We righted the canoe and returned home. Larry and I were a good canoe team. He was always the power man up front, and I would steer at the stern, never taking my paddle out of the water. The hurricane of 1938 put

Garber Brothers selected me for the hall of fame for winning the six-mile Tuppan Post Race, 1938.

a stop to our trips for a while. It sideswiped Staten Island, with water reaching almost to Hylan Boulevard, and hit New England directly, washing houses out to sea. The seas were choppy and the skies were overcast for weeks.

On March 3, 1939, I joined the U.S. Army at the 29 Whitehall Street recruiting station. I was sent first to cold Fort Slocum on David's Island in Long Island Sound, but I didn't remain there for long. Still seeking adventure, I signed up for Foreign Service and was assigned to the Fourteenth Infantry "Jungleers," which were serving at Fort Davis in the Panama Canal Zone.

Island Harriers Honored

TWO of Staten Island's outstanding long distance runners were honored at last night's meeting and dinner of the Staten Island Sportsmen's Club at Jack Lobosco's Idle Hour restaurant. They were, Richard Fisco of New Dorp High School, winner of the Tappen Post six-mile run on Sunday at Clove Lakes Park, and Anthony (Buddy) Fair of West Brighton, the first Island boy to finish in the 20-mile A.A.U. championship event. Fair finished fifth in the event won by Mel Porter of the Millrose A. A.

In the above picture, left to right, George Kearney is shown presenting the Blue-White Laundry Company trophy to Fair, while Fisco is receiving the Sportsmen's Club trophy from Charles Schiels, president of the club.

Receiving the trophy for winning the Tuppan Post Race.

Collecting Insect Life

Richard Fisco, young Oakwood entomologist, is shown mounting a few of his collection of 3,000 beetles. Young Fisco, who is also known as a runner, hopes to get a job in the U. S. Department of Agriculture as an entomologist.

Oakwood Youth Builds Up Hobby for His Life Work

Richard Fisco Has Collected 3,000 Beetles in Four Years

Most people have a hobby, but few are interested when they grow older in the hobbies that absorbed them in their youth. A few keep their childhood hobbies and build them into a life work. In the latter category is Richard Fisco of 411 Amherst avenue, Oakwood, 18 years old, who hopes to turn his boyhood interest into a career.

As is usual among boys, Richard for years was interested in natural history to the extent of bringing home frogs, toads, snakes and insects, much to the disgust of his parents, Mr. and Mrs. Joseph Fisco. Not that they objected to his liking for the crawling, creeping or flying animals, but they didn't enjoy having them around the house.

Even without parental encouragement, however, Richard continued to collect small specimens of wild life whenever he found them and his very persistence won his parents' respect and finally their approbation.

He first believed that he would concentrate on the study of reptiles, but in his excursions through fields and woods near his home, then farther afield on Staten Island and neighboring communities, he discovered so many interesting insects that they rather overshadowed his original love, the reptiles. He Staten Island's noted naturalist, William T. Davis, president emeritus of the Staten Island Institute of Arts and Sciences. Richard worked for a time as a volunteer at the St. George museum and Davis' enthusiasm for entimology communi-

cent of which he found on the land. Through Davis' guidance, learned to properly mount, lab and catalog his specimens.

The collector kills his insects wi a jar filled with cyanide fume then dries and pins them to mounting board. They are then go for study purposes indefinitely, p vided they are kept free of derm tes—a small type of beetle, kno as the "museum bug," which e dry animal matter. The odor camphor will discourage dermest therefore Richard pins his beetl into cigar boxes, so that the i can be kept closed and the ca phor can be confined where it w do the most good. Rows of cig boxes, rising tier upon tier, ad the sun porch of his home, whi he uses as a laboratory.

During the summer he colle adult insects and in the winter gathers moth cocoons, which stores until they hatch in spring. He has attempted to cr breed moths, and was successful the extent of getting them to larval stage.

Records New Wasp

Scientists, whether amateur professional, are always on lookout for something new and recorded, and Richard feels him fortunate to have been the first collect and record a wasp new Staten Island. This was Scolia dubia, which no one had found here previously. In studying the various stages of its life history, he said he came to the conclusion that it was of great value in aiding the destruc tion of the beetle, Cotenis nitida, which is called the fig beetle as it attacks figs and other fruits. Richard said this wasp lays its eggs on the beetle larvae and when they

Beetle Collecting' Chutist Has Wound, Silver Star
Ex-Islander, Buzzes Nazis

S/Sgt. Richard D. Fisco, 25, former Oakwood Heights resident now a Paratrooper veteran of Africa, Italy and the Western Front, has received the Silver Star Medal for conspicuous bravery Dec. 29, 1945, when he was wounded battling the German breakthrough in Belgium. He is the son of Mr. and Mrs. Joseph Fisco of 120-03-223rd street, St. Albans, L. I.

The soldier, whose peacetime hobby was entymology, collected 3,000 beetles and many other insects and snakes then. He has been collecting Nazi prisoners and decorations since he went overseas. In addition to the Silver Star he holds the Purple Heart, the Bronze Star, a unit citation, and the French Legion of Honor decoration.

After four operations in a hospital in England, the last Feb. 2, Sgt. Fisco returned to duty with his outfit Feb. 15, his parents say.

Last night, one radio sponsor sent 500,000 cigarettes to soldiers overseas in honor of the former Islander.

The citation reads, in part, "For gallantry in action Dec. 29, 1944, in the Belgian Bulge breakthrough. Paratrooper S/Sgt. Richard D. Fisco became separated from the rest of his company because of intense enemy machinegun fire. He organized a group of six men and engaged a nest consisting of three enemy machineguns.

"Although wounded by enemy artillery fire, Fisco continued his mission until it was accomplished. He displayed unusual leadership in the organization of the group and in leading it into an attack on the machinegun position."

He won the Bronze Star for heroic action Feb. 15, 1944, near Carano, Italy, when he and two other GIs, only ones uninjured in a seven-man patrol, returned to the American lines after killing 25 Germans.

A resident of Staten Island ten years, Sgt. Fisco was employed at the Barrett Park Zoo, West Brighton, as a laboratory assistant under the National Youth Administration. He had attended New Dorp High School, but left a short time before graduation to enlist in the Army in February, 1939. While on the Island, he was active in cross-country running, and won a six-mile race at Clove Lakes Park in 1938.

As a teenager I hoped my studies in entomology would lead me to Cornell and the Department of Agriculture.

William T. Davis, naturalist and historian, president emeritus of the Staten Island Institute of Arts and Sciences. He always welcomed visitors with goodies. Notice his pockets full of butterfly and cicada nets.

Chapter 3

The 14th Infantry Jungleers

Before leaving the States I went to see Carroll Stryker at the Barrett Park Zoo and asked him if he would accept reptiles from me. I was hoping to find some really great specimens in the Central American jungles. "Sure!" he answered.

We left New York on the *Hunter Liggett*, headed for Colón on the Caribbean coast of Panama. The first part of the voyage wasn't all that pleasant. We passed through a storm off Cape Hatteras and I became a little seasick. After that, things got better. On the boat I met Sgt. Bob Sink, who was returning from furlough to an infantry regiment at Ft. Clayton on the Pacific side. He immediately took me under his wing, calling me Chick and insisting that I visit him at his unit.

As we neared Colón the weather got warmer, and I was surprised to find the waters of the Caribbean a beautiful green. It was certainly nothing like the

Atlantic Ocean off New Jersey! The banana boats were loading at the wharf, and the waterfront was a beehive of activity.

Fort Davis consisted of four large, screened-in buildings surrounding a short-cut grass drill field. There were three battalions and a headquarters. I was assigned to K Company and issued vintage World War I wrap leggings (which were changed to laced leggings within a week) and a Springfield rifle. The Springfield's were very accurate, and I managed to qualify as a sharp-shooter, but not an expert. I kept trying to get my left eye behind the sight since it was stronger than my right.

Each company had its own mess. Our mess sergeant was gay. Perhaps for that reason we had the best mess in the whole regiment. Some of the local people, mostly San Blass Indians, did KP (kitchen police) duty. The mess hall is where I was unofficially indoctrinated into the Fourteenth Infantry Jungleers. We were eating, and I asked someone to pass me the black-eyed peas. A southern accent responded that they were beans, not peas. I responded, "Peas," and he said, "Let's go out on the green." He turned out to be the post's middleweight boxer. The mess hall emptied, and everyone formed a ring around us. We fought for a while, but it came to a sudden end. He said, "If you had caught me with one of those, you would have floored me." He offered me his hand, we shook, and the whole crowd returned inside to finish lunch.

My plan to ship reptiles to Mr. Stryker didn't work out. On my pay of twenty-one dollars a month I just couldn't afford to do it. Further, I would have had to put the cages at an outer edge of the golf course, right at the edge of the jungle, and hordes of mosquitoes awaited anyone foolish enough to venture there.

It rained a lot in Colón. The rain would fall hard, the water would rise rapidly, and then the rain would stop, the sun would come back out, and the high water would recede as quickly as it had come up.

The golf course was an important part of life at Fort Davis—both for the officers who played on it and the enlisted men who had to keep it in good condition. The course had armadillo holes all over it, which were a major impediment to play. Our colonel sent us out at night now and then with base-ball bats to take care of the problem. You never saw so many nature lovers in your life. Colonel Delemata, Gen. Ret. replaced that colonel, and the armadillo hunts stopped.

We maintained the golf course by "sprigging." On rainy days, wearing fatigues (ugly blue jeans) and carrying burlap sacks, we would grab clumps of grass, fill our sacks, and carry them to areas that needed grass. Within several days there would be a lawn that needed cutting.

I loved the jungle, and whenever I had some free time I would go out by myself looking for snakes. One day I heard what had to be a huge snake slither down a tree nearby. I couldn't see it, but I knew that it must have seen me. Bushmasters—big, poisonous vipers that can reach lengths of twelve feet—were known to be in the area, so I got away from there as fast as I could. Another time while I was out in the jungle alone I heard a huge roar behind me. I started swinging my machete into the brush to make noise and got the heck out of there.

Once, my friend Private Duncan and I helped ourselves to a dugout belonging to one of the locals and paddled out the Chagres River to the sea. A squall blew up, and we overturned. We held on to the canoe and kicked our way to shore, which was probably not the safest thing we could have done. I saw a boa not far away from where we landed and asked Duncan to get me a stick so that I could hold down its head. When I turned to reach for the stick, all I could see were the soles of Duncan's feet running down the beach. I managed to pick up the boa, which was full of ticks. I took them off and turned it loose. After that, I rejoined Duncan and we headed back to camp, which was on the other side of the river. There was a phone on our side, so we called the unit on the other side to come and get us. They came, took us across the river, and, thinking we had been AWOL, they locked us up. When they called our unit, Captain Cone told them to turn us loose and let us return. Going "over the hill" is a serious offense, but Captain Cone knew all about my jungle safaris.

I tried to keep running in Panama, but the heat was just too much. I ran the half-mile and mile, but I always felt burnt out because of the heat. There had to be a better way to stay in shape. We had a pool on the base, and we played water polo—I could swim better underwater than on top—and I lifted weights with another soldier named Anderson.

Captain Cone put me in for prep school for West Point. I think my IQ mark was very good. Unfortunately, when it was time for me to go, I was in the post hospital with a raging fever that wouldn't go down. They left without me, and I lost my chance for West Point. I asked the post doctor, a colonel, to let me out of the hospital and told him that I would get rid of the fever myself. I went over to the gym and worked up a heavy sweat, and sure enough the fever went down.

On maneuvers, contrary to what you might think, we wore wool shirts and campaign hats. On night operations in the jungle we wore white gloves and head nets to keep out the mosquitoes. The nets didn't work all that well. Someone was always coming down with a malaria attack. The combat intelligence unit to which I was assigned kept the trails open to the Pacific with bolos, machetes, and compasses. The work taught me a lot about mapping, which was to be very useful later. I ran messages between units during these night ops with just a machete for protection. When we stopped to rest for the night we would build "wickies," little huts that were made of black palm, forked stakes, and cross poles covered with palm branches, mosquito netting, and a shelter half. Packs of wild boars occasionally ran through the camps at night. The rest of the unit knew about my fascination with reptiles, so when Colonel Delemata (now Gen. ret.) found a snake in his wickie while on maneuvers, I got the call. I found the snake—a coral snake—in the colonel's bedding, caught it, and took it a long way off before releasing it.

Back on the post, we had nightly movies. The gadgets, as tickets were called, cost fifteen cents, and we had to be dressed in our khakis to attend. Our garrison shoes were of beautiful brown quality leather. Before the movie started we would listen to Judy Garland singing "Somewhere over the Rainbow" or maybe a rendition of "South of the Border."

Guard duty included a broad array of jobs. We had to guard our own prisoners, and we had to guard the base, of course. We carried twelve-gauge shotguns in most areas, Springfield rifles in others. One night, I was walking post by the stadium; there was a hill nearby with a beer garden at the top. I saw a large black jungle cat on a little dirt road at the bottom of the hill, looking up at the beer garden. I must have moved in readiness, because the cat took one leap and disappeared into the darkness. Walking the top of the spillway was an interesting post. If you fixed bayonet, you could get yourself a fish. Another outpost was along the old French canal. Two guards would man it. Even double mosquito bars would not keep the sand fleas out.

It was also our job to board and guard all ships passing through the Panama Canal. Usually seventeen of us would board with an officer, who would stay close to the pilot. On larger vessels, more than twenty of us would go onboard. We had telephone lines from the bridge to the engine room to ensure that responses coincided with orders. When the spillway was opened, a siren would sound and the water would rush down the Chagres River. We would get off in Gamboa, stop at the nearest base for eggs fried sunny-side-up, and then return on the *Micheline* the next morning. We even guarded Japanese vessels carrying the scrapped Third Avenue El, which was soon to be thrown right back at us.

President Franklin D. Roosevelt himself passed through the canal, disembarked at the Gatun locks, and proceeded through Fort Davis by motor vehicle to board the ship again in Colón. Our entire regiment stood at present arms along the motorcade route. We had been ordered to remove the bolts from our rifles. I believe Mrs. Roosevelt said that soldiers returning from Panama needed rehabilitation.

Certainly, there wasn't a lot to do in Fort Davis and the surrounding area in our off-duty hours. There was a Chinese restaurant that made chicken or iguana fried rice. Soldiers went into town and drank at the beer gardens to the tune of "Roll out the Barrels." Inevitably, some of them would end up in the hospital with their heads bashed in by MPs. Opportunities for shopping were limited as well. Still, there was a store that sold shrunken heads for ten dollars. They were about the size of a baseball and probably came from the Indians in the Darien. In 1939 half the city of Colón burned to the ground, and the army set up wall tents for the homeless.

Once a year, Captain Cone would take K Company on the *Deborah* with a keg of beer aboard. The ship would cruise down the coast about twenty miles, and the company would drink and swim in the clear, warm water. Some of us swam ashore to visit the San Blass Indian village.

I reached the end of my two-year hitch still a private. I returned to the United States as part of a security detail on an Italian passenger liner that the U.S. government had detained in Colón and was sending to New York. My next post was in the Guard Company at the Brooklyn army base.

Fourteenth United States Infantry

To all whom it may concern:

This is to certify that

Private 1cl RICHARD D. FISCO, 6973808, Company "K", Fourteenth Infantry is awarded this Certificate of Proficiency as evidence of his having satisfactorily completed a course of Instruction in the following subjects:

Combat Intelligence

Instructor: JOHN D. COPE,
Capt., 14th Inf.,
S-2.

August 26, 1940
Date
Ft. Wm. D. Davis, C. Z.
Place
G. A. SANFORD,
Lt. Colonel, 14th Infantry,
Commanding.

Combat Intelligence kept open the trail from the Caribbean to the Pacific with just machetes, bolos, and a compass. There were no roads. Below, a certificate of honorary citizenship of St. Tropez, awarded to me on August 15, 2004, the sixtieth anniversary of the "Second D-day."

Diplôme d'Honneur

DÉCERNÉ à M Fisco Richard

Citoyen d'honneur de la Ville de Saint-Tropez

S' Tropy Le 15 Aout 2004

Dr Jean-Michel COUVE
Député-Maire

Fort Davis '39 to '44: running track and lifting weights kept me fit in 1939, at age nineteen.

I lifted weights at the Brooklyn Army base in 1941 with
Pete Latkovich and Anderson.

Chapter 4

The 509th Parachute Infantry Battalion

Some of us who came off escort duty on the Italian passenger liner were assigned to the Guard Company at the Brooklyn army base. We wore MP armbands, but we were not regular MPs. We patrolled the base and the adjoining streets.

The Brooklyn army base would have been a great place to settle down. There was a large cafeteria and a spacious bunkroom. And my buddies Copeland, Anderson, and Ed Zinteck had accompanied me from Panama. Our chef, Pete Latkovitch, was tops. The base had an ideal setup for bodybuilding and weight lifting, and Pete, Anderson, and I exercised together. Pete had triumphed over polio and had built himself into a real bodybuilder. He had sixteen-and-a-half-inch biceps and a powerful overall build.

Sometimes we would go into the city for pasta to supplement the steaks Pete made for us as chef. I would bat the breeze with Copeland while he drank a few beers at some bar. I always ordered milk. Ed Zintek took me to polish places in Jersey where I was forced to dance. They were great times. I was enjoying life as a soldier.

Then came Pearl Harbor. Ed received a telegram from Schofield Barracks in Honolulu telling him that his brother had been killed in the Japanese attack. In January 1942 I decided to join the paratroopers. I hated to leave my good friends at the Brooklyn army base, but it just seemed like the right thing to do.

I needed a physical exam before my transfer could be approved. The doctor at the army base examined me for what seemed like an hour. He couldn't find anything wrong and seemed baffled to find me in such perfect health. I guess the cross-country running with the Staten Island Harriers and all the fitness training of the past few years had paid off. The doctor approved my transfer, and I headed south.

I started jump training at Fort Benning, Georgia. The training started with shock harness tower drops from one hundred fifty feet. Each man was strapped into the shock harness and then raised in a horizontal position face down. At the top, he had to pull a simulated ripcord and freefall for a short distance. After that, we moved on to the two hundred fifty-foot tower and real parachutes. We practiced jumping and landing from a twelve-foot elevation and front and rear tumbling. In order to qualify we had to make three jumps from the plane.

The planes used for training were old, and the engines spewed oil across the windows. For the first jump, we filed onto the plane and took seats on the benches that ran down both sides of the interior. When we reached the target area, we rose and snapped our ripcords onto the overhead static line that ran the length of the plane. One by one, in line, we went to the door and jumped, making sure we were in good body position so as not to tangle in the lines.

My first jump was almost my last. My main chute opened only partially, so I pulled my reserve cord. Then, like a stupid ass, I pulled my reserve chute back in after untangling my leg from the main chute. When I hit the ground, the sergeant came down on me like a load of bricks. Didn't I know that the reserve could have gotten tangled up in the main chute as I pulled it in?

The second jump was a little better, but not much. I got tangled up with another jumper, and we came down back to back. My head was positioned so that I could tell him when we were about to hit the ground so we could both pull down hard on the risers.

I was well aware of the English version of the French saying *jamais deux sans trois!* In this case, however, bad things didn't come in threes. On the third jump everything went smoothly. I made a perfect landing, standing up without having to tumble.

After I qualified, I was assigned to K Company of the original 504th Parachute Infantry Battalion. (The 501st was the initial experimental battalion, followed in sequence by the 502nd, 503rd, and 504th—all original battalions.) After qualifying, our battalion was transferred from Fort Benning to Fort Bragg, North Carolina, for further training. Before the transfer, we were formed into the 2nd Battalion of the 503rd Parachute Infantry Regiment—the first such regiment to be formed. The 1st Battalion was sent to the Pacific; the 2nd was sent to Europe.

We were all strapping young men, still boyish and carefree. Our company commander, Capt. William "Wild Bill" Morrow, was a big man—about six feet three. The advanced training we received at Fort Bragg was rigorous and exhausting. I participated in the first night jump ever made—and landed on some railroad tracks. The long marches and night operations meant going without sleep for twenty-four hours at a time. I didn't much like that.

For recreation, we visited Fayetteville, the closest town to Fort Bragg. At the Town Pump Restaurant we indulged in French fries, fried chicken, and beer. Some of the local men didn't appreciate our presence and went out of their way to show it. Pete Dudniack was knifed and slashed through the biceps. We had to go to court, but the case was dismissed with admonishments. The local girls were a bit happier to have us around. Sgt. Tom Crane, for instance, made friends with a local schoolteacher. He was one of those who didn't make it back from the war; he was killed in southern France.

We were now trained and ready—we thought—to be shipped overseas. The first part of that journey was to Fort Dix, New Jersey. I recall seeing Lt. Charles "Bull" Howland's wife and children waving goodbye to him as we left Fort Bragg in our open boxcar. Captain Howland was killed near Saint Vith in Belgium. He had his chinstrap fastened, and the concussion from an artillery shell snapped his neck. At Fort Dix, to my surprise, I ran into Dotty Johnson. I thought she was there to see me, but actually she was there to try to convince a soldier not to evade the service.

We boarded the *Queen Elizabeth* on June 4, 1942, and zigzagged across the Atlantic to Gourock, Scotland. At our speed of thirty-five knots the trip took only about four and a half days. The *Queen Elizabeth* must have been loaded with good food in New York, but we didn't see any of it. We were fed mutton all the way across the Atlantic. We tried searching the ship for something else to eat, but all we could find were sea biscuits.

From Gourock we went by train ultimately to Chilton Foliat, Hungerford, near Newberry in England. Along the way we saw thousands of children from London escaping the Nazi blitz. The ladies of Chilton Foliat welcomed us to a dance, where they fed us sandwiches that tasted like grass. I'm not sure what was in them, but I know it wasn't watercress. "Doing the Lambeth Walk" was all the rage, but, not being a dancer, I sat it out.

I took the train to London on weekends to visit my new friend Rose Pledger. I slept on the kitchen floor of her family's apartment, and her parents would feed me a share of their scant rations for breakfast. One day, I took Rose to the restaurant of the Flemings Hotel. It was quite a fancy place, but because I was in uniform I was permitted in. As I passed by the bar, the bartender exclaimed, "Ay, Yank, you weren't here during the Blitz, you know!" I reached over the bar with my left hand and grabbed him by the collar. I don't think Rose liked that.

My buddies and I met the mother of a British pilot who had been killed in action. She took us to the restaurant in her apartment building for steaks more than once. You can bet your boots that she cried tears of joy when she got to take the D-day boys to dinner.

We were attached to British Gen. Frederick "Boy" Browning's paratrooper units for more training. Life was tough from that point on. He thought we needed a lot of work, and he saw that we got it. We trained at Ilfraccombe, a village on top of some cliffs overlooking the Atlantic on the west coast of England. It wasn't a very friendly place to stay. Our boys were jumping out of second-story windows. I don't think the liquor was so good.

During our first three months in England we were on British rations, and I came to understand what is meant when someone says that an army travels on its stomach. Our rations gave us barely enough energy for daily training operations. I would linger at the back of the column and dash in quickly for some crumpets whenever we passed a teahouse. When our rations finally arrived from America three months later, it took men wearing gas masks to remove the mutton.

Jimmy Nunn and I had already started scouting, and we led the unit on night problems. Jimmy was a six-footer from Florida with blue eyes and light-colored, straight hair. He had a crooked right elbow—the result of tetanus when he was a child—but he didn't let it keep him out of the service. He didn't like it when I complained about things.

On one mission we were given orders to get from point A to point B. We chose a straight line that took us through a turnip patch. Jimmy had the wire cutters, and we got the men where they were supposed to go. The next day, though, there were complaints from the farmers.

Jim was in the kitchen when the American rations arrived. He took a slice of bread and toasted it—and was promptly put in the guardhouse. The jail was a one-story building with an open transom over the door. I used to climb up through the transom and bring a pail of ale in to the prisoners. I usually stayed awhile to visit and then escaped back out through the transom. It was all part of scouting.

We flew to Ireland on a training mission and jumped at Nuts Corner near Belfast. Quite a few of the battalion, Jim and me included, got arrested there. It seemed that a goose had been stolen, and the blame fell on us. (It seems safe to admit now that I shot it and Jim skinned it, and I buried it under a streambed when we were pursued). On our return to England we surprised the Royal Air Force by jumping on one of their bases. The commanding officers were aware of what was going on, of course, but we certainly put a scare into the rest of the men.

Finally, as our reward for five months of training, General Browning awarded us the red beret of the British paratrooper. We got along better with the British paratroopers than with their infantry. The paratroopers were a mixture of nationalities—Polish, Canadians, Americans, etc.—and we seemed to fit right in.

With our training finished, we were briefed on our upcoming mission to North Africa. Jim and I, as scouts, were to take out the German sentries at either the La Senia or the Tafaraoui airport outside Oran in Algeria, North Africa. We were issued long johns to deceive the "fifth column" (spies and enemy collaborators) regarding our destination. Wearing full battle equipment, we were taken to our departure point: Lands End at the southwestern tip of England. We took off at midnight and flew south 1,500 miles, preparing to jump on the morning of November 8, 1942, on the two airports. As we flew over Spain, one of the fellows called out, "Who's throwing cigarette butts out the door?" No one of course. The Spaniards were shooting antiaircraft guns at us.

We lost nine planes on the way. Those who jumped or landed in Spanish Morocco were interned in Spain. That's where Herb Coberly picked up the nickname "Poco." Herb had played college football for West Virginia and looked like a wide end receiver. He was a head taller than most of the Spaniards around him. The men were all released eventually and joined us in Italy.

Vichy French Dewoitine fighter planes shot down three of our planes. Our Lt. Dave Kunkle was the first fatal casualty of America's involvement in the European war. Two pilots were killed as well. Rather than our planned destination, the men in our group of planes all jumped on the Sebkra, a dry lake bottom on the desert miles away from La Senia and Tafaraoui airports.

Captain Morrow carried the American flag unfurled as we marched on our targets. Jim and I led the battalion, taking turns with the compass through the night. As we passed through a little village, we noticed a drum on wheels that was secured to a building. I asked a nearby Arab if it contained water. He said no. I tapped it; it was half full. We signaled, and the men brought up their canteens to be filled. Our path across the desert was littered with a snaking trail of long johns. A very old Arab man standing by some olive trees reached his hand out as we passed. I had some miniature boxes of Sun Maid raisins and gave him two, and he bowed politely in thanks.

We proceeded on to the airports and found that some of our landing force—plus some men from the 509th—had already arrived and taken the targets. No shots were fired. I was given the job of guarding a tiny building where Gen. Jimmy Doolittle, commander of the landing force's aircraft, was staying.

We repacked our chutes on the ground and prepared for our next jump, this time in Tunisia. I missed this jump because of an infected puncture wound received when I tangled with some barbed wire. I had red streaks going up my right arm. I asked Capt. Carlos "Doc" Alden if he could lance it and drain it, but the wound got worse instead of better. I ended up in the hospital in Arzu under the care of a pretty American nurse named Mary. While the rest of the battalion made the Tunisia jump, I stayed at Maison Carrée in Algiers. For some reason that I can't recall, Jimmy Nunn was with me rather than in Tunisia. In any event, the battalion soon returned to Maison Carrée, and we rejoined our unit.

As the first Americans to fight alongside the French 3rd Zuave Regiment, the men of the 509th earned the privilege of wearing the 3rd Zuave French unit's insignia—a prowling desert jackal and crescent moon with the inscription "here I stay." One of my most thrilling and unforgettable experiences was hearing the Marseillaise breaking the night silence amid the low-altitude bombing runs of German Heinkel 111s.

After Maison Carrée we were moved to a winery in Boufarik, where we slept on top of wine vats. Some of the fellows used siphons. Three separate photos were taken of the battalion at Boufarik, although none shows the complete battalion because some units were still returning from Tunisia.

Jim and I met a cabby who would take us into Algiers in exchange for some hundred-octane airplane fuel. It was a good deal for all of us; his car had never run so well—until the engine blew apart a few weeks later. Once we got to Algiers we usually overstayed the curfew. On one of those occasions we tried to sneak around the back way. It was about midnight, and we had to get over a six-foot picket fence. I made it okay. Jim, who was six feet tall, got caught by the heels and hung there, yelling at me to get him down. I was laughing so hard I could barely stand up. When I finally got him loose he started swinging at me, thinking it wasn't so funny. The next morning, Capt. Ernest "Bud" Siegel had us digging slit trenches for latrines, as usual.

Early one Sunday morning, Jim and I decided to go out for breakfast. We found a restaurant in a private home and entered. The Arab who was both chef and waiter said he had rabbit, and that sounded good to us. When he brought our plates and we saw long tails on the "rabbits," we drew our .45s and took out after him; fortunately, we didn't catch him. We were never sure if they were cats or rats, but they most definitely weren't rabbits.

I made friends with a little Arab boy named Zuluth who was about ten years old. I liked him because he was a fellow runner. He was always fast enough to outdistance the person he had just robbed. When I hadn't seen him for a few days, I asked around and heard that he was ill. I grabbed a couple of Hershey bars and searched through the village until I found Zuluth's hut. I think the Hershey bars brought down his fever.

As is usually the case during wartime, those good times didn't last. A more realistic location was found for us in Oujda, in barren desert land alongside a B-26 airbase. We pitched shelter halves over one foot-deep-foundations lined with sand-filled gas cans and settled in for a while. Still, things could have been a lot worse. Fresh eggs came at regular intervals in huge, straw-filled crates about a foot high and six feet long. Some of the fellows found some little gasoline-fueled stoves, and we turned out some pretty good meals. Occasionally a stove would blow up and set someone on fire, and we would have to roll the man up in a blanket to douse the flames.

Lt. John Dunn, a B-26 pilot and friend of my nurse, Mary, took Jim and me for a ride over the Mediterranean. John told us that the outlook wasn't very good for B-26 crews; most of them didn't return from their missions.

We made friends with some French wine growers who invited us for dinner on weekends. They would send a driver with two white stallions and extra shotguns, and we would ride shotgun on the return, guarding against robbers. The distance was more than two miles, and along the way we would pass Arab encampments with huge tents and beautiful horses. Some of these Arab men joined us for the dinners. We would sit in a large circle, eat fava beans, drink wine, and pass the bottle while we waited for our dinner of roast lamb to arrive. The wine grower's wife would make us any drink we asked for. She had all the makings. I always asked for Cointreau. I'm sure those people must have lost everything in the war between the French and Algerians that followed World War II.

Those good times soon ended, too. We loaded on "forty and eight" boxcars for the trip to Kairouan in Tunisia. It was a horrible spot. We dug deep holes in the desert sand and lay still at the bottom. The surface of the sand above us reached 158 degrees in that merciless sun.

On one occasion, Jim and I were walking toward the beach near Kairouan and came across a farmer raising chickens. We asked him if he would sell us one and he did, binding its legs before handing it to us. As we carried away our purchase, anticipating the delicious dinner to come, the chicken broke loose and took off for home, which by then was about fifty yards back. The Arab must have tied a slipknot so the chicken could escape. Jim raised his .45 and dropped the fleeing bird with one shot. We dug a hole in the sand, plucked the chicken, cooked it, and ate it on the spot.

On another occasion I thought I would "try a Zuluth" and see if I still had the endurance of a cross-country runner. About a half mile from camp an Arab was selling watermelons. I grabbed a big watermelon and took off for camp. The Arab was hot on my heels, but I made it, still carrying the watermelon.

Our training continued during this time. A British colonel about five and a half feet tall with a big red nose visited us in Kairouan and taught us how to shoot from the hip. He had taught FBI agents how to shoot during Prohibition. He fired two pearl-handled revolvers from the hip into some sandbags a hundred feet away and made a pattern no bigger than your fist. He said, "Face the target, the vertical raise, center it on your belly button, and squeeze. *!?$#@! his mother; that's what she gets for having a son." He told us a story about a man who got off a submarine along the French coast, entered a tavern frequented by Nazi pilots, killed six of them with six bullets, took all their papers, and got back on the submarine. He called the man in the story by another name, but he later admitted that he was the man. Inspired, Jim and I picked up our Tommy guns, a couple of hundred rounds of ammo, and a couple of cans, and walked a hundred yards into the desert to practice. What we had just learned came in handy later.

The 82nd Airborne came to Africa a few months after the 509th in preparation for the invasion of Italy. The 82nd's planners wanted to see what an eighty-two-plane dispersion would look like and asked for volunteers to make the jump. Jim and I volunteered. Each plane was supposed to carry one officer and one volunteer. It was to be a night jump. We flew out over the Mediterranean, turned around, came back in, and jumped on the north coast of Africa. Jim had an officer in the plane with him, but the officer who was supposed to be in my plane never showed up. I was alone in the back of the plane in the dark with dust blowing all around. I got the red light to stand in the door, and then I got the green light and went out. Everything was fine as I came down, but all of a sudden I wasn't falling anymore. My chute was tangled up in power lines. It was very dark, and I had no idea how far above the ground I was. I took a chance and turned loose—and touched lightly down. I must have been about a foot off the ground.

We filled the empty hours waiting for the jump in Italy as best we could. I played cards now and then; not being an experienced gambler, I lost most of the time and had to borrow money from Jim. Once, though, I was playing against Don Heron and Duke Williams, who always held the bank. We played blackjack, and I cleaned them out for eighteen hundred dollars. I gave Jim nine hundred and kept the rest to carry with me on the next mission. (That proved to be a wise move.) I didn't send any home, as I should have. Jim, on the other hand, sent most of his money home.

Our next move was the real thing. We flew to Sicily and landed for a briefing on our next mission. We were to jump forty kilometers (twenty-five miles) behind the Salerno beachhead onto the main road junction at Avellino, which fed the beachhead.

September 14, 1943, was a beautiful moonlit night. We bailed out, as usual in two groups. Half the battalion landed in Avellino, as they were supposed to do, the other half which was my group, landed in Montella about seven miles to the south. Montella was also a road junction forty kilometers from the beachhead, and since it also fed the beachhead was just as serious an objective, so the mistake wasn't a total loss.

We jumped from such a high altitude that I thought I was coming down between cliffs, it took so long to reach the ground; I estimated it to be about four thousand feet. As I descended, the cliffs gave way to a valley. The moonlight was so bright that the olive trees below cast long, dark shadows. About a hundred feet up the road below me, a scout car with four occupants was approaching. I slipped my chute quickly to the right, pulling down on my two right risers and drifting into the shade of the nearest olive tree. I grabbed the exposed grip of my Tommy gun, which I had arranged ahead of time with the muzzle protruding, and was ready to fire if necessary. The car went by, heading in a westerly direction toward the beachhead. I detached my chute, bundled it up, and hid it. Church bells started ringing. An Italian in the distance started toward me. I waved him away and started looking for anyone who had jumped with me. To my relief, the first person I ran into was Jimmy Nunn. He said, "Dick?" and I responded, "Jim?" You couldn't have been behind the lines with a better buddy.

We climbed for high ground, rested a bit, and then headed back down. A squad of 509 parachute riggers passed us but made no attempt to join us. One of them explained, "We're supposed to pick up chutes." Marion Shade, from Ohio, was bringing up the rear. He grimaced an apology as he passed, obviously disagreeing with the others in his group. The enemy traffic was heading east now, away from the beachhead. Obviously, they were looking for us. The enemy thought five thousand of us had jumped, but our battalion was only about five hundred strong. I honestly believe that our unit turned the tide at the Salerno beachhead. The 82nd Airborne had jumped on the friendly side of the lines rather than behind them, as the Germans were expecting them to do.

At the bottom of the valley we came upon an older couple cultivating their farmland. I couldn't speak Italian, but they pointed, saying, "Americano here" and "Tedeschi la" (Germans there). I recall being told by one of the Italians that one of our boys had been shot while hanging in a tree, helpless. We changed course for higher ground, found a little clearing, and rested.

I was sitting on the ground, my Tommy gun, on half safety, resting across my thighs pointing to the left, when three German soldiers appeared out of the wheat fields to the left about one hundred feet away. One of them sighted down his barrel at me and shouted something in German. My finger was on the trigger. The German couldn't see my Tommy gun because he was looking down the end of the barrel. With my Tommy centered on my belly button, my thumb moved the safety forward to "off safe." I called back, "Americano," for some reason giving the word an Italian twist, and squeezed the trigger. Perhaps I had stumbled on a professional gunman's technique: divert your opponents' attention when you kill them. All three folded up. They didn't dive for cover; they just folded up. Jim cranked his gun up and we got the hell out of there. I splashed into a stream, and Jim called over, "What are you doing this for?" I yelled back, "In case they have dogs."

About a hundred yards later we started up a steep, barren hill and I called ahead to Jim that I couldn't keep up. We each found a little hole and waited, ready to stand off any pursuers. No one appeared, so we rested a bit and continued up the mountain. I didn't understand why Jim was doing better than I was. He was in great shape, sure, but so was I. Later I realized I had been carrying too much ammunition. I had three thirty-round .45 caliber clips in each trouser side pouch pocket. Anyway, Jim had waited for me.

We found ourselves in a shady wooded area where a farmer was watching over about a dozen cattle. We asked him if he would squeeze us some milk, and he did. I think that spot is where I got the malaria. It was wet and full of mosquitoes. As we continued uphill through the rocky forest we heard bells tinkling, indicating the approach of a shepherd and his flock. We lay prone and frozen amongst the forest ferns. The shepherd and his herd passed by us several feet away. We caught up to him and asked for bread. He said he didn't have any.

The vegetation got thicker, and we came upon a house built into the side of a hill. We approached the couple that lived there; they were very friendly and invited us to dinner. They cooked pasta and chicken for us and put a small barrel of purple wine on the table. As we sat there we could hear vehicles passing by on the road just above. Jim and I ate with our Tommy guns across our knees. It was getting late, and the couple asked us where we wanted to sleep. I said, "In the barn." I handed the couple several twenty-dollar bills as we left the house. We went into the barn and lay down, but it didn't feel right. "Let's get out of here," I said to Jim. We left quietly, slipping through the darkness up toward the road, and rested in the gully alongside the road while vehicles passed by above us.

As we made our steady way toward the front lines, I made sure to distribute a twenty-dollar bill here and there. It's never a bad idea to have the local populace on your side. We eventually came upon Lt. John W. Teasley with a group of about twenty men and went along with them. A guide took us over the mountains. We had no food, but people along the trail handed us some bread now and then. We spent one night on top of the mountain, "spooning" together to keep warm. The descent seemed to take forever, but we knew we were being guided to safety. I think I had about three crumbs of bread left in my pocket by the time we rejoined our unit.

Ted Fina

Danny Brenner

Boufarik, North Africa. Above and below, members of Battalion 509 after returning from the jump in Tunisia.

Chalka

Sully

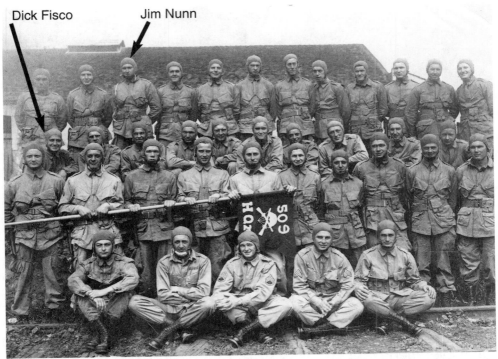

Dick Fisco   Jim Nunn

I am in the third row, first on
the left. In the top row, third
from the left is Jim Nunn.

Staff Sgt. Herb (Poco) Coberly
from the 509.

Before the first night
jump ever made. Sgt.
Crane is first on the left.
I am third from the left.

Jim Nunn, who was at
my side on all patrols.

Chapter 5

We Break the German Winter Line at Venafro

A little schoolhouse in Piscinola, on the outskirts of Naples, was our base camp for the next couple of months. When we got there, we were able to clean up and get our weapons ready for the next operation. One of the fellows managed to find a phonograph, and Tennessee Ernie Ford's "Sixteen Tons" soon made the place seem a bit more like home.

It was in Piscinola that we witnessed the worst tragedy that I personally experienced during the war. Some of the local children had gotten hold of a bazooka shell, and about ten or eleven of them were killed when it exploded. Children's bodies were lying all over. I saw a little girl about eight years old lying on the floor with a hole in the middle of her chest. The entire village echoed for days with wails and screams. I have never been able to forget the horror of that sight.

Our next mission was to break the German Winter Line at Mount Croce in Venafro. It took thirty-four days of fighting to do it. We left Piscinola at dusk in two-and-a-half-ton trucks and proceeded slowly through the valley at the base of Mount Croce. There was a cross on its summit. Off to our left, 155-mm long toms were croaking, probably hitting in the direction of San Pietro or Monte Cassino. We unloaded at the foot of the mountain and dug in under olive trees. The next morning we attacked. We took the top in about four hours. Jim Nunn and I led the attack. Lt. John Martin (Col. ret.) told us to head for the saddle, which was between a high knoll called Mount Corno on the left and Mount Croce on the right.

About halfway up I passed a Ranger. "Where are you going?" he asked. "We're heading for the top," I answered. We climbed a little farther and suddenly there was no one behind me, not even Jim. There had been a sudden change in plans. Col. William O. Darby of the 1st Ranger Battalion and Col. William P. Yarborough of the 509th must have talked it over and decided to keep the 509th from passing through the Rangers. The others in my unit had veered off to the right and were attacking up and around Old Orange Face, the vertical rock leading to the top of Mount Croce. I turned around to follow Jim, and we found ourselves behind the attack. If my unit had continued on our original path as directed by Lt. Martin, we probably would have cut off those trying to retreat from Mount Croce. Anyway, we somehow got to the top—I don't know how, in spite of all the eighty-eight shells splashing off of Old Orange Face on top of us. Among our casualties was our old squad leader, Sgt. Lehman "Snake" LeCompt Jr., who, despite his nickname was not a big fan of snakes. Back in England we would tease him by yelling, "Snake!" It was always good for a laugh.

Oddly, we saw a naked old woman on the mountain in enemy position. Jim and I returned later looking to help her. We were told that she had died and had been carried down the mountain on a mule.

Although we maintained control of the mountaintop, once in a while Colonel Yarborough would pull the men off Mount Corno and allow the Germans to retake the top, having zeroed in seventy-five's from halftracks at the bottom.

On one of our night patrols we were driven up to a point in front of the 45th Division on the right, which put us in front of the right flank of the 509th's position. As we returned, we found ourselves in the middle of a barrage of outgoing and incoming "mail" from one of our own batteries of 105s as well as 88s coming in. It was terrifying. We checked in at the 45th's command post to ask for a ride back to Venafro, but no one was moving while the exchange of artillery fire continued. One of our fellows, Joseph Laudacini, confiscated a jeep, and we drove back to our unit through the barrage.

At Piscinola, Colonel Yarborough formed the S-2 Battalion Scouts with seven of us. We found ourselves a place on the ground floor of a residential building on the outskirts of Venafro at the base of Mount Croce. The floor was dirt, but there was a fireplace and we kept a fire going. Colonel Yarborough had asked us if we wanted noncommissioned officer ratings when he formed the scouts, but we weren't interested. We should have said yes.

Our daily activities consisted of climbing over the top of the mountain through our front line and mortar positions to reconnoiter enemy positions. Lieutenant Martin (Col. ret.) was in charge of our group. He treated us well. He kept passes on his desktop in Piscinola so that we would never be caught without a pass when we went to Naples.

I had a nurse friend in Naples named Fritzie. It wasn't a romantic relationship; we were just very good friends and she was already married. One day we took a train to Pozzuoli and then a taxi up to the Solfatera. Also called Little Vesuvius, this volcanic crater is well off the beaten tourist path. Very few people have ever heard of it, much less seen it. The lava boiled continually right in front of us. After that we visited a nearby orphanage. The sight of those beautiful children in a war zone was difficult to comprehend. I had no money to make a donation, and that made it worse. We both went away feeling sad.

The men from my unit often went into Naples in search of recreation and diversion. One day, my buddies and I found a dance hall in the center of town and went in. My friends went to the floor to dance while I went to the bar and ordered drinks for the four of us. A big tanker came up to the bar and spotted the four drinks sitting there. The bartender told him the drinks were for someone else, but he went ahead anyway and downed all four of them. He was over six feet tall to my five feet eight inches, but I followed him out to the dance floor and patted him on the shoulder. The expected mayhem ensued, and I ended up with cuts in my fists from his teeth. I went to one of our hospitals afterward and presented my hands for treatment. When they asked me how it happened, I told them that a soldier bit me. They seemed to accept that explanation. They put heating pads on my hands and then forgot them, and the pads ended up burning my right wrist. I left the hospital with a big plaster cast on my forearm.

A day or two later I was visiting Fritzie in the building where all of the nurses lived when suddenly we heard screams. One of the nurses was being attacked. I rushed into her room and discovered that the attacker was one of our own lieutenants. I bashed him over the head with my plaster cast, and that was the only punishment he ever got.

On another occasion when my buddies and I were walking along a street in Naples we came upon a GI with a drawn pistol trying to force a young Italian woman into a building. I sneaked up behind and hit him over the head with my GI-issue semiautomatic .45 and then took his .45 Colt revolver away from him. How he got it I don't know. It must have been one of the weapons air-dropped to the Italian partisans.

Initially the S-2 Battalion Scouts consisted of seven men, which turned out to be the ideal number for reconnaissance patrols. Our job was to plot the enemy positions on overlays that we sent back to headquarters. I usually made these using my map training from Panama. I led the way on these patrols with Jimmy Nunn at my side followed by Danny Brenner. Albert Lewis and Joe Moffo with their Tommy guns brought up the rear. Joe always complained about bringing up the rear. Don Kammer with his carbine and Murph Trahan with his M-1 were in the middle. We were a good team. Ken Edney, a British paratrooper who had hitchhiked by plane from Africa to be with the 509th, soon joined us. He told us that his mother and sister had been raped and killed in Singapore.

Capt. Charles Howland wanted to see how we operated on patrol, so we staged an operation to show him. I decided to get to the enemy in front of our position by starting out in front of the 45th Division's positions in Pozzuoli. We started up the valley below the military slope of our own positions. After we had gone a short distance, I realized that we had exposed ourselves to the enemy's view from their side of the valley, and I told everyone to stand up in plain sight and return. Once the Germans thought we had abandoned our mission, we started up the right side of the valley below the military slope of the enemy. As we approached the top, I bent a trip wire at my ankle, stepped over it, and warned the others. A little farther and we were up on their ridge. We knew they had eight machine guns in line across the ridge. I spotted the backside of a dugout, stepped down into it, and surprised two machine gunners. I pointed my Thompson to my left and said, "To the right." They understood perfectly. They were grumbling as I handed them over to Jim, who was right outside. Ken Edney and I stood side-by-side behind the dugout and challenged the remaining seven machine gun positions to come out and fight. We were behind them and they would have to expose themselves. We had the drop on them and there were no takers. Our two prisoners were arrogant all the way back to our lines.

On one occasion we were sent out in broad daylight to retrieve a German antipersonnel mine. This fell into Jim's hand. We went over the top and slipped down to the bottom in the enemy positions. Jim discovered a trip wire attached to an antipersonnel mine; it looked like an old cheese box ten inches long and four inches square. We kept him covered while he detached the mine. He turned, put it inside his shirt, saying to me, "I put it where it will do the most good if it goes off." Just then, a platoon of Germans walked by from right to left about twenty yards away. We could have killed them all, but Jim had our mine and I decided to return without firing a shot. One of our fellows had to go. There was no paper, so he used the latest issue of *Stars and Stripes* and hung it on their trip wire after he went. Halfway down the other side, we had to pass Colonel Darby's dugout. Jim gave the colonel a peek at the mine, and then we continued down to Lieutenant Martin and Jim gave the mine to him.

On another of our daytime seven-man reconnaissance patrols, we managed to penetrate up into the enemy's position. There was vegetation all around us. The rest of the patrol was looking for a fight, not me. I agreed to their plan to attack in one minute, but the firing started before the minute was up. I couldn't see the others because there was a ten-foot rise between us. I had just seen a young German soldier slowly lower himself back into his foxhole. He was down and out of sight now, and I had let him go. He looked very young. As we backed down the mountain, Joe Moffo stopped to reload, and I yelled at him for doing it in a standing position. We all got out of there safely, although a bullet skinned me across the left wrist. Back over the ridge we went, and on down to Venafro to our house.

As we approached the house, we saw someone in an Italian or similar German uniform running away. I yelled after him to halt, but he kept running and started over a shed and a ten-foot wall. I drew my .45 semiautomatic and fired two shots from the hip, then pursued him over the wall and down the street until I caught up to him. He had been hit twice—once through the palm of each hand. When Doc Alden, got a look at the man's wounds, he joked, "Fisco probably held his hands to shoot him."

We made one night patrol with members from different units. I didn't like it; too much confusion. I was glad to return without any mishaps. On another night patrol, Jim and I went down close to the Germans' positions and just listened. Our own seventy-five's were hitting all around us and we could hear a young enemy soldier crying and an older one consoling him.

The weather was always cloudy and cold up on the mountain. The temperature was below freezing most of the time, and rain or freezing rain soaked everyone and everything. I wore wool socks under my leather jump boots, never changed them, and never had a problem the entire thirty-four days we were there.

A young Italian orphan named Giovanni joined us. He had lost both his parents. He came from Aqua Fondada, a village on the other side of the mountain and sang beautifully. He and I were out in nearby gardens one day scavenging for leftover vegetables while 75-mm shells were coming over from behind us. I ducked every time one went over, but Giovanni said, "Not to worry, not to worry; they're Americans."

Life goes on even in a war zone, of course. One day I was walking alone down the main drag on a little narrow street of Venafro. Eighty-eight shells were coming in every ten seconds. As I went by an open door, I looked in and saw an elderly Italian woman with a rolling pin in her hand stirring polenta.

Finally, after what seemed like a year instead of a month, it was time to return to Piscinola for replacements, rest, and recuperation. I believe we lost about nineteen men killed and more than double that wounded during those thirty-four days of mountain fighting. During that time we had captured strategic heights from which the enemy had been able to fire on our positions in the vast valley below.

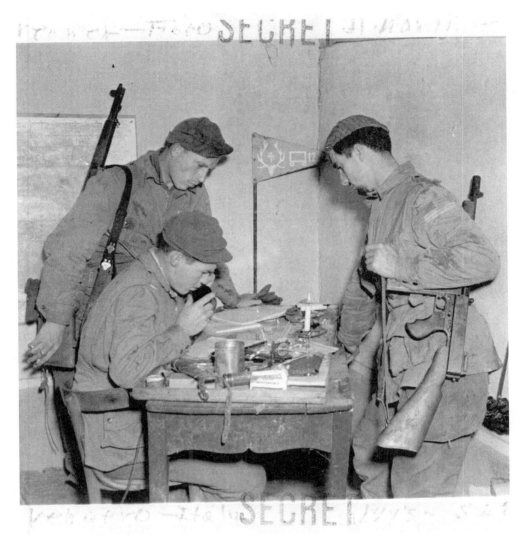

Venafro, Italy, December 1943. Lt. John Martin (Col. ret.) briefing Danny Brenner and me before patrol.

Captain "Cool" Doc Alden (second from left) escaped from the
Germans twice. To his right are John "Blackie" Johnson and Tom Hall.
Blackie Johnson gave me the half parachute to give to Louise.

Venafro, Italy. Lt. John Martin (Col. ret.) briefing Danny Brenner, me, Jimmy Nunn, Joe Moffo and Murph Trahan before patrol.

Chapter 6

Anzio:
"Draw Fire"

nzio would prove to be the most difficult of all our campaigns. We put in seventy-two days there, almost every one of them on the front line. Artillery fire coming down from the enemy's high positions around Cisterna pounded us constantly. After making some progress initially, we were stopped cold. We held the same position for about seventy days, unable to advance and unwilling to retreat. Sixteen lieutenants alone—half the battalion's young officers—were killed.

We had no priests with us. There was someone who may have been a minister, but he stayed way, way back behind the lines. We were never introduced to him, and he never introduced himself to us. The only thing I recall him doing was ordering Doc Alden to put purple coloring in the medicinal alcohol to prevent us from drinking it. Doc complied.

We went ashore at Anzio on January 22, 1944, after two British rocket ships had ripped up the beaches. The landing was easy; there was no opposition. I was first off the assault craft and up the casino steps, which are no longer there.

From Anzio we proceeded the short distance to Nettuna. A German soldier in civilian clothes was turned over to us, and we turned him over to Colonel Darby. We walked a short distance away and heard shots behind us.

Colonel Yarborough had enlarged the S-2 section to about fifteen men, which I thought was too many. We led the battalion in a wedge formation inland across the farmland. I heard a bolt click and yelled, "Hit the dirt!" just in time. Automatic fire swept over our heads, but no one was hit. We continued to advance and came on a ten-foot-deep dry irrigation canal. The gunner, fighting a rearguard action, had escaped up the canal.

In our advance through the farmlands we went through Campo Morto, two and a half miles from the Carano road. We saw people evacuating a farm-house that had an open staircase on the side. It could have been Saint Maria Goretti's home. Saint Maria Goretti died when she was eleven years old because she would not submit to Allesandro Saranelli and was stabbed fourteen times. Her body was—and still is—in Nettuna in the Shrine of Our Lady of Grace.

We kept advancing each day for about a week until we reached a point just short of the Carano road, where we dug in. We would hold a disproportion-ately large section of the beachhead for almost seventy days. When we were on patrol between the lines at Anzio we could hear artillery exchanges from both sides whizzing by overhead. Occasionally, Anzio Annie, a 280-mm rail-road gun, would chug along aiming shells at our supply ships.

In the early days of the beachhead, while we were still moving forward but had not yet crossed the Carano road, Colonel Yarborough called for scouts and Jim Nunn, Danny Brenner, and I responded. I was told to take one patrol out on the left flank to draw fire. Jim was to lead a reconnaissance patrol out toward the graveyard on the right flank. All three of us warned the colonel that the flat terrain made it too dangerous to draw fire. "I still want you to draw fire," he said. I asked the colonel if it was okay for me to head in the direction of a red barn about three hundred yards away, and he consented.

On leaving the colonel, I thought it best to ask for volunteers to come with me rather than the usual. Ken Barton, a West Coast radio announcer, insisted that he wanted to go. I wouldn't let him because he had two children. Another fellow came up to me and told me that so-and-so was afraid to go. I went up to so-and-so and asked, "Are you afraid?" He answered, "Yes." I said to him, "Stay back." He remained with the battalion to the very end, though—all the way through

Belgium. Danny Brenner, Murph Trahan, Joe Moffo, Ken Edney (the British paratrooper), Tom Dressel, and Jesse McNight went on the mission with me. Jesse removed the rear sight from his M-1; anyone within three hundred yards would be a dead duck. Neither Tom nor Jesse had been on patrol with us before.

We started off in four-foot-deep dry irrigation ditches, but the depth gradually tapered off to less than one foot. The bottom of the ditch was now lined with green mud. I smeared some on my face for camouflage. It took more than two hours to get close to the red barn on that bright, sunny day, and the ditch hid us only if we were in a prone position. I picked up the scent of moldy uniforms mixed with cigarette smoke and knew we were close. (Years later, I found out that I am allergic to mold.) Then I saw an unmanned machine gun at the base of a haystack; it was pointing right down our ditch.

I saw no way to draw fire except by attacking. I assigned Ken Edney to take out the two machine gunners, and I anchored Murph and Jesse at each end with their rifles to cover us. We five Tommy gunners attacked: Ken was on the left; Danny was to the right of Ken and left of me; to my right was Joe Moffo; and to his right was Tom Dressel.

Joe, who was out of my sight, in a hot house behind a row of small bushes, must have run into a hornet's nest. I heard the dying wails of at least a dozen of the enemy through the chattering of his Tommy gun. Joe was a short, burly guy with a powerful build and blue eyes—one splashed with coffee brown. He was one of four fighting Moffos from Bristol, Pennsylvania, and had been Col. Edson Raff's bodyguard in North Africa.

Danny, on my left, was shot through the left bicep and had his Tommy gun blown out of his grip. He passed by me, heading back and holding out his left arm as if to apologize. Joe was backing up on my right and stopped to reload— once again from a standing position. He was shot down. I made it back the twenty-five yards to the ditch. Joe raised his head and called in a weak voice, "Save yourselves, boys," and was riddled up off the ground by machine-gun fire. Ken Edney charged back from the haystack where he had killed the gunners. I yelled, "Kenny, no!" as he flew through the air and threw himself on top of Joe. The machine guns rattled again, and both of them were still.

Tom and Jesse had withdrawn, followed by Danny. I was sure that Ken and Joe were both dead. I wanted to go out to them but didn't have the courage to die. Murph, still alive, was lying with his head near my shoes. I called out, "Murph, do you have smoke?" Smoke was always your way in and your way out, but I had dropped my white phosphor grenade.

Murph called back, "Yeah."

I answered, "Throw it!"

"I can't!"

"Why?"

"I'm shot through the fingers."

I yelled, "Throw it anyway." I knew that the enemy had only a 6 percent chance of hitting us through smoke.

Murph asked, "Where?"

"Anywhere!" I answered. The grenade landed close to my feet and burnt my jumpsuit, but that didn't matter. We took off. A gentle breeze was carrying the smoke in our direction, obscuring us from the view of the Germans. We were receiving artillery fire from both sides in addition to small arms fire from the enemy. We made it back to our lines as the melting sun cast a golden glow across the western horizon to our right.

Colonel Yarborough had advanced our battalion across the Carano road, and some of the men had gathered around the tomb of Garibaldi's son. The tomb was a vertical tunnel about ten feet in diameter with a spiral staircase going down about fifteen feet. Men were huddled on the stairs taking shelter from the shelling. They had heard all the shooting but had no idea what was going on. That was the reason the colonel had wanted us to draw fire. We had shielded the advance of the battalion on the left front, as Jim and his patrol did on the right front. Jim told me they had also run into a skirmish. We had two dead and two wounded. No greater love hath any man than he give up his life for his friends. Joe Moffo gave his life for us, and Ken Edney laid down his life for Joe. They had courage beyond even a Congressional Medal of Honor. Many years later, I asked Father Val, a Dominican priest (of Mohawk Indian descent), whether or not Joe and Ken could have been assumed into heaven. His answer was yes. Personally, I think their actions were out of love that could have come only from Heaven.

The next night Colonel Yarborough sent out a twenty-four-man combat patrol to search for their bodies. The patrol found the haystack and looked all around, but there were no bodies. The enemy had also evacuated their positions. This was the first time I had lost anyone on patrol. I think the men always had confidence in me. I was always very stealthy and defensive.

Tony Sais had been a member of S-2 since Venafro but never participated in the patrols. He was usually in an outpost position. One day at Anzio, one of the S-2 men ran toward me calling for me to come quick, that Tony was yelling for me. I saw Tony circling around, looking confused; I called to him to get down as I approached. At Anzio, you did not stand up behind the front line. I guided him down to the medics—Jack Zenker and the others—waved my Tommy gun in their direction, and said, "Take care of him; he's not a phony." Sure enough, the next day Tony returned, back to normal.

The S-2 scouts were assigned to an outpost located in the farmhouse of Fernando Spiragia, about two hundred feet across the Carano road in front of our lines. Our job was to observe the German lines from the second floor. I asked Murph to keep watch with the binoculars in the dark, especially just before dawn. One morning he suddenly called out, "They're having breakfast." We looked and, sure enough, the enemy troops on the front line were puttering around in their foxholes making breakfast. I checked the coordinates, picked up the phone, and asked the British artillery behind us to lay down bursts five feet off the ground between the two coordinates I gave them. They did, and their accuracy was unbelievable. The next morning the enemy was at it again. They must have thought the firing was an accident. The British hit them again, and that was the end of the early-morning breakfasts.

One morning a P-41 belly-landed in between the lines in front of our observation post. Jim and I ran out to rescue the pilot. As we approached, we saw that the pilot had gotten out of the plane and was headed toward the enemy line. We called out to him, and he turned back in our direction. He told us that he was out of ammunition and had crash-landed. We guided him back, and Jim asked the colonel if he wanted the bombsite removed. "Yes. Definitely remove it," was the answer. Here again, Jim had the courage and technical know-how to do it. I covered him and called out, "Jim, check his ammo trays while you're at it." Jim got the bombsite out and found that the ammo trays were full. Jim brought the bombsite in to the colonel but made no mention of the ammo trays. What character! As far as I know, Jim got no recognition for all that he did.

I always thought the Protestants were better than the Catholics, but we were given an ace in the hole—confession!

I remember as a teenager hitchhiking to Burmingham where a teenage boy called me "brother" and took me to his home where we ate his mammy's biscuits.

One of our daytime patrol objectives was to determine the enemy's position in the vicinity of the graveyard to our right front. The graveyard was about two hundred feet square and had high walls. The entrance to it was on our side of the lines. It was midday under a bright sun. I recall stepping about an inch to the right of a two-and-a-half-inch-square pressure plate for one of our mines as we started out. We entered the graveyard. I could hear the enemy talking behind the rear wall and thought it best to get out fast before they started pitching hand grenades in at us. I asked the men to keep twenty-yard intervals. About halfway back to our lines, Albert Lewis tripped a mine and a piece of shrapnel went through his wrist. Incoming mortar fire started. I doused Albert's wrist with sulfa powder and bandaged it, then led the men out of the minefield, retracing each of our steps to miss the mines. When we got back, I took Albert to the medics. They said there was nothing further they could do, that I had done a good job. I don't think Albert ever regained the use of his hand. I was given a Bronze Star.

Later, I discovered that a piece of shrapnel had gone through the plastic blood shed kit I carried in my left breast pocket and had settled in the pocket. It was about half an inch long and a quarter inch in diameter. The plastic box that saved my life was about two and a half inches square and five-eighths inches thick and had contained a map, a tiny compass, two gold pieces, and other survival gear when we jumped in North Africa. I had lost the gold pieces to some Arabs because I thought they were francs but had kept the box; this made up for my stupidity.

I had found a black leather jacket that could have belonged to a German tank officer. It was about an inch and a half longer than the jacket of my jump-suit and very warm. I wore it the entire time at Anzio, although I knew I would be a dead duck if the Germans caught me wearing it.

One day while the S-2 scouts were in our normal location in a farmhouse about two hundred yards behind our front lines, we saw six Tiger tanks coming down the Carano road from left to right. I quickly called Colonel Yarborough on the phone to let him know. The Tigers shot the place up and then left. We had a 57-mm gun facing them, and one of the tanks split its barrel with a shot right down the middle of the barrel. As Jim and I were walking along the Carano road one day after that, two M-5 light tanks came along and stopped. One of the tankers opened the hatch and asked, "Are any Tigers around?" We called back, "You're in a bowling alley." They turned and took off in the opposite direction.

Strategically, our most important position was on our right flank in low hills to the right of the cemetery. Before dawn on February 29, 1944, Capt. John R. Martin (Col. Ret.) of B Company called for my crew to come and reconnoiter in front of his position while B Company relieved C Company. I reported back that I could feel for him, but I couldn't reach him; the enemy was out there just a short distance away. I didn't see Captain Martin again until after the war. When I spoke to him years later, Colonel (as he was then) Martin did not recall me telling him that. I probably said it so quietly that he couldn't hear me. The attack, when it came, overpowered his greatly outnumbered force. I saw the hills covered with green enemy uniforms. Captain Martin was wounded and captured, and the rest of his company was either killed or captured. The 3rd Division on our right flank plugged the hole for us until we could take over.

Our dead had to be picked up in front of the lines. Nick De Gaeta would go out at night with a three-quarter-ton open truck and bring them in. At least there was no problem finding enough to eat at Anzio. We would just go out and cut a steak off a cow that had been killed by artillery.

We left the beach head and the battalion returned to Naples on April 1, 1944, greatly depleted in strength. On the next mission, I would be a platoon staff sergeant, as would Jim Nunn.

I later learned that in coming to this part of Italy I had in fact been coming home. My son, Richard J. (J. for James after my buddy Jim), did some genealogical studies and found to his surprise—and mine—that the Fisco's originated not far from Venafro, the very area where the 509th Parachute Infantry Battalion fought from November 10 to December 13, 1943. My grandfather, Mariano Fisco, was born in 1838 in Piedimonte d'Alife, now Piedimonte Matese. Mariano, a tailor, came to the United States with three of his brothers. They arrived on June 24, 1891 at Castle Clinton, Battery Park. This was nine years before Ellis Island was even operational. His name is listed in the records of immigrants on Ellis Island. Legend has it that Hannibal's elephants passed through d'Alife on their way to Rome.

There was a German headquarters in this area. The Nazis revenge-bombed the town and then massacred 127 men, women, and children (probably including some Fisco's) with rifles in the caves of Pietransieri in 1943. The former headquarters is now a ski resort.

R E S T R I C T E D

VI   AWARDS OF BRONZE STAR MEDAL.

    Under the provisions of Army Regulations 600-45, as amended, a Bronze Star Medal is awarded to the following-named enlisted men:

    RICHARD D. FISCO, (6973808), Private, Infantry, United States Army. For heroic achievement in action, on 15 February 1944, near Carano, Italy. Entered military service from St. Albans, Long Island, New York.

For rendering first aid to a scout on patrol while under fire. I entered the service actually from 411 Amherst Ave., Oakwood Heights, Staten Island, NY.

1st Lt. Sexton and Pvt. Logan, both killed in Anzio and buried in Nuttuna, Italy.

Chapter 7

Southern France, The Second D-Day (Dragoon): We Retake the Chateau at La Napoule

The unit's final stay in Naples lasted about a month and a half, and then we moved to a rest area at Lido di Roma. As staff sergeant, I assembled my platoon when we arrived there and instructed the men not to go on the beach because it was mined. Within ten minutes, it seemed, mines on the beach killed two of my men. Capt. Ralph R. "Bing" Miller called me in and asked me if I had warned my men. I was one of the four platoon sergeants who had warned his men. I felt terrible about it, but things like that happen when you have all new men. They didn't know me, and, aside from brief training, I didn't know them, except for one wise guy. Time was short, though, and they didn't get all the training they needed.

Thinking that we would be at Lido di Roma for a while, we removed partitions from the bathrooms and set up tables to form a mess hall. That pleased Nick De Gaeta, who was in charge of the mess. We made frequent visits to

Rome, walking by the Coliseum where early Christians had been put to death and under the Arch, a memorial to Constantine's victory at the Milian Bridge.

Right after we arrived, I started getting chills and fever every other day. A nurse visited me and sent me to the American hospital downtown, where I was diagnosed positive with malaria. The medical officer ordered me to take five tablets of Atabrine, synthetic quinine. We had all been instructed to take one Atabrine a day, but I hadn't been taking them because I was afraid of what they might do to me. The bitter tablets made me nauseous, and some men who took them had more severe problems. I obeyed orders, though. Strangely, I didn't vomit and the pills helped the malaria. In later years Atabrine was withdrawn from use.

Several days later, First Sergeant Tony Dorsa asked for volunteers to enter an army track meet. I said to Tony, "Put me in the longest race you have." The six-mile race started and ended at the Mussolini stadium. I was doing pretty well, but two limeys who were letting me set the pace were dogging me. I thought I knew where the finish line was, but I kicked too soon. They passed me and I came in third. My buddies were there to cheer me in with cognac.

I met a blonde named Anita in Rome and spent some of my free time with her. One day when we were out together we passed by a large grocery store and heard screaming and crashing inside. The pasta ration was being handed out, and the shoppers were going berserk. I raised my pistol and pointed it toward the ceiling, but I didn't have to fire a shot. They all quieted down. I asked Anita to tell them to form a line. They did, and for some reason they let Anita get in front. Another time we were at a very large circular plaza that was surrounded by restaurants and bars. I summoned a horse and carriage for Anita and myself. Instantly a mob formed and charged us. Just as instantly the bars emptied and GIs came running to our rescue.

I have never tasted a better pizza than the ones I got in Rome. They were very large with very thin crusts covered with peppered marinara sauce. We stayed for several months and enjoyed ourselves immensely, never visiting, of course, the most interesting historical sights; not even the Vatican. Even though most of us thought that we wouldn't make it through the war alive, religion was not on our minds; at least not on mine. That came later.

I drilled the platoon in the usual manner during this time, but I think it went in one ear and out the other. In hindsight, I think my training should have been more intense. There should have been more discipline. Anyway, I knew they would find out the hard way. Those of us who had been in combat were probably on the easy side, knowing what they would have to go through, instead of the opposite.

Usually I would go to town with Jim, Danny, and Don Kammer. Once, Nick De Gaeta came with us. He didn't drink, and we got the bartender to give him some kind of drink that wouldn't taste of alcohol. He felt great until he started feeling bad. Jim and I got into trouble in Rome, and the MPs locked us up. Unfortunately, the MP Sergeant was an old acquaintance. "I remember you two from Belfast," he said. "You're going to rot in here." I pleaded with him to let me make one call to my battalion; he finally consented, and we were permitted to make the call. The adjutant, Lt. Bill Sullivan, answered the phone. We called him Sully because he was one of us; he had come up through the ranks. Colonel Yarborough gave the word, and his two scouts were out of there within the hour.

Our next mission was the invasion of southern France, an operation designed to relieve the pressure on the Normandy beachhead to the north. We took off from the airfields at Fallonica and Grosseto, north of Rome, at four-thirty in the morning on August 15, 1944. The Red Cross ladies offered us doughnuts as we boarded the planes, but I passed. Doughnuts were the last things on my mind. Our objective was Le Muy, several miles inland north of Saint Raphael.

We would be jumping just before dawn. I liked to stand in the door looking down at the countryside on our flights. On this night we were flying over clouds, but once in a while I could see through them to the water below. We were getting close, and I turned and told the green new lieutenant, Ferris Knight, who wore a beautiful red walrus mustache and had never seen action before, that we had been flying over water the last time I was able to see through the clouds. The light turned red, meaning "stand in the door," and Lieutenant Knight said, "Sergeant Fisco, what shall we do?" I hadn't seen an opening in the clouds in several minutes, but I knew that Le Muy was only about twelve miles inland; I had no reason to think that we were not over land. Just then, the light turned green and I said to the lieutenant, "Let's get it!"

As I descended, I prepared for water landing by slipping up into the seat of the harness and releasing the leg harness straps. This way, I could throw my arms upward and slip free and clear of the harness when I hit the water. The tops of the clouds below were solid white. As I passed through the clouds, I saw that I was indeed over water. We wore Mae West life vests, but we also carried at least a hundred pounds of arms and supplies. I screamed out to God to please bring me to land. Immediately a gust of strong, warm wind hit my back and blew me toward land. It was probably the *sirocco* coming from North Africa, but as far as I was concerned it was a breeze from Heaven. I pulled down on my two front risers and slipped landward. I landed on the steps of a villa and sprained my right ankle slightly. Since I had prepared for a water landing, there were no leg harness straps to support me, and my legs buckled under me. Sgt. Harvey Southerland of my company landed in water chest high.

Like the Avellino jump and the North Africa jump before it, this operation was one big blunder. The battalion was split. A Company, with Captain Siegel, and HQ Company jumped in Le Muy, the objective. The other half of the battalion—including my Company B, with Capt. Ralph Miller, and C Company, with Capt. Jesse Walls—jumped in Saint-Tropez on the French Riviera.

Captain Miller and sixteen men, including First Sergeant Tony Dorsa, drowned. They were in plane number one and had been given the green light over open water. The pilot must have been flying through dense, low fog. Captain Miller was the best jumper in the battalion, having jumped hundreds of times with the riggers. Since he couldn't see the water below him, he did not prepare for a water landing as I had done. The same must have been true for the other sixteen men in his planeload. Evidently, by the time they saw the water it was too late for them to inflate their Mae Wests. The life vests would probably have been ineffective anyway because of the heavy weight the men were carrying. Neither their bodies nor any of their equipment was ever found, although in later years I heard of an article of Captain Miller's being auctioned off in France. Captain Ernest ("Bud") Siegel and I have talked about it over the years, and he finds it difficult to believe that no trace was ever found of them because there were numerous fishermen in the area.

After eleven months of fighting in rugged terrain in Italy, where the enemy was always above us, landing in the Côte d'Azur of southern France was like jumping into Heaven. When I touched down there was just enough daylight to identify friend or foe at a short distance. My first encounter was with a tall young Frenchman carrying a bottle of wine. He greeted me and offered me the bottle. I refused and told him that I had to fight. Years later, I learned that this young man was François Coppola, age fourteen. His mother had sent him out with the wine to welcome us. He would become adjoint to most of the mayors in Saint-Tropez. When we were introduced years later in Saint-Tropez, I described my experiences there and mentioned that a young Frenchman had offered me a drink from a bottle of wine and that I had refused. His face lit up and he responded, "That was me."

As I moved inland, I came upon my first lieutenant, who was wounded, and about a dozen men from my company. I had now lost my captain and my senior lieutenant; Lieut. Ferris Knight was a green lieutenant who had never before seen action.

Most of C and B companies had jumped in the Sainte Anne area of St. Tropez, Colline de la Potence. (The 18th century-old Sainte Anne chapel is open only three times a year, and one is for the candlelight procession and ceremonial mass celebrating the invasion of southern France on August 15, the date of the Assumption of the Blessed Virgin Mary.) Some time later, Captain Walls and C Company were involved in the surrender of the German forces inside the citadel fortification. Sgt. Boggs Collins was sent forward to accept the surrender from a German colonel. When the colonel refused to surrender to a sergeant, Boggs raised his Tommy gun and said, "You'll surrender to this." The colonel and the remainder of the German detachment capitulated. The navy was offshore, ready to fire if needed.

As I said, HQ Company and A Company had landed on the intended objective in Le Muy. When a British colonel with his paratroopers failed in their attempt to take Le Muy, Captain Siegel and A and HQ companies of the 509th took it on the orders of Colonel Yarborough. The British colonel and his detachment were sent back to Italy.

The companies from Le Muy and Saint-Tropez converged at Frejus. From there on, we followed the coastal road, RN7, all the way to Nice. The first battle against rearguard action was for the château de La Napoule. We passed through Saint Raphael, climbed a four-hundred-meter mountain, descended, and then ascended up into the enemy positions. We attacked down the bald slope into machine-gun and small mortar fire, probably 40 mm. My two machine-gunners, Luksis and Knapp, took off to the left and began to set up the machine gun right out in the open. I yelled out to them, "Bring that gun back! We're still attacking." They paid no attention and set the gun up about 150 feet away. Snipers killed them immediately.

The unit in front of us was holding us up. Lieutenant Knight turned to me and said, "Sergeant Fisco, what do you think we should do?" "Continue right through them," I answered. The other unit was now under the cover of the forest, only about twenty yards away. "I'll have to get permission to move ahead," he said. I called to the remainder of the platoon behind me to protect themselves by piling stones around themselves. I surrounded myself with small boulders and lay down on my left side with my Tommy gun in my right hand cradled over my right hip. One small mortar had been firing repeatedly from a very close distance. I could hear it fire, and then hear the shells land. Then I heard one round go off and said to myself, "If I get over this one, I got the war made." I felt the pressure wave that preceded the shell. It landed on our Canadian radioman about six feet away from my head. His legs below the knees were still standing there, but the rest of him was gone. The shrapnel shattered the stock of my Tommy gun. One piece of shrapnel went halfway through the barrel, but I wasn't hurt.

Finally, the lieutenant told me that we could move ahead. I called to the men to move out. No one moved. I went back to find Victor Osborne, the medic, with his intestines on top of him. John Reiner was wounded. Between the dead and the wounded, I lost about a third of my platoon. That's when I started smoking cigars.

After the battalion had taken the ridge, which had been well fortified, we proceeded on foot farther along the coastal road. There was a huge dead, bloated German soldier lying face-up in the road. I almost kicked him as I walked by. It was a good thing I resisted. I later learned that the body was booby-trapped.

From then on, we were on and off trucks, stopping to fight the rearguard action and then moving ahead. Everywhere we went we were barraged with cheers, kisses, champagne, cognac, and wine. One of our stops was Antibes. The enemy had moved ahead, so we rested. We anchored one man at each machine gun and went into town. There was a dentist nearby who had two daughters. Jim made friends with one of the daughters, named Danny, and I borrowed a bicycle from the other one. I had never ridden a bike before. Going downhill, I put the front brakes on first, flipped over, and was temporarily knocked out. My upper lip was cut and bleeding, so I went to a nearby doctor. His prescription: grow a mustache. One of my eyes was bloodshot from the ordeal as well.

By the time I got back to my unit after having seen the doctor, I found that they had moved out and I had to catch up. From there all the way to Nice, it was on the trucks and off the trucks, French people waving and shouting, and more wine and champagne. The French Resistance kept us informed of when and where we could expect to meet with rearguard action.

We crossed the Var River into Nice on August 30. The river was shallow because it had not rained. That was good, because the retreating Germans had blown up the bridge. That night in Nice we stayed in a hotel. The next morning we proceeded on foot up the Moyenne Corniche, the middle road. We passed two women sunning in the tiny swimsuits for which the Riviera was famous (they would later be called bikinis). We continued on our way up to the Grande Corniche to Tête de Chien, the mountain overlooking Monte Carlo below.

There was a fort there that the Germans had occupied but vacated after heavy shelling by our navy. When we received instructions to advance to the fort, I took three men with me and we drove up in an old black four-door convertible; I wore a Maurice Chevalier-type straw hat that I had found. The fort was vacant. I wandered among the rocks below it and found an opening that looked down on peaceful Monte Carlo, enjoying its neutrality. The next day, mines were detected along the dirt road we had taken up to the fort.

We positioned ourselves, as I recall, at a monastery, where we stayed for a couple of days. The day or so after we entered Nice, we went up the hill to Cimiez. I went into a very small bar with a couple of 509th buddies. The bar was packed with military representatives from many different countries, including England and Ceylon. The Senegalese were reputed to cut enemies' ears off and hang them on a string. We sat down at a table, and right away there was a huge explosion. The .45 Colt revolver that I had taken from the GI in Naples had slipped out of my holster, and it went off when it hit the floor. The whole bar emptied out. Not a single person remained except the bartender, who had come out from behind the counter prepared to run for his life too. I went out on the sidewalk and tried to call the others back, but they just kept on going.

We were all getting tired of army rations, and the men had been trading their canned food to the French for fresh food. Lieutenant Ferris Knight wanted us to give our canned goods to the French rather than exchanging them. In any event, we needed supplies, and Lieutenant Knight asked me to take a driver and go down to Nice to get them. On the way back I met Monsieur Rubens, of the Rubens Brewery, driving a car carrying an icebox filled with beer. He took us to his brewery and gave us three cases of six percent beer (the public could buy only three percent alcohol). I promised chocolate for his children (and later returned with it) and took the much-appreciated beer back up to the platoon along with the rest of the supplies.

Then it was down the mountain, back through Nice, and up the Var River valley on National 202 heading for the Maritime Alps and Lantosque, some forty-five kilometers away. We stopped for the night below the village of Colomars at Pont de la Manda. There was a small wooden chapel nearby, and some of us entered to drop our packs. The church was empty. I walked up to the altar, there was no tabernacle, knelt, and thanked God for bringing me this far alive.

That afternoon, I was ordered to take seventeen men and liberate the village of Colomars just above us. I avoided taking the road and instead took the men up in a straight line. It was almost dark when we arrived, and villagers told us that there were no Germans there. The entire village turned out to greet us. They brought out a barrel of wine, and there was music and merriment. The villagers danced, and some of our boys may have danced as well; I don't recall. We were in a cleared area studded with olive trees on the edge of the road that passed through the center of town. I sat at the base of a tree waiting for everything to quiet down. Since the battalion was not moving out until the next morning anyway, I thought it safer to spend the night in the village and descend at daybreak. On returning the next morning, though, we found that the rest of the battalion had been awaiting our arrival and the officers were not pleased with my decision.

We drove on up to Lantosque, which became our center of operations for the next two months or so. Once we got off National 202 the roads got scary. There were hairpin turns, called *lacets* in French, and steep, precipitous sections through tunnels following the Vesubie River.

For the most part we were in high country. Lantosque, our battalion head-quarters and the gateway to the other mountain villages we controlled, was only four hundred forty-three meters high. La Bollene, the next village was at an altitude of seven hundred meters. We launched patrols from there to attack the Germans in Turini, altitude seventeen hundred meters. The next village was Belvedere, eight hundred meters, then Saint Martins Vésubie at one thousand meters. Four or five miles past Saint Martins was the Mercantour range, with peaks above three thousand meters.

I led several patrols up to Turini from La Bollene. Staff Sgt. Jim Nunn's unit had taken positions overlooking all the approaches to Lantosque. I developed a low-grade fever and was sent to our medical officer, who could not determine its cause. Doc Mullins sent me for further examination at the medical center several miles away. They did not find anything obvious, nor have any doctors since then. Ever since the war I have awakened once or twice a month with violent chills, no fever, that last about ten minutes. Doctors have no idea what causes them, but I think they are from the malaria I picked up in Italy.

I returned to the unit by way of Nice, where I stopped for a haircut in a little shop on the Mediterranean side of the Rue de France. As I was leaving the barber's chair I glimpsed a beautiful young French girl walking by. She was dressed in a pretty yellow-and-white cotton print dress with short sleeves and a pleated skirt that ended right at the dimples of her knees. I quickly paid the coiffeur, not waiting for change. The young girl had a good lead on me, but being an old roadrunner I quickly closed the gap. Being a runner had also given me a critical eye for shapely legs. I was definitely a legman.

The only thing neat about me that day was my haircut and my boots. My jump suit was shiny from wear, and my baggy pants had huge, sagging side pockets. My jacket, with its staff sergeant stripes, had four large pockets and a zippered slot in front of the neck that held a switch and hook blade. (I always made sure that was in place. Back at Fort Bragg, one of the fellows got hung up in the tail of the plane on a training jump. He cut himself loose with the switchblade, pulled his reserve, and made it down okay. Then he went to town on his motorcycle and got killed.) I had an army-issue .45 Colt semiautomatic holstered on my right hip and a holstered .45 Colt revolver (the one I took from the GI back in Naples) sticking out of my left trouser pocket. I was still sporting the large blood clot in my left eye from the bicycle episode in Antibes.

As I caught up to the young woman I called out in my one-year-of-high-school French mixed with a ten-months-in-Africa accent, "Ou allez-vous, mademoiselle?" To my surprise she stopped, turned, smiled, and answered me. I looked into her large, beautiful, clear brown eyes and said to myself, "This is my wife." I was twenty-four and a half years old, and until that moment I had had no intention of marrying anyone.

"Comment vous appelez-vous?" I asked her.

She answered, "Louise Cecchetti." Her beautiful, coppery chestnut hair was flowing to her shoulders. I complimented her pretty dress. She said that she had made it herself and was on her way to answer an ad for work as a seamstress.

I found out later that her previous employer, Mr. Tomas, was a prominent designer of women's clothing in Europe. The French had torn his factory apart after we had liberated Nice on August 28. They accused him of entertaining Italian army officers when the Italians occupied Nice, just before the Germans moved in.

Louise had started learning her trade by picking up pins in Mr. Tomas's atelier. Under the guidance of Mr. Tomas, she became a wizard at cutting as well as sewing.

I asked Louise if I could see her again and if she would give me her address. She said, "Oui," and I copied it down. I then did something very unusual for a paratrooper. I took off my original jump wings and pinned them onto her dress at the breast, being very careful not to touch her body. I had to lift the fabric in order to close the clasp safely. Years later, she told me it would have been curtains for me if I had made a wrong move.

When we parted, I was frightened that I would never see her again. As we were about to leave each other, I reminded her, "Demain soir?" She responded, "Oui," and smiled as we parted in different directions. I wanted to go with her. She later told me that she thought I looked like a gangster.

The next evening, John "Blackie" Johnson, the 509th's medic, drove me down to Nice in a medic vehicle. Blackie gave me half of one of our camouflaged nylon chutes that he had recovered on the jump and told me to give it to Louise. I don't know what made him do it. Neither of us had any idea of her creative ability and the speed with which she could make a dress. I brought it along with a carton of cigarettes for her father.

The winding, treacherous road to Lantosque followed the Vesubie River, which had cut its way through solid rock and carved out a bed hundreds of feet below the road. In order to stay to the right while driving down the blind turns we found ourselves within a foot of vertical rock that overhung the road in many places. It was more than a bit scary to be on the passenger side that night. Eventually, though, we were in downtown Nice, population about three hundred fifty thousand. Blackie had no problem finding 18 Ave Notre Dame, the apartment house where Louise's family lived. He pulled up to the curb and parked. All old apartment houses in Nice have elaborate entrance doors. This one was no exception. We passed through two huge, hand-carved walnut doors, entered a marble-and-tile hallway, and went straight back to a door leading to a courtyard and the family's ground-floor apartment. A white chicken pecked away at the ground, paying us no heed. We didn't have to knock. The door opened and Louise welcomed us in. She introduced me, and I introduced Blackie.

I met her mother and father. Her little three-year-old brother, Roger, his blonde hair in large curls, was clutching his dad's leg. Nine-year-old Henri was sitting on the steps leading to the second floor, doing his homework. Jeanot, age fifteen, walked in behind us. I found out later that he attended meetings of Franc-Tireurs et Partisans, a resistance organization in Nice. It was a dangerous activity. Louise told me she had seen a young FTP lad walking toward a bridge where she knew there was a German sentry. She heard shots; he was killed.

Louise was delighted with the parachute. She spread the panels of light green and dark green and immediately visualized what she would create and how. I still have the dress.

Her dad was a bit awkward with a full-length cigarette and tried to keep his stern composure when the children teased him. He worked in construction, especially on the bridges spanning the many ravines in the area. Louise's mother took care of the family. Both she and Mr. Cecchetti were caretakers for the apartment house.

GIs are seldom without chocolate bars and chewing gum. I had two chocolate bars sticking out of my pockets, and I gave them to the boys. Their eyes lit up. They had refrained from asking and were shy about taking them, but first Roger and then Henri accepted.

I asked Louise if she would go out to dinner with us and if she had a friend for Blackie. Yes, she said, there was Susie. Jeanot was dispatched around the corner to bring Susie to the apartment.

Blackie voiced his concern about the ten p.m. parking curfew, which was strictly enforced by the MPs. No problem. Jeanot swung the two gigantic entrance doors inward, and Blackie drove the Jeep inside. Jeanot closed the doors behind the Jeep, and the four of us went out to dinner. On a few other occasions, we stored the Jeep in the firehouse around the corner.

Several nights later, when I went for another visit, Louise's mother had dinner ready. The white chicken was nowhere in sight, and Louise's eyes were red. Only after we had finished dinner did I discover that the delicious *coq* we had eaten was Louise's pet chicken.

As I got to know the family and their friends, I learned that times had been both difficult and perilous for them. But that hadn't stopped them from doing what was right. The Cecchettis' neighbor, Madame Pochi, who had an antique shop on the corner, hid a Jewish family so the Nazis could not send them to a concentration camp. Louise's mother would stand in line for food for them. Louise's aunt was married to a Jew. He hanged himself from a tree in front of their home in Nice when he learned the Nazis were coming to get him.

I started seeing Louise on a fairly regular basis and spent quite a bit of time with her family. I learned that Louise's mother saved rainwater in a rain barrel in the corner of the courtyard to wash Louise's hair. I also learned that people from the theater would occasionally come to Louise's home trying to persuade Louise to audition for roles in the movies. Louise's mother always turned them away.

Louise told me that one night during the German occupation, before the

Allied forces arrived in Nice, she and Susie were taken at bayonet point to peel potatoes for the Germans. They were ordered to return. Susie did, but Louise did not. She also told me of being awakened from a sound sleep by the sound of our planes flying overhead on the morning of the jump. She knew they were not German planes because the engines didn't sputter. The whole family was so excited that they couldn't go back to sleep.

Occasionally Johnny McDonald, who became friends with Susie, would accompany me on my visits to Nice. At the time, Louise was so thin that I would take her from restaurant to restaurant trying to find enough food for her. Many establishments were short on supplies, and getting enough to eat was often difficult. On our dates, Louise and I would either go to the movies, which I didn't much care for, or stop at one of the numerous cabarets. One evening, Johnny and Susie were with us in a restaurant and I was drinking cognac. Louise said, "You take one more and I'm leaving." I took one more and she went home. They told me that I tried to poke out a horse's eyes on my way back to her house.

On another occasion, in a cabaret on Jean Médecin at the corner of Notre Dame where we stopped for a drink, a soldier who had overindulged threw a lit cigarette at our table, then stood up and charged at us. I put out my left fist and he flattened out. We got out just before the MPs arrived.

Occasionally Nick De Gaeta would drop off a carton of our best rations for Louise's family. The flour, sugar, and coffee were difficult—if not impossible—to find elsewhere. One day, I noticed that they had not yet started to use the rations. Perhaps they were afraid someone was going to come and demand their return. I told them to go ahead. After that, Louise's mother would make gnocci, which I loved. Nick also saved the leftover bacon grease for me, one can at a time. I bought Louise a fox fur coat with those cans of grease.

By this time, Louise occupied most of my waking thoughts. One day in Lantosque, after a few drinks, Joe Laudicini and I decided to drive down to Nice. He had "borrowed" a Jeep on the Moyenne Corniche that had a cushioned right front seat. It must have been at least a colonel's Jeep. I sat in the right front on the floor; having removed the cushioned seat for fear that the Jeep might be recognized. Blackie Schwartz and George Broderick were in the back seats. When we crossed the Vesubie at Saint Jean la Rivière, Joe swerved and hit a two-foot parapet on the left side of the bridge. I found myself alone in the Jeep. The other three had been catapulted sixty feet down the riverbank. I climbed down to them and helped George back up. The other two made it up by themselves. I commanded a passing civilian truck to stop and ordered the driver to take us to the medical center in Cimiez, Nice. Joe had about a dozen stitches sewn in his scalp. Blackie was badly shaken up and slept that night in a small-attached bedroom in Louise's family's apartment. George suffered a serious spinal injury and never regained the use of his legs.

Shortly after that episode, I made friends down in Nice with Monsieur Mignon, who agreed to take me up to Lantosque in his car. The first trip was a long one. The wood fire that powered his car went out halfway up, and he had to rebuild the fire. When we arrived in Lantosque, I gave him a can of gasoline. From then on, whenever he drove me to Lantosque I would replenish the gas.

Once he drove Louise up to Lantosque to see me. When Louise stepped out of the car, a shell hit nearby. She was wearing the parachute dress, and Captain Siegel confronted her and asked where she got the parachute. He tried to get her address, implying that he intended to investigate. One of the fellows standing nearby told him that she was my girlfriend. He apologized, and Louise and I walked to where we could sit and talk on a low wall nearby. Then M. Mignon got his complimentary gas and drove her back to Nice.

During this period, my visits to Nice were curtailed for a while. Lt. Harry Pritchett had offered me a two-day pass, and I had asked if he could make it three days. Over three days would be a furlough. I had been in the service five years and never had a pass, and I asked for just one more day. Lieutenant Pritchett, who had not been with the 509th very long and did not know me well, turned down my request. I stayed three days anyway, and when I returned he had me confined in a little garage in Lantosque under the custody of Sgt. Bob Erickson while I awaited a court-martial.

During my confinement Robert Lee (Bobby) Holcomb Jr., who had been with me several times to Louise's house, asked me if I would mind if he took Louise out to dinner when Johnny went with Susie. "Go ahead, Bobby," I told him; "all's fair in love and war." He was later killed leading the battalion's attack before Saint Vith in Belgium.

Charles and Maria Auda ran the bistro that fronted the garage in Lantosque where I was confined. Their one-year-old son, Paulin, was very ill with a high temperature, and the attending physician had given up on him. I asked the Audas if they would allow our doctor to give Paulin penicillin, which was very new at the time. They agreed, and Doc Mullins also consented and administered the penicillin. The next morning Paulin was back to normal. Many years later, I visited Lantosque and found Paulin, now in his fifties and a very strong and healthy man.

The battalion moved again, this time up to Piera Cava. Our new location was a very short distance from Turini, where the Germans were operating out of caves. Once again I was confined, this time pending a court-martial. My "jail" was a four-foot-high chicken coop under the front porch of a house. I was put to work sawing logs while awaiting my trial. I wasn't present, but when the trial was over, Captain Howland came by and said, "Fisco, if it wasn't for me they were going to hang you." I wasn't hanged, but I was reduced to private.

The snow was deep in Piera Cava, but fortunately an infantry unit came and relieved us. The night before our departure, Monsieur Mignon brought Louise up for a visit. The platoon was staying in a house, and Louise stayed overnight. The next morning, in heavy rain, the platoon loaded up on a truck for the return to Nice. Louise got in the back of the truck with me. Captain Siegel got out of the cab, came back, and told Louise and me to get in front. He went back and rode in the rear of the truck with the men. Back in North Africa, in Kairouan, Captain Siegel had made Jim and I dig a six-foot by six-foot by six-foot hole as punishment in lieu of a court-martial. We had come a long way together.

In Nice, our battalion crossed back over the Var and then drove inland up into a rest area at La Gaude, in the Maritime Alps at the foot of the Baou de Saint Jeannet, a very high vertical cliff above the town of Saint Jeannet. We slept in tents.

I could still visit Louise in Nice, although it meant crossing the Var River. Most often, my visits with Louise coincided with Johnny McDonald's visits with Susie. Johnny had jumped with the Pathfinders, whose mission was to guide us in. One special evening the four of us ate at Christy's (later called Brasserie Victoria) on Blvd. Victor Hugo. During dinner I proposed to Louise in French. I'm sure my French was not as good then as it later became, but she said yes. Many, many years later I asked Louise if she recalled my proposal. She didn't remember it at all. I think she may have been in the habit of saying "yes" to most of my comments, even those she didn't understand. Anyway, I thought she knew what she had agreed to and I set about getting the engagement and wedding rings.

Johnny and I went to the jewelry store on Avenue Jean Médecin in search of a *bagge de fiancaille* (engagement ring). The jeweler was not interested in money. He pointed to two showcases and said, "For four cartons of cigarettes you can take your pick." I chose a small pearl-and-diamond engagement ring. The government controlled the cost of the gold wedding rings, and each had to be weighed and paid for. I think they cost me about fifteen dollars each.

Abbé Pontremolli, who had been Louise's pastor and one of her school-teachers, arranged our wedding date. Initially he chose a date after December 8, 1944, but when I found out that the battalion would be leaving on December 9 for Viller Cotteret, northeast of Paris, the wedding date was changed to December 8. That day is the day of the Immaculate Conception, on which no one is permitted to be married, but Abbé Pontremolli waved his hands and said, *"C'est la guerre."* Jimmy Nunn was my best man. In those days, non-Catholics were not allowed to stand as best men in Catholic ceremonies, but once again Abbé Pontremolli waved his hands and said, *"C'est la guerre."*

Louise and I were married in the chapel of Nôtre Dame, a huge, beautiful church at the foot of the Avenue Nôtre Dame on Jean Médecin. There was a little suspense when Jim fumbled for the rings. Twenty-five years later, Louise and I visited Abbé Pontremolli, who had by then retired. "I'm glad to see at least one of my weddings worked out," he told us.

The wedding dinner was at Louise's home. Ken Barton, Jimmy Nunn, and a few others were present along with Louise's family. That night we stayed at the Mediterranean Hotel.

The front line in Antibes, France, fall 1944. I'm driving and Nunn is the passenger.

In Lantosque, France. The owner of the bistro, Charles Auda, poured the drinks and supplied us with pasta. Bobby Holcomb, front left, was killed in St. Vith, Belgium, leading the attack. Behind him, an Italian partisan who was killed in Turini on patrol. In the back right is Marsh. I am holding the bottle.

TROUPES AÉROPORTÉES EN INDOCHINE

*1ᵉʳ Bataillon
de Parachutistes Coloniaux*

CITATION

Le Chef de Bataillon MONIEZ,

Commandant le 1ᵉʳ Bataillon de Parachutistes Coloniaux

Certifie que le Caporal CECCHETTI Jean

a été cité à l'ordre de la DIVISION
par OG n°64 en date du 29.7.1954 du Col CREVECOEUR, Cdt. les
Forces Terrestres du LAOS.

TEXTE:

" Chef d'équipe de voltigeurs. A fait l'admiration de
tous par un sang-froid extraordinaire et un total mépris du
danger. Le 8 Janvier 1954, à BAN NA KHAM (province de SAVAN-
NAKHET - Laos), a d'abord participé à l'assaut furieux donné
sur les lisières Nord-Ouest, puis, avec le même calme, le
même courage, a assuré seul, la protection du décrochage de
son groupe.

" A continué à donner dans les opérations qui ont suivi
la preuve de sa haute valeur de Chef et de Combattant ".

CETTE CITATION COMPORTE L'ATTRIBUTION DE LA
CROIX DE GUERRE DES T.O.E. AVEC Etoile d'ARGENT.

S.P. 76.036, le 20 Septemb...

Louise's brother Sgt. Jean, a French paratrooper, was killed in the
Dien Bien Phu (Indochina) battle and awarded a citation for leading
his men and holding off the enemy's violent assault.

Chapter 8

The Battle
of the Bulge:
We Retake Sadzot

The next morning December 9th the battalion moved by train to Chateau Francois 1er Villers-Cotteret. I sent Louise a telegram as soon as we arrived and she came up to see me. We spent every moment together that we could; never knowing how much time there would be for us. The trains were all occupied by the military, and when Louise boarded, the MP Sergeant said to all, "This is a GI's bride. Hands off." Louise played cards with the soldiers all the way there.

A butcher had told me of a vacant upstairs apartment in an old house owned by a very old lady, and I arranged for the two of us to stay there. The rooms were dusty, and Louise started cleaning as soon as she arrived. We were there only for a couple of days. One morning Louise awoke very early, about six in the morning, crying. She didn't want to tell me why, but finally she said, "I dreamed you were wounded in your left arm and your wedding ring was changed to your right hand."

It was very early, but for some reason I decided it was best to get back to the battalion at the old château. As I approached, I saw ten-ton open trucks at the gate with their motors running. The guard said, "Fisco, we're moving out." I dashed back to Louise and told her, then returned to grab my backpack and weapon and load on the truck.

Louise returned home through Paris, stopping at her aunt's. On her train trip from Paris to Nice the conductor tried to confiscate all the cigarettes and other luxury items she carried in her luggage. She told him off, letting him know that her husband was an American soldier.

It was snowing as we drove through the night, and we all huddled under a tarp. I was in the front of the truck next to the cab. We were heading into the Battle of the Bulge. Now that I was married, I had to decide whether or not to continue giving the Germans hell. I thought for a while and then decided I would.

The enemy was all around, but we managed to get through. We unloaded and reloaded onto two-and-a-half-ton trucks and proceeded into Manhay. We jumped off the trucks shooting. The snow was deep. Tanks were shooting it out all around us. We pushed the enemy back about one hundred yards. There may have been two divisions coming at us. I saw the barrel of a Schmeisser submachine gun protruding from the back of a tree trunk. I was facing my target and had the vertical raise, centered on my belly button; all I had to do was squeeze the trigger. His burst kicked up the dirt about ten feet in front of me. I had killed him as his body came into view. He had the windage but didn't live long enough to get the elevation. I don't know why but I was always so calm whenever there was a shoot-out. I'm not a calm person.

I was digging in with another paratrooper in the dark. We were encountering heavy small-arms fire. I started to tell him when to start and stop, but I gave up since he was always moving in the right direction. The bullets were coming in behind him and then in front of him as he shoveled. Someone called out to pull back because another of our companies was replacing us. I picked out a star to orient myself and decided to go back a ways and then cut over to the road to avoid German-manned American tanks. I found myself in Capt. Jesse Wall's C Company, which was also being pulled back, and I made it back to our location. The rest of the company returned, depleted in strength.

Our battalion was ordered to dig in and rest in a strategic position on top of a hill east of the village of Clerheid, above the Grandmenil Erezee Road, overlooking the level farmland of Sadzot and Erezee. We didn't know it, but the enemy had overrun the area. German troops had broken through Sadzot and were threatening our corps area's 105-mm howitzers. At about four in the morning we were called out to counterattack and retake Sadzot. The date was December 29, 1944.

Captain Walls ordered me to lead the attack. We descended our hill. As I crossed the road, I saw hundreds of our infantrymen taking cover in the gully that ran alongside it. I wondered if they noticed that I had fewer men following me than there were of them hiding along the road. We attacked with two tank destroyers and four M-5 light tanks.

As I advanced I came across a disabled American tank, and I jumped up and fired what remained in its machine gun. Ammo was short. Before the attack, all our ammunition had been collected and redistributed, seventy rounds each. I had had to give up my six thirty-round clips. I was alone at this point. C Company was right behind me, now forming a skirmish line. On continuing, I saw a hand sticking out of the ground. I grabbed the hand and pulled, and out came a live GI. Next to him was another GI, also buried and alive. They were from the 87th Mortar Battalion and had hidden themselves from the Germans in a compost heap.

Other companies of our battalion were advancing on our right. There was B, A and HQ. We pushed the enemy out of the open farmland and toward the wood line just ahead. Captain Walls was with most of the company off to my right out in the open and back a little. He called out to me, "Fisco, I'm making you sergeant as of today. Take us in."

I called back, "I'll take you in, Captain. Get the men out of that open field and follow me." I was in a narrow, shallow gully alongside a very small dirt road. The captain had been in a dangerously exposed position that was fenced in for livestock. As we moved up into the wood line, the four M-5's came up. I sent two of them around to Captain Walls, who was in the woods off to my left, and told the two M-5s with me to alternate in front of us and push through the woods. We pushed the Germans out. I saw Staff Sgt. William F. "Bill" Withem go down about seventy-five feet off to my left. I could tell he was dead before he hit the ground.

One of the M-5 tanks came to a stop in front on a rise in the ground. The driver raised the hatch and was killed instantly. The enemy counterattacked, as they always did. I was in a prone position behind a tree, looking around its left side. I emptied a thirty-round clip, and then started to reload, shifting to the right as I did. Something that felt like a baseball bat hit me in the left elbow. Lt. Joseph Viteritto, who was at a tree behind me, called out, "Fisco, you're hit." I answered, "I know. In the left elbow!"

I started back, and one of the 509ers helped me. I don't remember his name, but I think he had a mustache. He held me up by the right arm and walked me back. The pain was terrible. The bullet had traveled eight inches up through the length my left elbow and exposed the nerve. Medic Joe Hoben met us. He shot me with morphine in the left shoulder right through my jump jacket and then took me to the medics. I told them I was thirsty. They couldn't find any water to give me. I said, "My canteen." They checked it; it was frozen. In his book *Stand in the Door*, Charlie Doyle said that the temperature that day was zero degrees Fahrenheit.

I remember nothing after that until I woke up at night on a cot on the floor of a large warehouse in Liège. Hundreds of wounded GIs lay all around me, so many that the cots were almost touching each other. I had an itch under my left arm. When the male nurse passed by, I managed to whisper loud enough for him to hear me. I asked him if he could please scratch me under the left arm. He said, "Sure." On examining me he found my cot full of blood. They immediately carried me down to surgery, giving me blood plasma on the way. I started to revive on reaching the operating room. I guess they started tying off veins. The wound was about eight inches long through the length of the elbow.

I asked why my wedding ring had been changed to my right hand. The response was that it would have stopped the circulation and that they had had a difficult time removing it. The next thing I knew, I was on the floor of a depot awaiting a train to Paris. From there I would be flown to England. A Frenchman was standing nearby in the depot, and I asked him to send Louise a note telling her that I was wounded but okay. He took down Louise's address, and Louise told me later that she received the note. Although I didn't find out until later, Louise was in Paris the day I went through in an ambulance. Marty Galuskin, who had been wounded as well, was with me on the Red Cross train to Paris. On the way, German fighters strafed our train.

The 509 received an Airborne HQ citation for assisting in slowing the enemy thrust toward Liege and from cutting the Grandmenil Erezee Rd. I spent three and a half months in a hospital in England before returning to France. My cast was removed, and I asked my surgeon, a Dr. Smith from Texas, if it was okay for me to move any part of the arm. He said, "If you can move any part of that arm, go right ahead." All the weightlifting I had done back in Panama and at the Brooklyn army base paid off. I quickly started pulling and pushing my left forearm, gripping it with the right hand. The progress was noticeable. Every morning the nurse would stuff about three feet of Vaseline gauze through the wound above and below the elbow to prevent rapid healing. I was given pain medication, but it didn't always work very well. One night the pain was severe and I couldn't get the nurse to come. I got up and walked to the back room where the nurse would be and found her sitting on the lap of one of the male nurses. I asked her to please bring me my medication.

I needed a shave, but all I had was an old double-edged razor. I tried sharpening it on a leather belt, but that didn't help. I was also thinking that a good, stiff drink would be nice. I heard about a pub a short distance from the hospital. I put on a raincoat, made a hole under the fence, and sneaked out under the wire carrying a small container under my coat. I went to the pub several times. Usually, I would sit at a table and then go up to the bar a few times for Scotch. I would put most of the drinks into my little container, have one for myself, and carry the rest back to the ward. On my last trip there were two Englishmen at the bar talking loudly and without much good to say about Americans. In his book *Bloody Clash at Sadzot,* Bill Breuer said that I punched a major. Obviously it was a typographical error. I have never punched any officer. In the army regimen we were disciplined and had respect for officers. My left arm was in a sling. I walked up and belted one of them with my right hand. He turned out to be the mayor. Anyway, I was court-martialed in the hospital, again without being present, and fined. I guess the nurses turned me in for bringing scotch in to the other wounded men. They weren't like the American battlefield nurses in Italy.

I was hospitalized for about three and a half months. The soldier in the bed next to mine told me that he lay wounded on the battlefield, under fire, until someone came and picked him up and carried him to a Jeep. That someone was Gen. George Patton. I have always thought that we should have listened to General Patton and kept on going right through Russia. Then there would not have been any iron curtain.

Dr. Smith wanted to send me home with eighty percent disability. I told him that I had left my French war bride in France and would like to return to my outfit. I talked him into letting me go back to France with my wound still oozing fluid, and even though I could hardly use my arm.

When I got back to France, I was put in the 505th Parachute Infantry Regiment of the 82nd Airborne Division at Suippes, France. The handful of 509ers left after the Battle of the Bulge were all disbanded and placed in the 82nd. There was no love lost between the 82nd and the 509th. I really don't know why. We had more battle awards than they did, but that shouldn't have made a difference. I believe that Gen. Matthew Ridgeway, the 82nd airborne commander, was responsible for disbanding the 509th. I heard from Bob Erickson that General Ridgeway had wanted to integrate the 509th into the 82nd earlier, but Col. Yarborough refused to give in. This may have been the root of the problem. Good for General Yarborough. We used to call the 82nd the 82nd "Chairborne" Division. I wish I could change my official discharge from the 505th Parachute Infantry Regiment to the 509th Parachute Infantry Battalion. I think it's possible. Charles Doyle said it was. I believe General Yarborough was responsible for forming the new 509 regiment.

While I was at Suippes I heard that furloughs to Nice were available, so I applied for one. I was refused and told to come back next week. I did, and the same thing happened. This went on for several weeks. First I was told that I needed more time overseas, which was ridiculous. Then I was told that the furloughs were being given to those with medals. I told them I had medals, but I still didn't get a furlough to go to Nice.

Finally, when the 82nd was being sent to occupy Germany, I went on sick call. The medical officer was a colonel. When I rolled up my sleeve and exposed my still-oozing wound, he said, "What are you doing out of the hospital with an open wound? You stay back here. You're not going into occupation."

So I stayed in Suippes when the 82nd left. I sent Louise a telegram, and she joined me for a thirty-day honeymoon. We stayed at Monsieur and Madame Gaston Loche's house. Our mattress was made of feathers one foot deep. I found out later that I am allergic to feathers, dust, and mold. I never noticed it at the time.

Sergeant Lucky would drive Louise and me each day in a Jeep to visit the old Battle of the Marne positions where our boys fought in World War I. The trenches were still there, the soil was yellow gravel, there was nothing green and the villages were still buried. There was no grass. What a horrible war. The poppies around the graves always stirred your emotions.

Lucky was in charge of the whole rear echelon, including the prisoners of his own 82nd Division. The prisoners would save some of their food for Louise. Soldiers had no problem getting enough to eat, but food was in short supply for civilians. Mr. Loche constantly nagged us for *ravetaillement* (groceries). He didn't want money, just food. Lucky took care of that.

One day Lucky drove us back to the post in the Jeep. Gen. James Gavin flagged us down. Lucky promptly stood up and saluted with his shirttails hanging out. General Gavin told him, "Put those shirt tails back in and go and get back into proper uniform." Then the general addressed me: "Who is that woman in the Jeep?" I answered, "That's my wife, sir." He asked, "Where did you get permission to marry her?" I answered, "I'm out of the 509, sir." He said, "Oh. Get back in the Jeep and take her where you were going and get back."

I had never driven before, but I slid behind the wheel, grabbed the gearshift, and headed back to our house, bucking and grinding the gears the whole way. I had to drive through a bunch of gypsies; anyway, I did what the general told me to do.

The 82nd Division returned, and the men with the most points were being sent back to the States to be discharged. I had the most points of all; I think it was more than one hundred fifty-seven. My father used his printing skills and made a poster with my photo and the number one hundred seventy, and it was posted on the wall of the Cambria Heights Bar and Grill back home (some of my time in the regular army had counted toward points). Before I left, someone from the 82nd Division handed me my Silver Star, which should have been presented to me at a formation. Capt. Jesse Walls had given it to me for Sadzot.

I accompanied Louise to Reims to put her on the train for Paris and then Nice. She had one suitcase. We went from door to door in Reims trying to find a place to stay for the night. Everyone who answered my knock closed the door in our faces, thinking that Louise was a prostitute. I was told by a GI to see the town major (a US lieutenant). I found him. I explained everything to him, telling him we needed a place for the night and that Louise was my wife. I started to show him our papers; he waved them aside and said, "You don't have to show me anything. I can tell by looking at you." He gave us the address of a place where we could stay the night. The next morning I accompanied Louise to the train. It was raining. It seemed like it always rained when we parted. I wouldn't see her again for eight months.

I returned to the post and left for the States the next day, stopping at what I think was Camp 20 Grand. The departure camps all had cigarette brand names. The fellows in my tent had a big soup pot boiling over a fire, throwing in old shoes to make soup.

Nick De Gaeta returned with me on the same Liberty ship the "Marine Devil". As usual, I was a bit seasick on the return. I had my semiautomatic .45 with me one day when we were standing at the rail. I showed it to Nick and told him I was going to heave it. He said, "Give it to me. I'll take it." I threw it into the sea. I had had enough killing.

Last Name	First Name	Middle Initial	Serial No.	Grade
FISCO	RICHARD	D.	6973808	PVT.

Organization	Foreign	Others
COMPANY "C", 509th PARACHUTE INFANTRY BATTALION		

Headquarters	Station or APO	G.O. No.	Section	Date
HQ, XVIII CORPS (AIRBORNE)	109	7	I	18 JANUARY 45

Type of Award	Posthumous	DO NOT WRITE IN COLUMN BELOW
SILVER STAR	NO	

Oak-Leaf Clusters	Number	Posthumous	
			Type of Personnel
			Country Serving

By Command of	Amended	Revoked
MAJ. GEN. RIDGWAY		

Major Code

Type Organ

Parent Unit No.

P. U. Type

Residence

Arm or Service

Grade

Component

Nativity

Race & Citizen

CITATION

For gallantry in action on 29 December 1944, near Sadzot, Belgium.
Private FISCO, while acting as first scout for his company, became
separated from the rest of his company because of intense enemy
machine gun fire. Subsequently he assembled, on the right flank of
the company, ten men who had been similarly separated from the
main body. With this group, Private FISCO engaged a nest consisting of three enemy machine guns. Although injured by enemy artillery fire, Private FISCO continued on his mission until it was
accomplished. Private FISCO displayed unusual leadership in the
organization of the group and in leading them into the attack on the
machine gun position.

Entered military service from New York City.

Citation Date

Day | Month | Yr.
Award

Recomm. | Recv'd
Approval Date

Day | Month | Yr
Citation Station

Approval Station

Posthumous

Foreign Award

Country | Type

WD, AGO Form No. 0-
1 October 1943

To: Machine Records Branch, AGO

I earned a Silver Star for leading the attack on Anzio on December
29, 1944. C company retook Sadzot.

Left to right: Cpt. Carlos Coolidge "Doc" Alden (he escaped the Nazis twice), Lt. Morton Katz (Col. ret.) and Cpt. Charles Howland. Katz and his kittens were in charge in S2 scout at Venafro. Howland wanted to see how S2 operated on patrol at Venafro. We captured two for him. He was killed at St. Vith.

On honeymoon in Suippes, France, May of '45. Louise holds a bunny named Suippe Pea. The bunny died the day Louise left. She had been feeding it.

Louise in her wedding dress on our thirty-day honeymoon.

Chapter 9

A Confused Gun Fighter Returns

After a pass to visit home, I was discharged from the U.S. Army at Fort Dix on June 17, 1945. I was lean and tough, and my skin was weathered brown from exposure to the elements. When I received my separation papers I was asked to reenlist, but I declined because I was now married. With my separation pay of six hundred sixty-nine dollars and thirty-nine cents in my pocket, I headed to my parents' home in Cambria Heights, Queens.

First, though, I stopped off in the city to shop for presents. I think I spent most of my separation pay on a yellow gold wristwatch with diamonds and rubies and a twelve-carat gold necklace and bracelet for Louise, along with pocketbooks for my mother and Louise, and a bottle of whiskey and box of cigars for my father. I almost missed my stop at the train station in Saint Albans. I threw everything out the window and then slid out myself as the train pulled out.

My dad was a serious horseplayer and a member of the Doghouse Club at the Cambria Heights Bar & Grill. He kept statistics and charts, and he knew the results of all the horse races from one year to the next. One day he said to me, "Rick, let's go to the track. These three horses won years ago on the same day: Lord Boswell, Chief Barker, and Star Pilot." He called his friend Charlie, who drove us to Belmont in his limo (my dad didn't drive). All three horses won. Dad parlayed all his money each race. I bet ten dollars on each race. He picked another winner in the fifth race, and I picked a winner, Fire Warden, in the last race. Dad won more than six hundred dollars and couldn't wait to tell his friends in the Doghouse Club all about it.

I longed to have Louise with me, but her arrival date was still indefinite. She had been pregnant when I had to leave her behind but had a miscarriage. I was so worried about her that I could barely function. I was having a drink at the local bar on a Sunday morning when a neighbor who was a banker walked in after mass to have an aperitif. He sat by me and said, "Rich, are you worried about when Louise is coming over?" He got out his pocket missal and opened it to a page that showed Jesus crossing the Red Sea. He said, "You have to read between the lines. She'll be here the first week of January in 1946." I was skeptical, but you never know who is praying for you and what might happen.

I decided it was time to search for employment. I had a wife to support. My first visit was to the Staten Island Institute of Arts and Sciences in Saint George on Staten Island. Mr. Leng offered me an assistant curator ship for $1,700 a year. I thanked him, declined, and then asked if I could look at Mr. Davis's insect collection on the top floor. On inspecting the boxes of insects, as I used to do regularly, I found that dermestid beetle larvae had invaded many of the boxes and were destroying the collection of mounted insects. I was very concerned. Mr. Davis was responsible for naming many insect species of cicadas and the collection was a very valuable one.

I left the museum and went directly to the American Museum of Natural History in New York City to see Dr. Chapin. When I notified him of the condition of Mr. Davis's collection, he told me he would immediately have it moved to the American Museum. Dr. Chapin also noticed a bald spot the size of a quarter on the back of my neck that had been there since I had a haircut in Italy. He scanned the pages of a book he took down from a shelf and told me to put iodine on the spot.

I had another reason for visiting Dr. Chapin. I was hoping he could help me fulfill my ambition to study entomology at Cornell University. I had known

Dr. Chapin through the monthly meetings at the Staten Island Institute of Arts and Science I had attended before entering the service. I used to take over Mr. Davis's job of making coffee for the group. I told Dr. Chapin about the death of Peter Crowe who was killed on the tail gun of a Flying Fortress. He knew about it. He wrote me a letter of introduction to the Entomology Department at Cornell, so I decided to give the matter some serious thought. I compared the government's allocation for schooling to the cost of Cornell and decided it was insufficient. Looking back, I wonder if I made the right decision. Louise could have done some sewing and I could have worked part time while I was in school.

Louise arrived the first week of January 1946, eight months after I returned to the States and right when the banker had predicted. She had made repeated visits to the American embassy in Marseille, staying overnight at a convent each time. Finally, when the paperwork came through, Louise left for her aunt's home in Paris from the Garre de Lyons. This aunt's husband was Jewish and hanged himself when the Nazis came for him at his home in Nice. From Paris Louise left from Garre D'Orsay for Le Havre, where she boarded the *Marques du Comilla,* a two-stacker.

They stopped at the frontier port of Bilbao. Here passengers were momentarily discharged. Portugese customs inspectors checked the papers of those going to America. They threatened not to let her onboard until the last minute, poor thing.

I paid about $700 to the Thomas Cook Agency for her trip, borrowing the money from my father. Ironically, a week later all the GI war brides were brought home on a Liberty ship free of charge.

When she was in Spain, Louise noticed people staring at her. She finally approached someone in the hotel where the Thomas Cook travel agency had booked her and asked why everyone was looking at her. It was because of the bobby socks she was wearing, the person told her. In Spain, only loose women wore them.

Although I was worried that she would be seasick, Louise had a pleasant voyage. The ship had a stopover in Havana, which she really enjoyed, but it wasn't very good preparation for winter in the northern United States. When she arrived in New York it was ten degrees Fahrenheit and the ship took half a day to get into the pier because the river was frozen over.

A neighbor had driven me to meet Louise. She was beautiful and had gained weight on the voyage. She had not gotten sea sick like the others and had even eaten their food. We stayed upstairs in the finished attic of my parent's house at 120-03 223rd Street, Cambria Heights, Queens. Louise tried hard to be a good daughter-in-law, but there is always friction when two women share a house. My friends loved her. Everyone said that they had never seen a woman so beautiful and so friendly. She spoke English perfectly in one year but with an accent. She said she watched people's lips. The first week, my mother sent Louise to the butcher for a chicken, and Louise asked for a "kitchen."

We wanted a place of our own, but there were no apartments available for returning veterans. My mother helped me buy a bedroom set with a beautiful vanity. I joined the 52.20 Club, the government's one-year monthly allowance to vets, and we moved to a single room in Jamaica. When our son was born we moved back in with my parents.

Louise developed terrible itching all over her body when she became pregnant; I had to help her scratch continually. The problem was PUPPS (the acronym for Pruritic Urticarial Papules of Pregnancy), a condition for which there is still no effective treatment, and she was told that it would most likely reoccur with each succeeding pregnancy. Our son, Richard James—the James after Jim Nunn—was born October 22, 1946. When Jim's second daughter was born to his first wife, they named her Melinda Louise (who is the editor of my story) after Louise. Although we had planned on a big family, Louise would have no more children.

Still looking for a place of our own, I heard that barracks were being erected for veterans in Jackson Heights, Queens. We filled out an application. So did many other vets, and our chances didn't look good at first. I told the individual in charge, "You better have a list and you better make sure you have our name at the top." I don't know how much good that did, but we were finally accepted and moved in. For the first few nights, we used the stainless steel kitchen sink as an improvised cradle for our son, and then we placed his crib in the bedroom. I put up Howdy Doody wallpaper and we purchased a Taylor Tot stroller. Louise and I slept in a hideaway bed in the living room. Our bed was against Smitty's wall (Emanuel Smith, an attorney, and his wife, Bee). The apartment's heat came from a permanently installed heater that was fed kerosene from the outside.

For a while we had a Peeping Tom in the barracks that would stand on the kerosene storage drums at the rear bathroom windows and peek inside. Jim Wilson, a neighbor (82nd Airborne, discharged), walked down to the office with his shotgun to complain and try to scare the manager into action.

The sidewalks in the barracks were about ten feet wide—wide enough for vehicles—and each building had four units. This was the era of the baby boom, and there was hardly a unit without children. A cabby who lived at the end of the block was always speeding through. I let him know that he was endangering the lives of the children, but he kept it up. He was tall and lanky, over six feet to my five feet eight, but I weighed about one hundred and sixty pounds and had a twenty-eight-inch waist I caught him getting out of his car, and we went at it. He finally called it quits and we never had any problems thereafter.

The Lagutskis—Eddy, Reba, and their three children Peggy, Carol, and Eddy (Butchy)—lived directly opposite us on 14th Walk. Little Carol had something lodged in her throat one day and had difficulty breathing. I picked her up and ran to the doctor's office about a block away. When I got there she was breathing clearly. Evidently the running had dislodged the object.

A peddler used to pass through the barracks with his vegetable truck. I happened to be watching one day and saw a little girl being run over by his right rear wheel. She was wrapped around the tire and dropped off when he moved forward. Then she got up and walked away. No one would believe me when I told them what I had seen.

I got a job with Union Boot, the only men's shoe factory in New York City. Mr. Lolinski was the owner. After we had worked overtime for an hour or so he would give us a shot of whisky and a ten-dollar bill in addition to the time and a half he paid us as we walked out. Mr. Nurk, my supervisor, gave me a ten dollar increase each week and Charlie Pescarmona (previously a designer with I. Miller) was my foreman in the upper shoe leather end of the cutting department. Charlie introduced Louise and me to Mr. & Mrs. Carbino. Mr. Carbino made custom-made shoes, and Mrs. Carbino was a French dressmaker who worked out of the couple's apartment in lower Manhattan. They had worked for the theater in Hollywood. We all became good friends and they were godparents to our son.

Charlie had a stroke, and I was asked to take over his job. There were seven upper leather hand cutters, and I had to allocate leather to each one. The cutters were all Russian Communists who belonged to the CIO and received a fabulous amount of money for about twenty-five hours' work per week. I worked under the GI bill and got a hundred dollars a month subsistence pay. When the CIO went on strike, Mr. Lolinski decided he would rather go out of business than give in to the union, so he closed the factory and we were all out of a job. I worked a couple of weeks for a shoe company in New Jersey, but they paid me with rubber checks.

Next I applied for employment with Pan American Airlines as a parachute packer. The young woman I spoke to there was also surprised to find out that the commercial airlines did not provide parachutes for passengers. The airline hired me anyway, but not as a parachute packer. I typed billing and customs clearance documents—despite my hunt-and-peck typing ability, which I had picked up when I was studying entomology. I started working for Pan Am at La Guardia Airport in 1947 and would remain with them until 1949.

Working for Pan Am had definite perks. A woman used to come in late on Saturday night, just before flight time, to ship dresses to Havana. I would rush to type the waybills and declaration papers for customs and get the shipment on the flight. In return she would give me a handful of Havana cigars, each with a nine-cent tax stamp. They were so good you could eat them. Still, it wasn't the best job in the world. George Yasunas, a fellow employee, used to tell me, "What are you doing working in this place? Get a good job." I think George was the one who turned me toward the NYCFD.

Training for the NYCFD at the barracks near Jackson Heights, Queens, with my son, Richard.

Chapter 10

The New York City Fire Department

I started training for the New York City Fire Department at the barracks during my off hours. I secured planks vertically to metal clothesline poles to practice vaulting a wall. I lifted weights and practiced running around our barracks carrying a hundred pounds. In 1949 I passed the physical and was appointed to the NYCFD.

I was honored to have gone through probationary training under Chief McGinty. When we were up on the scaling ladders he would call up to us by our number; mine was 81. After my training I was assigned to Firehouse Engine Company 261 with Ladder 116 in Long Island City (37-20 29th Street) near the Queens Borough Bridge. During my twenty years with the department there was hardly a building in our district that didn't have a fire or an emergency of some sort. Most of the structures were factories and residential buildings. The biggest fires were usually in Greenpoint, Brooklyn where we responded on a second alarm.

One fire that I particularly remember involved several blocks in Greenpoint. I was manning the deck pipe of a hose wagon when the three-story building in front of me collapsed. I scrambled for protection under the rig, unaware at the time that a building usually falls no further than within one third of its height. We moved hand lines into the buildings and were there all night long. When we were relieved at daybreak and I came outside, I found that I couldn't see in the daylight. I was exhausted, and the subway ride down to the medical office seemed to last forever. The X-rays they took showed spots on my lungs. The hospital people always frightened Louise because they exaggerated about my injuries on the job.

We were called once to the scene of an apartment house fire and explosion caused when a man attempted to commit suicide by blowing himself up. The man survived the explosion but was trapped in the cellar with the whole building caved in above him. While Rescue Company and Ladder 116 stood by, the Engine 261 men (they called us feather merchants—because of our long black rubber coats, I guess), Stanley Kulesa, and I made our way down to the cellar. We slithered down beneath a large pipeline that was still blowing gas and found the man. We tied a bowline on a bight for his legs and a clove hitch around his chest under his arms and dragged him (he weighed about 170 pounds) to an opening that led above, then threw the line up and asked the men waiting above to haul him up. Capt. Duncan Cameron of our Engine Company 261 submitted a report of the incident to Chief Charles Shea requesting awards for us, but Chief Shea pigeonholed it because giving us awards "would not have looked good with the Rescue and Ladder companies standing by." The man who started the fire later died of his injuries.

We did all sorts of things to amuse ourselves while waiting to be called to a fire. Physical competitions were favorite activities. The radiators in the firehouse were pretty high, and Stanley Kulesa could jump up to the top of one from a standing position. I think I used to be able to hold my head in a bucket of water the longest. Mario Maraschino, who drove Ladder 116's hook-and-ladder truck, was a gunsmith on the side. He used to ask me to check the triggers for creeps when he had finished because I had a keen touch and was able to detect them.

Firefighting is a dangerous and stressful occupation, and many firemen develop physical problems as the result of the beating they take on the job. We didn't have self-contained masks in those days, and mucous would hang down about six inches from our noses when we "took a feed" (ate smoke). I was wearing the mask with a filter canister at a supermarket fire. You were supposed to get out when the canister got hot. I got out too late. Freddy Sawicki, the chauffeur of the pumper saw that I was not myself. He told me to sit down on the curb. I was taken to the hospital with carbon monoxide poisoning. Freddy had nine children. They were heading up state when they realized one was missing and had to return for him.

I remained with the department, though, and reached the rank of lieutenant. I developed chest pains at one fire and was hospitalized; cardiograms showed pericarditis. I was put on light duty for three months. One of the F.D. medical officers told me that I probably had arthritis—at age forty-seven? At the time the Heart Bill was in effect, and any heart problems automatically resulted in three-quarters tax-free retirement instead of taxable half pay. I received only my service retirement, though, which was one-half of my $15,000 lieutenant's pay.

Anyway, Louise made me leave the department after twenty years. She had always said, "Twenty years and you're out!" Good for Louise. It was the right thing to do. I'm still kicking at eighty-six. The chest pains went away after about twenty years.

We weren't living in the barracks all this time. In 1952 we moved into Pomonok, a middle-income apartment development on Kissena Boulevard in Flushing, Queens, opposite Queens College. Our son, Richard, started first grade at Saint Nicholas of Tolentine after having finished kindergarten at the barracks. Louise modeled hats on 57th Street in Manhattan while Rich was in school.

Rich's nighttime routine included eating half a banana before he went to sleep. One night while Louise was giving Rich his banana, he started crying and said, "The sisters told me you and Daddy are not going to Heaven because you're not receiving communion." Touched, I answered, "There's no problem. The missionaries are coming next week. We'll go to confession and begin receiving communion."

The mission priest was Father McDermott, an Augustinian. On the last night of his visit Father's last words to us were, "Your lives will be beautiful." His words penetrated my heart, and I immediately understood that a beautiful life would not be all peaches and cream—at least not for me. I liked adventure. I went to confession the last night of the mission and waited outside for Louise. She came out and I asked her, "Did you go to confession?" She shook her head. "Why not?" I asked. "Go back in there; he doesn't know you from Adam." She went back in. When she came out again, I asked, "Did you spill the beans?" She said, "Yes." We both went home free. After that night, I was drawn like a magnet to any place where there was a tabernacle with Jesus. I could feel His presence even from the outside the building—through the back wall of Saint Nick's or any church.

A few days later, I was sitting on one of our newly purchased twin beds trying to get my wedding ring off because my ring finger was swollen. The ring was the same thin gold band that I had purchased during the war in France with Johnny McDonald. Father Murphy happened to visit, walked into the bedroom, and he caught me trying to get my wedding ring off. We all had a good laugh and finally got the ring off with soap and water.

In 1955, when Dicky was nine, Louise took him to France for a month. I saw them off at the dock, but I stayed behind because I wanted to use my vacation from the NYCFD on a trip to the West Coast when they returned. The ship had a German crew, and one of them made a point of harassing Louise about the wounds he had received, as if his injuries were her fault.

Louise and Dicky stayed with her family during the visit to France. They slept in the upstairs bedroom, and Louise's father and stepmother, Marie, slept in the bedroom downstairs. (Louise's mother had died in September 1948 while vacationing with cousins in Montone, Italy.) It was a difficult time for Louise's family because her brother Jeanot had recently died in Saigon in 1955 from wounds he received at Dien Bien Phu.

Louise's youngest brother, Roger, was four years older than Dicky. The two boys did not get along very well, so Dicky started hanging out in the wine store, helping to fill the bottles and breathing in the fumes. Dicky was an adventurous boy, just as I had been; one day he was discovered in the back of a delivery truck heading for Paris. A tussle with the family dog ended with Dicky being bitten on the lip. Apparently, Dicky got too close to a bowl of grenadine belonging to the dog, and the dog bit him. The family took him to a doctor, and the doctor told him to grow a mustache—the same thing the doctor in Antibes had told me after my bicycle accident! Louise and Dicky had a wonderful time in France, but Dicky came home very spoiled.

Within a week of their return I started my vacation and we were on our way to the West Coast. We stopped off to see Lucille and Murph Trahan in New Orleans and went out for a fish dinner at Lake Pontchartrain. We continued west, dropping down into Mexico at Del Rio, Texas, and coming back out in El Paso. When the Mexican men saw Louise, they said, "Guapa, guapa" (pretty, pretty). While we were in Mexico I bought a lasso and a bottle of tequila for a dollar each. When we went through customs in Juarez, the customs officer asked us what we had to declare. I answered that we had just one bottle that we had purchased in Del Rio and kept going. Suddenly I realized that the customs officers were sighting their pistols at us. Louise screamed for me to stop. They made us get out and empty all of our baggage, then went through everything; Louise's underwear was all over the place. Finding nothing, they left us to put our belongings back together and leave.

Going through Texas I did something stupid and picked up a hitchhiker. I watched him closely in the rearview mirror, and something about him didn't seem right. I didn't like my son sitting in the backseat with him. Fortunately, I was able to convince him that we were about to stop for the day, and he got out.

We went through Arizona in torrential rains, never stopping until the skies cleared and the desert opened up in front of us. The organ pipe cacti were a beautiful sight in the sizzling sunshine. We had to get out of the car to take photos. I put the car in park and placed a stone on the accelerator to keep the water circulating so it wouldn't overheat. (our 1950 Dodge had no air conditioning). We crossed the desert and stopped at a Best Western in Indio, California. I still remember how good that swimming pool felt!

From Los Angeles we drove to San Francisco to see my brother Marty, the family's great success story. Finding our way around was a challenge, but a kind driver told us, "Hang on to my tail" and got us pointed in the right direction. Marty was very industrious in everything he did. He owned the best liquor store in San Francisco, then the best delicatessen, and he played in a large orchestra. Ultimately he went into antiques.

After that, with my vacation half gone, we turned for home. On our first night of the return trip we stopped about 10:00pm in Yellowstone National Park. I went out to find something for us to eat and saw several large white dogs. The next day I learned that they were coyotes. After a couple of days at Yellowstone we continued toward home, stopping in Wyoming to watch a rodeo. We visited a post office to mail some postcards and saw a wanted poster with a photo of the hitchhiker I had picked up in Texas. He was wanted for burglary and auto theft. The last day of the trip, Louise and I took turns driving the last nine hundred miles to Pomonok.

Firefighters were not officially allowed to hold outside jobs, but I earned a few extra bucks caddying at North Hills Country Club. I also started giving driving lessons for the Lexington Auto School in Manhattan. One night when I was teaching, a blizzard blanketed the city. I had given my last lesson at nine p.m., but the school's owner wanted me to take out another student—right in the middle of the blizzard. When I said no and told him that I had to go home, he fired me. I went home and told Louise the news, and right away she started the De Ville Driving School. I was the chief instructor.

I used a brand-new 1957 gold swept-wing Dodge for the lessons. It was an enormous car—twenty-two feet long—with persistent transmission problems. We called it "the Big Slipper." I had dual breaks installed for giving driving lessons. The Big Slipper replaced our old car; the 1950 Dodge Club Coupe that Louise had called "Betsy." I sold it at the firehouse to Tony Vecchone for three hundred fifty dollars. Its chrome never rusted.

Jack Zenker, a former 509th medic who owned a print shop in New York, printed Louise's advertising flyers. I used to slip them under the doors in apartment buildings. During the war, Jack had submitted two of my Purple Heart applications. While the 509th was in France, Jack met Hélène Lery, a courageous young woman who helped the 509th in the fighting along the coast around Cap d'Ail by passing information to Sgt. Boggs Collins. Hélène fell in love with Jack, but after the war she married Michel Lery, who had been in charge of a large sector of the FFI during the war. Michel was a good man, but he died young. Hélène remained madly in love with Jack even after he returned home and married Pauline. Louise would pass along Hélène's love letters to Jack, with the full knowledge of Pauline. Sadly, Jack died prematurely of a heart attack. While he was still living, though, Jack and Pauline always came to the 509th reunions.

One day about this time Louise and I had one of our worst arguments ever. I had gone into New York City to purchase a dressy raincoat. I found it, probably in Gimbels or Macy's, and headed toward the subway station near Central Park to go back home. Since I hadn't used much time finding the raincoat and I had heard that they played chess in Central Park, I decided to walk over and take a look. I played frequently with our neighbor, Frank McVey, who was a chief in the NYCFD. His wife, Ada, and Louise were good friends. I also played chess at the firehouse. I was an average to good player who knew most of the opening moves.

I sat down and played a fellow in Central Park and mated him in five moves, probably by accident. Just to take me down a notch, the regular players decided to put me against the best in the park, a Russian. He had just finished a game, so we went at it. I had never seen the moves he used, including pushing all his pawns at me, but I played him to a draw.

I lost track of time when I was playing, and Louise was furious when I got home. I had never known her to be jealous or wonder what I was doing. She must have thought that I had been misbehaving and was using the chess playing to cover it up. She didn't believe me until I narrated all the moves from the games. I still have the raincoat, but I never wear it now.

The De Ville Driving School kept me busy and gave me interesting stories to bring home to Louise. One day I was giving driving lessons to a young French-woman and had just had her do a back park. She raised her skirt and said, "What do we do now?" I responded, "Roll down your window, give your hand signal, and pull out." When I told Louise about it later, the story got a big laugh.

I taught the sisters at Saint Nicholas of Tolentine in Flushing, too. Although I would have done it for nothing, the sisters insisted on paying. I charged forty dollars for eight hours, giving the lessons an hour at a time. The Sister Superior, Edward Marie, told me one day, "Mr. Fisco, I remembered everything you told me. I was driving in this heavy traffic in New Jersey and I kept looking straight ahead where I was going."

I replied, "Sister, what were you doing driving in New Jersey with a New York State learner's permit?"

She exclaimed, "Oh, no!" and chuckled. At the end of her lessons, Sister Superior Edward Marie gave me a small plaque of the Blessed Mother and a little card with a picture of the Guardian Angel and a prayer on the back. I occasionally asked Sister spiritual questions after our lessons. I said," The Martyr's were in consolation?" She said," No they were not." I asked her how to avoid problems with women. She answered," Don't let the eyes meet."

At this time in my life I found myself turning more and more to my religion. Spiritual gifts started to manifest themselves. In a vision I saw a third of a Rosary rotating. The Blessed Mother was telling me to say the Rosary. In another vision I saw the heavens, void of any atmosphere, dimly but beautifully illuminated by particles of gold that surrounded Heaven itself. Beautiful music was playing. The Blessed Mother was telling me I would have to be pure of heart to get to Heaven.

One night God interrupted my sleep. I felt his grace pour through me and then saw a stained-glass window. It was weeks before I knew what it all meant. Then I received a card from Lucille, Murph Trahan's wife. The card was printed with a stained-glass window, and inside was a newspaper clipping telling me that my war buddy Murph, a deacon, had died of cancer. Our Lord, the creator of the universe, had reached out to me. I was awed and humbled.

When I was promoted to lieutenant in the New York City Fire Department in 1958, I began to be detailed to different companies. I put in a couple of weeks on the *Firefighter*, a fireboat berthed on the Hudson at the bottom of Manhattan. I spent a few weeks at Engine 32 around Wall Street. The streets in that part of the city were so narrow that accidents were almost unavoidable. When we returned from one run, the chauffeur grazed a car parked at a corner diagonally across the street from the firehouse. Hoping to avoid an accident report, a procedure I was not familiar with, I instructed the house watch to keep an eye out. Sure enough, the car was hit again and then a third time in the same place. Obviously, the fire department wasn't solely responsible for any damage to the car.

Then I was detailed to Ladder 6, a busy hook-and-ladder company near Canal Street on the Lower East Side. Soon after reporting in for duty one evening, we responded to a fire in the diamond center on Canal Street. Smoke was seeping up through the ground floor from the cellar below. The merchants, confident in the ability of the New York City Fire Department to put out the fire, kept their businesses open. The building was more than a hundred feet deep, and Ladder 6 moved right in. One man went to the roof; the rest of us put on our Scott packs and descended to the cellar from the first floor at the back of the building. The Scott packs didn't last much longer than ten minutes if you were breathing hard from exertion.

After forcing a couple of doors, we reached the scene of the fire at the front of the building in the cellar. All I had to do was hold the flashlight. The big truckies really knew their jobs and were experienced firefighters. I once saw one of them carry two children, one under each arm, through fire in a burning tenement. The engine company was having a hard time stretching the lines all the way to the back, down the stairs, and then all the way to the front of the cellar where the fire was. By this time, the fire had taken hold on the first floor and the merchants had lost their confidence and were closing their shops. We had to use hose lines now on the first floor. The water we were shooting into the building flowed out to the street, and jewelry was floating down the gutter. Finally, the fire was under control and we were ordered to "take up."

When I got home to Pomonok, I discovered what looked like a large diamond stuck to my trousers. I showed it to Louise and then flushed it down the toilet. I knew that there were bound to be accusations of diamond theft, and I didn't want to be involved. We responded to a fire in the building at Queens Plaza a couple of months after I was permanently assigned to Engine 261 as a Lieutenant in my old company, and after the fire, the owners were missing money. Roger Lanahan, the deputy chief, asked Captain Lynch of Ladder 116 and me if any of our men might have taken anything. The deputy chief and I were old acquaintances. I had caddied with him at North Hills back when he was still a fireman. The owners found their missing money weeks later in one of their places in Upstate New York.

Back then, firemen weren't always treated with the respect they deserved. When I was detailed to a firehouse in Redhook, Brooklyn, during elections, for instance, the people would build bonfires in the street, pull the alarm box, and then throw stones at us when we responded. I expect they behave better after 9/11.

Whenever I was reporting in for the six p.m. to nine a.m. shift at the firehouse, I always stopped at Saint Patrick's on 29th Street. The church was always empty at that hour. I would kneel at the communion rail about six feet in front of the tabernacle at a side altar, where the lighted red candle indicated that the Blessed Sacrament was present. One night while I was kneeling, a sudden strong wind swirled around the tabernacle. It lasted for only about a second. Startled, I looked to the rear of the church to see if someone had opened the door. There was no one there. I thought if it were God he knew he would frighten me. I stayed a little longer and then left. When I thought about it, I wondered if the wind had been another message from God. One night not long before that, I had been on my way to work the six-to-nine shift when I encountered a bleeding and apparently drunk vagrant near St. Patrick's Church. I wanted to take him to the firehouse to get help for him, but my 1950 Dodge Club Coupe had a mohair interior and I didn't want to get blood all over the car. Louise would have been very upset. I was more worried about that than being ridiculed by the "brothers" at the firehouse. I stopped in front of him, we looked at each other momentarily and then I continued to the firehouse on the next block, passing Saint Patrick's. Later I was ashamed that I had failed to help him. It was probably Jesus.

I had some serious sins to confess. I decided to go to the Franciscans, I think they were on 38th Street. I confessed my sins and the priest told me , "Get out!" I left and returned the next day at the same time and to the same confessional. I think it was the same priest because his voice was familiar. I confessed the same sins and he absolved me from my sins. I tell you this so that you will know that not even a Catholic priest can dissuade you from your Catholic faith once you know God. Thereafter I could never remember what the sins were. God always erases the sins we confess. I think this time He thought it best that I also forget them. Another time when I went to confession, I told the priest that my wife and I were living a chaste life. He laughed.

During these years, I was able to put my knowledge of nature and especially entomology to good use. I became the nature merit badge counselor to Boy Scout Troop 351 at Saint Nick's school. Father Alfred E. Murphy, the troop moderator, and I would accompany the troop on overnight camping trips to Ten Mile River and other spots. I would take the troop into the woods and "sugar" for moths by painting tree trunks with a mixture of stale beer and molasses. It sounds awful, but the moths loved it. Later that night we would go out with flashlights and look at the insects that had been attracted to the mixture. Those we wanted to keep we popped into a jar with a piece of cotton saturated with carbon tetrachloride. I later learned that at least one of those scouts went on to a career in entomology.

In 1962, Louise and I applied for a seventeen thousand dollar, no-cash-down GI mortgage on a Williamsburg cape house in Wantagh, New York, and were approved. I had been a lieutenant in the Fire Department since 1958. We were awaiting the closing, but we still needed almost a thousand dollars to pay for the closing and a refrigerator. One Sunday we went to mass at Saint Nick's, as usual. At the side entrance to the church we saw a young boy being lifted up to a revolving wire basket so that he could draw the winning raffle ticket for a one-thousand-dollar prize. We stopped momentarily to watch. The boy pulled out a ticket and handed it to the priest—and our names were called out. I had forgotten all about having bought the chances.

The Fisco family had grown to five when we moved into our new home in Wantagh: Louise, Dicky, me, a puppy, and a cat. Someone next door to the fire-house had a Dalmatian that had given birth to a litter, and we couldn't resist. We named her Tina. The cat was a stray that Louise and Rich had found under a car in Pomonok. I warned them that the vet who examined the cat had said that she wouldn't live long, but Louise and Dicky insisted on keeping her. We named her Tammy. She was cross-eyed and played games, including red light, green light, one, two, and three. Later we acquired Bijou, our Siamese.

Jesus said, "My Father has many mansions." All I asked for, though, was a little bungalow for Louise, Rich, and me with flowers all around and room for all our animals. The property at 1736 Roosevelt Street in Wantagh was a hundred by a hundred feet. Louise put in beautiful flowerbeds all around it. I cut the grass and dug a rose bed for her. My specialty was the windows. I sanded them down to bare wood, then soaked them with linseed oil and painted them white. The neighbors called me Rembrandt of the windows. We hung blue angel wallpaper in the kitchen, and I installed Vermont slate floors in the kitchen and entryway. The interior walls were plaster over which we either painted or wallpapered. The front of the house was fieldstone, and there was a beautiful dogwood in the front yard.

Our new parish was Saint Jane Frances de Chantal. I went to confession to Father Joseph Kennedy about once a week. I wanted to make a vow to say the Rosary every day for the rest of my life. Father Joseph advised me not to, but I insisted. I was able to say it for about thirty-five years—until 1987 when we moved to Virginia and Louise was diagnosed with breast cancer.

My religious faith continued to strengthen during these years. One night while I was at the firehouse, God awakened me and in seconds showed me the chronological course of my journey in faith, from Consolation to Dryness to Hatred and back to Consolation. I don't understand the hatred, but hopefully I will die in Consolation. In another dream I heard the beginning of Saint John's gospel, "In the beginning was the word and the word was with God." It was a male's voice, very clear, like a New Yorker with no accent that I could perceive.

Roosevelt Street was a lover's lane. I called the county and asked them to put in more streetlights. They installed several additional lights, but the kids still used the road for a lover's lane. Fed up, I would go out to the car, tap on the window, and ask if they could please go somewhere else. I reminded them that children passed by on their way to school and saw the things the lovers left behind. They were all courteous and left whenever I went out and asked them to. Eventually they moved their activities elsewhere.

One summer night when I was working at the firehouse Louise was sound asleep. The screened windows were all open. Tina started barking and Louise yelled at her to be quiet. The next morning Louise discovered a wallet in the backyard and learned that the police had been chasing a burglar in the neighborhood. Later we found out that Tina was deaf. I don't know how Tina heard the burglar; I'm just thankful that she barked when she did.

One night after Louise and I were each in our twin beds, I called over to her and asked, "I wonder how you can tell the devil?" A voice came from within me saying, "By his smile." I asked Louise if she had heard the voice and she said she had not. I never mentioned it to Father Kennedy. I continued to receive messages, although only once did I hear the voice of someone who had already died. I don't think I saw Uncle Pete in Brooklyn no more than ten times in my life. He weighed about 250 pounds and could really bang out the old piano tunes. About ten years into being a practicing Catholic, and the second year in our Wantagh home, I was awakened by the voice of Uncle Pete telling me, "Don't worry, Rich." Louise had been having stomach pains, and my son was going through the difficult teenage years. The words were very comforting, and I had a mass said for Uncle Pete and Aunt Eunice just in case he was in purgatory. I could take a hint. Now we know for sure that those in heaven know the details of what goes on here on earth.

Rich and I had our differences as he got older, as most fathers and sons probably do. To put it mildly, I didn't care for his attitude. I asked a priest— not my confessor—what to do about it, and he told me to punch Rich. I did and yelled, "I want my son back!" Years later, after he became a Scientology minister, Rich asked me why I had punched him. I answered, "A priest told me to, and I thought of Abraham and Isaac." He asked, "What was his name?" When I answered, "Father So-and-so," Rich said, "Oh, him?" Something about the way he said that made it obvious that the priest had made advances toward him. The devil was playing the angles, but God turns evil into good.

Both my parents had high blood pressure and died of strokes at age seventy-two. Mom, who was two years older than Pop, died in Florida while she was living with my sister, Theresa. A palm tree fell on the house during a hurricane, and Mom suffered a fatal brain hemorrhage. My father died in a small hospital; I think it was on 82nd Street in Manhattan. I held his hand as he faded away and asked him to squeeze it if he heard me. He squeezed it. I said to him, "Pop, say hello to God for me when you see him." I never heard from my dad after his death, but I did see my mother once. Years later, at Saint John's Church in Brunswick, Maine, after receiving communion I saw my mother crying. I immediately asked for a mass to be said for her. When my dad died, I had a dilemma. I wanted a funeral mass with communion served, but I had to choose between the two funeral homes owned by different members of the family. I chose Uncle Brizzi's, not the one owned by Aunt Eunice, Uncle Pete Frunzi's widow, and her sons.

My dad left us four children ten thousand dollars: five thousand to me in a passbook savings account and the remainder, in three other savings accounts, to my two brothers and my sister. My father had put fifteen hundred dollars aside and asked me to give it to Rose, a black woman who had fed and cared for him. The attorney had asked me and I had given him my approval to give it to her. Aunt Eunice was angry about both of my choices. At the funeral I said to her, "Aunt Eunice, Uncle Pete (she called him Petey) is in Heaven." She said, "What?" I said, "Yes, and he told me not to worry."

Rich had gotten all A's at Saint Nick's school in Pomonok, and when it came time for high school he was offered a scholarship to either Bishop Loughlin in Red Hook, Brooklyn, or with the Franciscans. Louise preferred Bishop Loughlin; I preferred the Franciscans. Louise won. Rich, who at about six feet two inches was big for his age, was stabbed in the leg while he was at Bishop Loughlin. After we moved to Wantagh, Rich attended public high school. His French teacher would mark certain answers wrong that Louise knew were right. Rich did not want us to bring it to the teacher's attention, so we didn't.

Rich started college at Dowling in Oakdale, which was farther out on Long Island. His marks fell off, and he was drafted. Knowing that he would almost certainly be sent to Vietnam, he asked us if he should go. I told him I had no firsthand information indicating that he shouldn't go. I did tell him to always carry smoke. "It's your way in and you're way out." To further protect him, Louise and I had him enrolled in prayers at Mother Cabrini's Shrine in New York.

Rich served as a helicopter door gunner with the Ghost Riders 189th Assault Helicopter Company in Pleiku, Viet Nam, from 1967 to 1968. I pinned a map of Indochina on the wall of the basement of our Wantagh home and kept track of where he was. I flagged his position in Pleiku. We wrote to him, of course, and he would write home to us asking for soap. He didn't tell us what he used it for, but I was thinking *demoiselle*s. We sent him the soap along with other goodies.

In his next to last month in the country, Rich's helicopter was returning at night from the "Greek missions" in Cambodia. The helicopter went into a spin and crashed in the jungle. It had been sabotaged. His knees and teeth were injured. He helped the two pilots and the other door gunner get out and turned off the engine. They stayed by the chopper that night, because the Viet Cong rarely attacked at night. At dawn, they decided to try to make it back. The two lieutenants wanted to cross the river, but my son insisted on going uphill. Fortunately, they agreed to follow him. As they started up the hill, the Viet Cong were crossing the river behind them and heading right for the downed helicopter. As my son's group got to the top of the hill, they heard a chopper overhead; their company commander had come looking for them. Rich threw his coded smoke bomb to signal their whereabouts, then helped the other three up. After that I'm sure he breathed a sigh of relief.

Rich remained in Vietnam, but his knee wasn't healing. Penicillin didn't help. Worried, I called Senator Bobby Kennedy's office in Washington. Rich could have come home but refused and finished his year. When Rich finally did return to us in Wantagh, we put Welcome Home signs all over the yard. We were fortunate. Many boys in our neighborhood didn't make it back; one was a doctor's son. Rich wore three "Friendly Bracelets" that had been given to him by Montagnards. Among the photos he showed us was one of him giving a bath to a young Montagnard boy. That solved our curiosity.

Rich went back to Dowling, but this time I told him he was on his own. He had let his grades fall the last time and had been drafted as a result. I thought it would mean more to him if he had to pay his own way through college. I don't know how he did it, but his marks went back up and stayed there. While he was in college he met his future wife, Vicki Machcinski. They became engaged and were married in the Catholic Church in Vicki's home parish. I wrote to the Vatican for the papal blessing from Pope Paul VI for their union, and received it.

I officially retired from the NYCFD on January 6, 1970, but the unused vacation time I had accrued allowed Louise and me to leave for France in December 1969. Louise left her work at The Casual Shop in the Walt Whitman Shopping Center, an exclusive dress shop on Long Island, at the same time.

PHOTO 8-14-44
SGT. DICK FISCO 509
PCT. BN.
14 Aug 1944 LIDO de ROME
NIGHT BEFORE JUMP
IN S. FRANCE on
Aug 15

Face your target, the vertical raise, center it on your belly button and squeeze. Photo taken by Ed Wojick two days before the jump into Southern France. Me, in proper position, shooting from the hip. Wojik was killed two weeks after the jump.

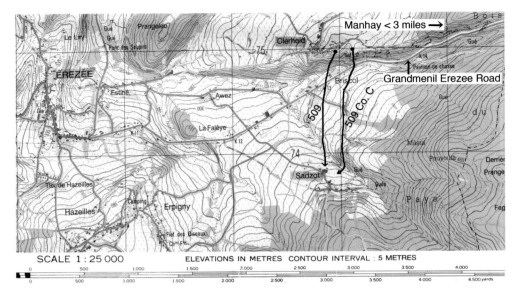

Put as close to page 72 as possible

This map shows the 509 retaking Sadzot on December 29, 1944.
See Chapter 8.

The Gimbels sale girls in New
York promised my father they
would photograph me for free
when I was discharged on
June 17, 1945.

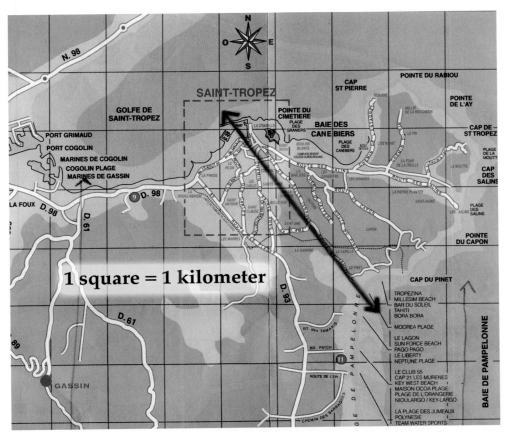

Map of Presqu'ile, St. Tropez, showing three kilometeres as the maximum distance to jump for any planes heading southwest across the peninsula. Mr. Coppola agrees with with me that the B and C companies flew in from the east and were thereby afforded the whole length and depth of the pennisula, reducing the risk of jumping at sea. See Chapter 7.

Wantagh, Long Island. Louise, standing in front of our Williamsburg Cape in the 1960s.

Louise, relaxing during a MONY TOP Club trip.

Louise asked the captain of the Michelangelo how he expected our dogs to "hold it" for fourteen hours, when he certainly wouldn't have been able to do so. We were then given keys to the kennel so we could walk our two dalmations.

Louise purchases François, our mini-poodle, at Chateau de La Garoupe at Cap D'Antibes.

Loiuse, 1990, in full remission at 133 Aire St. Michel near Mt. Chauve.

Louise, holding Coco, sits with Kiki, our beagle Fiston, and puppy
François (in chair) at the Hotel Les Gazoullies in Juin Lapin, 1990.

Our puppy mini-poodle, François.

François at two years, groomed by me. Chandler's Warf, Portland, Maine

Coco the Himalayan blue point as a kitten in Charlottesville, Virginia, 1987, Willow Lake Manor House.

The dress Louise made at age seventeen from a camouflage parachute used on the jump on August 15, 1944. "Blacky" Johnson gave me the parachute to give to Louise when he drove us to Nice, for my first visit with her at 18 Ave. Notre Dame.

The skirt that Louise took six months to knit. She could never find a top good enough to match.

My sister-in-law, Maryse, makes me a
board full of gnocchi in Nice, France.

Melinda Louise Conner,
editor of this book, is
Jimmy Nunn's daughter.

Me and Nick DeGaeta on Via Roma, Rome, 1943.

Me and Nick DeGaeta, Veterans Day at Capt. Bud Siegel's,
Long Island, before 1992.

Veterans Day at Bud Siegel's.

The guardian angel card that Sister Superior Edward Marie of Saint Nicholas of Tolentine gave me in the '60s. See pages 91 and 145.

8:00 a.m., August 15, 2004, the 60th anniversary of Operation Dragoon in Southern France. Rescue boat crew. I'm holding François with Mr. Coppola on my left. The crew showed me where we jumped on St. Anne Hill in St. Tropez.

Capt. A Company Ernest "Bud" Siegel and Sgt. Nick DeGaeta, entertaining with 509 songs at a reunion.

Colomar greets me. In mid-September 1944, as staff sergeant, I was sent (along with seventeen other men) by Lt. Ferris Knight B Company 509 to liberate Colomar. We were on our way to Lantosque.

The day we requested Captain Miller's monument. Left to right: Ed Monroig; American Legion Riviera Post 0005 Commander John H. Willms; me, holding François; Mr. François Coppola; Dr. Bourrier, the first deputy mayor.

Coco, at just a few months old, survived a rare blood disease.

Kiki in the washing machine. Her curiousity finally got her into trouble when she burnt her paw on the stove in France.

Coco on the kitchen floor of the Willow Lake Manor house..

Courageous Maggie. Notice the bandage on her front paw. She was the victim of a hit and run in Sag Harbor.

Fiston (Little Son) on the left, Jody on the rights. Jody was a very intelligent Lab.

Our house in Charlottesville, Virginia.

Louise's flower garden.

Louise and me on the mower that Lowe's delivered at 6:00 am.

The stream.

The stream becomes a river.

Louise feeds her friends and their babies.

Louise taps a tune for Coco.

The kitchen.

Louise's doll collection.

Our dining room.

The living room.

The upstairs divide between rooms. Olga chandelier we left with the house on resale.

Twin beds in our bedroom.

Upstairs guest room.

Second guest room.

Our bathroom.

Bathroom adjoining the small bedroom, which originally served as the servants' quarters and was also my office.

Old fireplace mantel in the cellar.

Wine cellar.

I built this gate.

Draining the back of the garage. A black snake came in with me.

Me with our friend, Father Murphy, from St. Nicholas of Tolentine. Tammy, our cross-eyed domestic cat, also appeared for her final blessing.

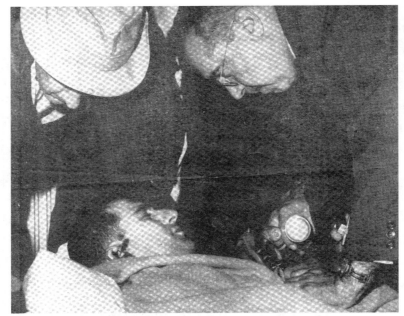

Carbon monoxide poisoning at a supermarket fire.
Filter-type masks were in use at that time.

Chapter 11

Retirement and Moving to France— Three Times

Now that I was retired, Louise and I planned to move to France permanently. We sold our house in Wantagh and had a yard sale. Within an hour and a half everything had been sold, including a Shaker rocker, two other rockers—one of which I had refinished the day President John Kennedy was assassinated—a new Wakefield dining room set, and an American-made love seat. What we didn't sell, including a VW fastback, we gave to Rich and Vicki, who had rented a little cottage in Oakdale. Before leaving for France, we managed several visits with them. Vicki was like my own daughter.

We had Tina, our Dalmatian, and Bijou, our Siamese. Tammy had been ill and gone into Tina's box to lie down. We took her to the vet and she died that night. Princess, a champion-bred Collie was given to us by my sister, Theresa. It was too hot for her in Florida. She was so beautiful that she made Tina look bad. I gave her to a firefighter who had performed mouth-to-mouth resuscitation on a dog to save its life. I thought he would take really good care of her. When I went over for a visit, though, I found Princess tied up out on the porch. I didn't have the humility to take Princess back. I should have (another mistake in my life I had to live with). The only reason he wanted her was to breed her but we had never given him her papers.

I was forty-nine when we left for France, and Louise was forty-two. Our only income was my seven thousand dollars per year pension, half of my lieutenant's pay plus twenty percent WWII disability pension for my wounded left elbow. We had made a decent profit on our house. We had purchased it for seventeen thousand dollars and sold it for twenty-six thousand dollars. I was shocked to discover that the new owner flew the American flag we had left behind, upside down though. We shipped personal things ahead, such as paintings and other things that would make us feel at home.

We said good-bye to Rich and Vicki and sailed on the *Michelangelo* along with Tina and Bijou. Our life in Nice didn't begin on the best possible note. Louise's brother Henri had reserved an apartment for us at La Madrague that fell considerably short of our expectations. It was infested with cockroaches— I killed seventeen every night. We ordered twin beds from a nearby store, but when they were delivered the edges of the box springs were torn, and we sent them back. The storeowner was furious, but he replaced them the next day.

We had a pretty little balcony on the third floor with beautiful pink blooming laurel trees on the street below. I went out by myself with the *fillet* (a little shopping bag) and purchased a bottle of wine, *baguette*, and the makings for lunch. I came home with a load of obsolete pennies that the merchants had unloaded on me, an easy mark. We still enjoyed our lunch immensely. Thereafter I examined my change carefully.

I immediately started looking for another apartment. I started on the Promenade near the Negresco Hotel and worked back west along the promenade, checking with the concierge in every apartment building I passed. Finally I found a brand-new apartment building in Fabron on the Promenade that had a vacant apartment with two bedrooms (called a *deux piece*). It had beautiful grayish white marble floors and an inside elevator. From our balcony we could see Corsica on a clear day, and we had only to cross the Promenade to be on the Mediterranean beach. The rental agent was a World War II veteran and former paratrooper. I think the rent was seven hundred francs a month.

Apartments in France come without light fixtures and kitchen appliances, so acquiring those was our next step. We purchased a beautiful chandelier and a massive, three-inch-thick oak table and chairs from an antiques dealer, M. Freemontier. We were on the first floor (the second floor in the United States). Louise's brother, Roger, an interior decorator, made us lace draw draperies for the apartment that went beautifully with the marble floors. There were a couple of drawbacks to our apartment. After we were settled, we discovered that the mosquitoes were terrible and traffic on the Promenade made an awful racket.

We became members of France Etats Unis Club, and I joined the American Legion, Riviera Post 5. The post commander was Ted Bessenger. Jacques Chirac, who later became the president of France, gave a speech on the beach next to a monument erected in honor of the invasion of southern France. To my surprise, he never even mentioned the Allied forces. Anyone who didn't know better would have concluded that the French had been entirely responsible for the invasion. Madame Du Coeur, the president of France Etats Unis, and other French members of the club sent letters of protest.

We purchased a Citroën D-Super (the slang term for it in France was Crapaud-Toad) on credit and drove it to Venice on our first long trip. I looked down at the speedometer and was shocked to see that we were going one hundred forty-five kilometers per hour (about ninety mph). The ride was so smooth that I hadn't noticed our speed. I didn't mention it to Louise, who was knitting with her head down. We took a ride on a gondola, and even Tina came along.

At home in Nice we particularly liked going to auctions. At one auction alone I bought a large tray full of Baccarat crystal for about twenty dollars and beautiful old plates for our old wild cherry *bahut* (sideboard). I also bought a marble and mahogany *coiffeuse* (small vanity table) for a hundred dollars for Louise. I tied the *coiffeuse* on top of the D-Super and brought it to our apartment at the Saint George.

One day as we were driving on the Promenade in the Citroën, we blew the left rear tire right in front of the Negresco Hotel. Louise got out the book of instructions, and I followed her directions. I put a jack underneath, removed part of the fender, pushed another lever that raised the car automatically, exchanged tires, and we were on our way in minutes. Only someone who has seen the traffic on the Promenade can appreciate that feat.

Before we moved to France we had received an invitation to a wedding in Vincenza, Italy, from a friend of Henri's named Silvio, who was a purser on Al Italia and had visited us more than once in Wantagh during his stopovers in New York. Since we were already in Europe, we decided to go to the wedding.

On our way through Vincenza we noticed a sign along the road indicating the presence of the new 509th Parachute Infantry Regiment. We didn't want to disrupt our trip, though, so we didn't stop.

The wedding was in a seventeenth-century church. The bride was beautiful, as brides should always be, and Silvio was so handsome; they made a charming couple. They were awed that we had come all the way from America to go to their wedding. On our return to Nice we went up to Cimiez to see the ancient ruins of Les Arenes de Cimiez.

Vicki's dad, Mr. Machcinski, paid for Rich and Vicki to visit Nice, and they stayed at the Hotel Les Fusains. The four of us decided to drive to Geneva in the Citroën. We had to go through the tunnel under Mont Blanc in order to get there, and the road was spectacular and awesome—and scary. It was overcast, and we couldn't see the top of the mountain. I couldn't imagine even attempting to climb it.

After we got home we went to the racetrack at the hippodrome in Nice. There was a long line at the entrance, and a Frenchman cut in front of us. Rich immediately went up and stepped in front of him. The man was very angry; apparently, it was okay for him to cut in front of us but not for us to do the same. Father Joseph Kennedy once told me before leaving for France to stay in the middle; that is so true.

After Rich and Vicki left, Louise's brother Roger insisted on driving us on a trip—anywhere we wanted to go. Louise asked me what I preferred, and I said I'd like to go back to the château de La Napoule, just this side of Saint-Tropez, where I lost one-third of my platoon. I wanted to see what it looked like in peacetime. So Roger drove us there. We walked up to the area where my unit had fought. New villas had been built on the former battlefield, and one of the owners came out to see what we were doing. I told Louise to tell him that his flowers "were cultivated with American blood." She told me to hush. We went back to Nice after that, stopping off for some *soup de poison* and bouillabaisse in one of the seafood restaurants in La Napoule on the way.

I loved Nice and our apartment. There was always something to do or somewhere to go. I fished for octopus quite a few times on the beach across the street from our apartment. Fishing for octopus isn't exactly like fishing for fish. I used a piece of wood tied to the end of a long string. The wood was about four or five inches long with two big hooks at the end where I put my bait. I would bait my lure, sling it out about fifty yards, and then drag it back in slowly. You have to beat the octopus against a rock to kill it. I caught one octopus that was about a foot and a half long with his tentacles stretched out and gave it to Louise's cousin Olga Ramoin to cook for us. She kept it for about two weeks, and I finally asked her what was taking so long. She told me she had to hang it in the refrigerator that long to tenderize it before she could cook it. The wait was worth it; the octopus was delicious.

On the day I caught that octopus the Tour de France was going by on the Promenade up above and I had my AE-1 camera. I quickly took a photo of the octopus and then ran up to photograph the bicycle racers as they went by. Louise's brother Henri once raced in the Tour de France. I don't remember where he finished, but I think it was about twenty-seventh. He was quite an athlete. He also played soccer. I asked him once how often soccer players trained. "Twice a day," he told me, "morning and afternoon." I guess there is a reason why they're so good.

There are dangerous caterpillars in Nice called *chenilles*. They are dark brown and about an inch long. They spend the winter in thick webs in trees, and then leave the webs in the spring, moving very slowly in a single line attached to each other like a train. Animals that lick them may die. I carried lighter fluid and matches in case I ran across any, and I did several times.

Traveling through southern France was great fun. We often drove Louise's dad and stepmother around in the surrounding mountains, visiting some of the bridges crossing ravines that her dad had worked on and dropping in on cousins who lived in the neighborhood—and there always seemed to be some. Louise's cousins Olga and Paul and Aldo and Elvire were among our favorites. Aldo was a bridge builder. We visited Giraud and Palmire, in a little village above Nice called the Jaïnes. There were no toilet facilities at the Jaïnes. They washed clothing in the outside tub commune. Girard policed the roads. He was very thin and short. Their doctor told them la poule est tros grand pour la coque (the hen was too big for the rooster). We visited artists' exhibits, too; Matisse's works were in Nice and Picasso's in Vallauris.

One day we went to Ville Franche and had lunch in an excellent restaurant by the water. The high stonewall that bordered the beach had beautiful climbing bougainvillea flowers in bloom. We ate mussels with pasta, wine, French bread, and salad. Our beautiful D-Super Citroën was parked outside. It seemed so perfect. Then Louise started to cry. We had been living in France for seven months, and she was homesick and wanted to return to the States. So we did.

Rich and Vicki rented a little cottage for us near Dowling College on Long Island, where Rich was still a student. Rich and a friend met us at the pier with a rented truck. We would return to France, of course; our hearts were always in both places. We had brought back our furniture, paying four hundred dollars in freight. We were in the cottage for only a few days before we moved to a nice apartment nearby at Birchwood on the Green. We placed a couple of ads, sold the dining room set to pay for our next trip to France.

Dowling College is housed on the former W. K. Vanderbilt estate. Rich's graduation was held in a big, beautiful building with a mahogany-finished interior. The high, winding stairs and openness of the hall struck a note in a retired firefighter's mind. I said to my son, "Tell the Dean it should have sprinklers." Either Rich didn't tell him or he didn't listen; only months later, the building burned to the ground.

We acquired a second Dalmatian from a pet shop. We felt so sorry for her, stuffed in a cage with her rear end sticking out, that we took her home. We named her Pistache. I couldn't work because Pistache had to be walked at least a dozen times a day.

Life in Birchwood on the Green was good. We enjoyed visiting Rich and Vicki in their cottage, and clamming and fishing for snapper from their boat. We visited the Vanderbilt museum. Louise invited Father Bruno, from a nearby parish, for dinner several times, and we took him here and there occasionally. But eventually France called to us once more.

The second time we went to France to live was from Birchwood on the Green. We had the two Dalmatians, Tina and Pistache, and our Siamese cat, Bijou, with us on the *Michelangelo,* but no one would give us permission to walk our dogs. Louise took care of that. On being greeted by the captain as we entered for a banquet, Louise pointed her finger up at him (he must have been six and a half feet tall) and said, "You can't go fourteen hours without pee-peeing." Thereafter we got the key to the kennel. To our dismay, we found that the seaman who was supposed to be caring for the dogs had never even changed their water, it was like jelly. I was very upset; I had given him a five-dollar tip.

When the ship stopped at Naples, we learned that there was going to be a strike. We would be unloaded at Genoa and bussed to Nice. That posed no problem for Louise and me, but we were worried about our dogs. Louise insisted on a seat on the bus for each Dalmatian, and she also insisted that the bus driver stop when we signaled so that we could take our animals out when they needed to go. We stayed overnight at a beautiful hotel on the beach on the Italian Riviera and the next morning took the bus to Nice.

This time we were headed for the Castel Provinçal, an apartment house development at the west end of Nice that Mme. Decarlis, who owned the Agence de Fabron, had reserved for us. Our brand-new apartment was on the ground floor at the corner of the building. It was the last of the apartments to be rented because its location made it the one most likely to be robbed. There was a little road winding around it leading to the underground parking area. The entrance to our apartment was through the back door and the garden. We knew that our Dalmatians would be no obstacle for the thieves; they would just throw in poisoned meat for them to eat, so we didn't leave the dogs out at night.

We had unexpected visitors right after we moved in. We kept Bijou's food on the floor in the bathroom, and one day we returned home to find a four-inch-wide trail of *formis d'argentine*—ants—running in through the window, down to the floor and across the floor into the bathroom. Louise was up to the challenge, though; she just wiped them off with a wet rag to get rid of them.

Our neighbors were M. and Mme. Papazian, an elderly retired couple. He had owned a mathematics school in Paris. I asked him one day if it was possible to win at roulette. He said yes, indeed, and wrote out a page-long formula. Unfortunately, I don't know what happened to it. The builder of our new apartment asked us what we would like to have planted for privacy, and we picked cypress, knowing that it would form a hedge across the entire back-yard. We made several trips up to Mont Chauve, picking up pieces of lava rock about one and a half feet long, carrying them home, and placing them all around the edge of the backyard as a wall for Louise's roses. The apartment was nice, but the terrace was our favorite spot. We kept two baskets for the Dalmatians there so they could be outside with us.

We loved so many things about Castel Provinçal. There was a fig tree in the back across the road that had wonderful figs. It was always a race between us and the local children to get them from the tree as they ripened. The washing machine made its own hot water and worked very well. The marble floors were beautiful. The hole in the toilet bowl seat was a problem, but the builder from whom we rented the apartment finally agreed to install a new toilet bowl seat. After having lived at the Castel Provinçal for the best part of the year, though, I started thinking about going back to the States again. I was walking with Louise down in Nice and I mentioned to her that I thought we should go back and I should get a job to build us some social security.

When we docked in New York, our son was there with a truck to carry our things back to Oakdale again and put our belongings in storage. We moved into a small cottage until we could decide where we wanted to settle.

Raccoons had always been a problem at Dowling College. Every morning we went outside to find the lid off our garbage and garbage strewn around. Determined to put a stop to the mess, I tied a string from the lid to a bell at the head of my bed. Whenever the bell rang, we would peek out and give the raccoon something to eat. One night the bell didn't ring, and we found a dead raccoon in the road nearby the next morning. We went out and bought a shovel to bury the raccoon. When our own raccoon returned the next night, we breathed a sigh of relief.

Early in the first ten years of being a practicing Catholic, I offered God my brains. Then I tried to take them back. One day as Louise and I were returning from a walk with Tina and Pistache, we noticed a cat stranded up in a tree. We continued home, but I returned to try to rescue the cat. This old paratrooper in his early fifties climbed the tree. I kept calling to the cat. It kept climbing higher and further away. Finally I reached a point where the branches would not support my weight. I decided the heck with the cat and descended. On reaching the lowest branch, about ten feet from the ground, I let go and did a rear tumble. I hadn't realized that the ground sloped downward and away, escalating my tumble. When I finally stopped rolling I didn't know where I was—or who I was. I saw railroad tracks and a path and decided to take the path. When I encountered a man, I called out to him and asked for help. I told him I thought I lived in one of those apartments nearby, pointing my finger. He took me to what I thought might be my apartment and pushed the doorbell. When Louise came to the door, I said, "Who are you?" An immediate trip to the hospital followed.

My memory started to return right away, and I had completely recovered it in twenty-four hours. That's when I told God, "I take back having offered you my brain." I don't think you can take back things like that once they've been offered, though. The amnesia left me with occasional transient spells, two in 1985 and three in 1986. The neurologist I saw didn't think the spot that showed in a brain scan was related, and in any case it eventually disappeared.

One evening at Oakdale we played cards with Rich and Vicki, completely unaware that their marriage was in trouble. The next morning, to our horror, they separated. We had known nothing about what was going on between them. Apparently, even the papal blessing I had secured for them wasn't enough to keep them together.

Tired of being unsettled, I scanned the classified ads every day looking for a place to rent. Louise and I had talked about buying a place that would bring in some income, and we even looked at a ten-room hotel up in Redhook, New York, for forty thousand dollars. But Louise didn't want to be tied down that way. Actually, I think she was worried that I would have refused to rent rooms to unwed couples, which I would have.

I started looking at ads for places in Sag Harbor, farther out on Long Island. When Louise asked why I was looking so far from the city, I told her that I wanted a place that we could rent whenever we went to France. We eventually rented a duplex at the Harbor Close condominiums just across the street from the bay.

While we were living there we were charmed by a Russian Afghan hound, the leader of a small pack of dogs that would come to the back door of our ground-floor apartment. Louise would remove ticks from him and give him a treat. He was a very smart dog. One day while he was walking with his master along the water's edge, Louise passed by and he pretended not to know her. That's how smart he was. He would lead the other dogs to the water but never went in himself—he would just stand there with his feet in the water.

Now that we were in Sag Harbor we decided to buy a house, but we couldn't seem to find the right place. We bought a duplex penthouse for fifty thousand dollars and then bought a smaller apartment that we sold for a modest profit to the young couple that had been renting it. We thought it would be good for them, but they divorced shortly thereafter.

I still wasn't ready to look for employment because Pistache had to be walked about a dozen times a day. Finally, in 1972, I started with Mutual of New York as a life and health agent. We bought a 1972 Pinto and I worked out of MONY's Melville office about seventy miles away. That meant that I had to commute at least 140 miles every day, in addition to seeing prospects in different areas, some as far away as upstate New York. My market was retiring New York City firefighters, who would take the maximum option pension and cover it with life insurance instead of taking the fraction of the maximum that would go to their wives if the men died first that way, if their wives predeceased them they would retain the maximum pension. I worked for Mutual of New York for fifteen years.

Our new apartment overlooked Sag Harbor and was less than a hundred yards from the water. I put in a redwood deck in removable sections, and we had a fifteen-foot awning installed. Then I made and hung eight beautiful three-foot redwood flower boxes that Louise filled with petunias. I also put in oak flooring on both floors myself.

We put an ad in the paper to sell some furniture, and Arthur Baron, a local antique dealer and auctioneer, responded. We refused to sell below our asking prices, but Louise wound up working for Arthur at the auctions and in his large shop. She was quite knowledgeable about antiques, and was always straight with the customers. Arthur would point a finger up in the air behind certain customers' backs with the Italian salute, but Louise would pay no attention to Arthur and to his surprise she'd make a good sale. Louise's new job solved the dog-walking problem, too. She could come home for lunch every day and walk them. That was certainly a relief.

Although I drove long distances, I never stayed out overnight, even through blizzards and other foul weather. And I always brought something home a treat for Louise—bagels or some treat from Nathan's or her favorite diner. The IRS continually called me down to explain my mileage.

In 1974 we moved to France once again. I kept my job with Mutual of New York, planning to work out of the company's office in Frankfurt, Germany. We boarded the *Michelangelo* with Tina and Pistache, our 1972 Pinto, and metal footlockers loaded with our personal belongings.

The *Michelangelo* anchored offshore in Cannes, and Louise's cousins, Liliane and George met us. Our realtor, Madame Decarlis, had rented Villa Les Glorioses in Nice for us on the Corniche Fleurie. The rent fluctuated with the value of the dollar, but it was usually right around two hundred dollars a month. The bed was a large hideaway that rose up into the wall when it wasn't in use. We were accustomed to twin beds, and Louise immediately declared me persona non grata. "Find yourself another place," she said. "You're not sleeping in here with me." I found a tiny room in the back of the villa with a very small bed. At its head was a wooden shelf holding some books and other objects. The very first night I slept there the shelf fell down and missed my head by a hair. After that it was safe. Can you imagine God chuckling?

We made a new friend, a seven-inch gecko that hung out on the wall of the basement. I dug a small vegetable garden at the back of the villa, and a gardener took care of the front. Weeds seemed to grow almost a foot a day. I asked the gardener to do the backyard as well, around my garden. He called the owner's rental agency and explained, "Mr. Fisco likes the back, but the owner likes the front." In the end I wound up doing both, carrying bundles of weeds every day. I found one or two small snakes under stones, but I don't think they were the vipers found in the area. There were foxes, though. We could hear them barking at night in the ravine just below the villa.

Whenever I left Louise at the villa while I went to attend a meeting at the Frankfurt agency. She would stay at the Hotel Les Fusains with the animals. On arriving in Frankfurt, I asked an elderly gentleman for directions to 1315 Schlastrasse. He was no help at all, and I was starting to get rather frustrated when a young man noticed that I was having trouble and offered to help. He gave me the directions I needed, and I asked him what was wrong with the elderly man I had been talking to. "He is deaf," the young man answered.

The manager of the agency was a retired army colonel. The meeting lasted just one day and I returned to Nice, very pleased with the outcome. I achieved more rapport with the Germans in a single visit than I had gained in years with the French, perhaps because our German heritage is such an integral part of American culture. It looked like the best market for insurance sales would be with the military in Toulon, where the U.S. Navy had anchored. That was too out of the way for me, though. I had come to France hoping to avoid the long commutes and long-distance travel my job in the States had entailed. I told Louise that we had to go home because I wasn't selling any insurance and money would be running out before long. We sold the 1972 Pinto for fifteen hundred dollars and returned to Sag Harbor with the rest of our belongings.

I continued selling for Mutual of New York after we returned to Sag Harbor. We bought a Thunderbird, and I put almost two hundred miles a day—about forty-five thousand miles a year—on that car in the course of my work. We also acquired a third dog. Louise was transferring a little beagle from the vet to the Animal Rescue Fund Kennel, and he looked at her so pitifully during the drive that she brought him home. We named him Fiston, which means "little son" in French. The first thing he did was pee-pee on the TV when he heard a dog's bark coming from the set.

One day I broke down about seventy-five miles from home and Louise had to come and pick me up. She had been preparing supper, and while she was gone, Fiston got up on the counter by way of a chair and table and ate everything—the whole meal plus bananas, skins and all. He was just burping when we got home.

Abbé Merlin celebrating Mass at Saint Antoine de Ginestière. His little dog can be seen on the floor at the left side of the altar. I told him I loved Louise as much as I loved God. He said I should love God the most.

Chapter 12

Virginia:
The Willow Lake
Manor House

In 1987, after back-to-back ten-inch snowfalls, we decided to sell our duplex penthouse in Sag Harbor and move south to Virginia. We sold the condominium for a hundred and fifty thousand dollars making a hundred thousand dollar profit. I had made many improvements, including installing oak floors, a redwood deck, an awning and flower boxes that Louise had kept filled with petunias.

Before anything else, though, we needed to rearrange our finances. I had run up thirty-five thousand dollars on charge cards with all our trips to France. Louise had saved up forty thousand dollars from working at Baron's Antiques, so I asked her to pay off my five or so charge cards. She was reluctant, but she did it. I kept my American Express card, because it had to pay in full each month, and cancelled our other charge cards. Visa and MasterCard wouldn't cancel the charge for two years. I haven't run up a credit card bill since. I would retire from

Mutual of New York and pick up a twenty-five thousand dollar lump sum on retirement.

We had been taking almost weekly trips to Virginia looking for a home, staying at a motel in Keysville. On one occasion we walked the two black Labs, Jody and Mega, along with Fiston, the beagle, in open farmland near the hotel. A herd of cattle up on a small hill nearby came down toward us. The cows were black with white faces. All of them stopped and stared at Louise, completely ignoring the barking dogs. Somehow they knew what we did not yet know that Louise had terminal breast cancer.

We didn't find what we wanted around Keysville, so on the next trip to Virginia we went to Charlottesville. A real estate agent showed us the Willow Lake Manor House, which had been empty for several years. It was one mile from downtown Charlottesville on Route 20 and came with about four and a half acres. It had five bedrooms, four bathrooms, and two screened porches that we knew our cat, Kiki, would love. I thought it had definite possibilities, but it would need a lot of work. The three-quarter-inch stucco exterior badly needed painting, and the tin roof needed work. The kitchen had big holes in the floor. The floors would need to be replaced and the interior painted throughout. The house was solid, though, and all of the walls were straight except for the front wall, which slanted inward at the top, intentionally. The wall studs were sturdy four-by-seven hand-hewn oak, and the floor beams were solid old oak. The huge living room had a beautiful fireplace that needed a flue pipe. We worried some about the cellar and possible flooding. Virginia gets a lot of rain; four or even eight inches can fall in a single rainstorm. Further, the property had a little stream that would need to be kept open. A charming little bridge crossed over the stream about halfway between Route 20 and the house. This was the home I had always wanted for Louise. We decided to take it and agreed on a price of one hundred fifty thousand dollars. And then the work began.

We moved into the house in the winter of 1987 right after the two ten inch snow falls which they also had. A sixty-foot trailer carried all of our things down from Sag Harbor, including some antiques Arthur Baron had given us. Bright red cardinals dotted the snow along the sides of the little stream as we drove up the driveway; it was a beautiful sight. The renovations were both costly and time-consuming. We had five contractors working and three painters—two outside and one inside. The chimney man put in a new lining but I didn't like it. He had started it too high up the chimney. It didn't come all the way to the bottom inside, leaving space for heat to escape. It had to be redone we didn't use it. The plumber was the best worker of all. He did the hardest work in the crawl spaces and put in the sump pump in the cellar at our request. Later, when the cellar was finished, I painted the walls with white Therma-Seal, and we had a Ping Pong table and wine room, with shelves I kept fully stocked.

The young painter working inside took a beating when he worked in the upstairs room that we had decided to make our master bedroom. He closed himself in the room and told us to turn up the heat, and then he stayed inside and scraped the Howdy Doody wallpaper off the walls. After he got the walls smooth, he painted them a beautiful light green. That bedroom had a fireplace that used the same chimney as the living room below. We put in our twin beds, and our two Labradors and the beagle would come up on the beds with us at night. Opposite our bedroom were two large guestrooms, each with a double bed.

A carpenter put a new floor in the twenty-eight-foot kitchen, and we had Italian tile installed over it. New solid cherry cabinets gave the room a bright elegance. There were two bedrooms downstairs: a large one and a small bedroom off the kitchen that I was going to use as an office to continue in insurance, keeping track of my old clients. It was probably originally designed to be the maid's quarters, but it made a nice little workspace.

Louise was in charge of the inside decoration. She made all of the drapes and curtains for the entire house. The outside was my domain. I ordered a power mower from Lowe's and got started. There were snakes all over the place, mostly black snakes. Having been an amateur herpetologist when I was young, I didn't worry about them. One black snake that must have been living inside and underneath our stone terrace had to go, though. He was probably friendly because he thought we knew he was always there. When we saw him near the garage I put on gloves, picked him up, and carried him across Route 20 to Carter's Mountain. I was careful handling him because even nonpoisonous snakes can transmit nasty bacteria when they bite. Another black snake that got into the cellar had to be removed too.

We had a diviner come with a forked stick to check for water under the house. He located three small streams. I searched downstream and found where the drainpipes came out and kept those open. I got into the stream with a cordless hedge clipper and kept it open, too.

Louise and I replaced all of the screening on the two porches. Replacing the spline strips that held the screening in place was a truly tedious job. I wanted strong screens in place, though; because I worried that a wild animal would charge Kiki through the screen. After we acquired another cat, Coco, the two cats would lounge together in one of the two outside screened-in areas.

Our real estate agent had told us that Louise could sell her antiques from the garage, a barn like structure that I stained red inside and put in really good condition, even replacing rotting wood around the doors, but when Louise went down to town and asked the town council for permission, they refused to give it to her. And while our realtor had told us that six special permits had been issued to people to sell antiques from their homes, the council said they had done no such thing. That worried me a lot, because I had been counting on Louise having a source of income if something should happen to me.

One evening at sunset, Louise and I were resting on the front porch after a hard day's work. I had changed the rotting porch steps to redwood and repainted them gray. Jody, Mega (I called her Maggie), and Fiston were with us. I had put a stretch gate across the stairs to keep the dogs on the porch. I thought I heard a car drive slowly by on Route 20 and then stop. Moments later, both Jody and Mega leaped into the air and started barking. Someone was coming up toward the stream, but he took off when he heard the barking. I didn't turn the dogs loose, good for him and the dogs, but I did go down to see who it was. He was back in his car and driving away behind the trees before I could get there. The house had been vacant for several years before we purchased it. Since it was almost dark and we had not put the lights on, he probably thought that it was still vacant. He must have been a young person to have run the fifty yards back to the road so quickly. That convinced me that we needed a fence around the property. The front was already partly fenced, and I continued the fence around the back, using a posthole digger for each fence post.

There were apartment houses up on the hill behind us across the road. We connected to the city water and sewer systems that ran through our property. The apartment developers owned Willow Lake, which adjoined our property and occasionally overflowed onto it because it was at a slightly higher elevation than our land. The whole property sloped down toward the stream. When it rained, the stream would widen into almost a river. The water would come up about one-third the distance from the stream toward the house. After I got it cleared out, the water would pass on through and flood the lands below. Keeping our stream open helped alleviate overflow from the lake into our stream, and the melody from the crickets, katydids, toads, and bullfrogs at night compensated for any runoff we did get.

I had planted a tomato patch with about twenty beefsteak plants behind the house on a level piece of earth surrounded by six-by-six-foot creosoted beams. Louise froze some for the winter, but we had so many tomatoes left over that we kept a basket full on the edge of the road that led to the apartments with a little Help Yourself sign.

Relations between the apartment people and us were generally good, although we did have some differences. An elm tree killed by Dutch elm disease was lying on the apartment grounds. Besides being a menace to our own elms, it was an ugly sight. I asked the apartment owners to remove it, but they didn't. A fungus causes the disease. The European carries the spores and native Elm Bark Beetle and the disease can spread from tree to tree by the roots as well. It spread to the three great elms that towered over our house, and eventually we had to have them taken down. They were a great loss. During the hunting season, wild turkeys from Carter's Mountain would flock over to our property and perch all over them.

After two years—and about a hundred thousand dollars invested in our home—Louise became seriously ill. She had noticed the first lump in her breast right after we moved in, not long after the incident in Keysville with the cattle. One night as we were about to go to sleep she asked me to feel her breast, saying that she felt a lump. I couldn't feel anything, but she was sure it was there. She went to the doctor shortly thereafter, there was a lump and the doctor decided to do a biopsy. We went back later for that, and Louise had decided to have a complete mastectomy if it was cancer. President Reagan's wife, Nancy, had had a complete mastectomy, and Louise, who admired her, thought it would be the right thing to do. I waited downstairs by the phone. I knew what Louise wanted, and when the doctor called down and told me it was cancer, I told him to go ahead and do the complete mastectomy. The doctor gave Louise no chemotherapy afterward, though, nothing at all. I believe that was a huge mistake.

Twenty-three months later, Louise took a turn for the worse, and on August 31, 1989, the doctor told her that her cancer had metastasized to the liver. He gave her one-month to live, six months if the medication worked. I believe the average life span with breast cancer is seven months once it has metastasized.

It seemed that every summer afternoon was punctuated by a big thunderstorm; some were very violent. We belonged to nearby Holy Comforter Catholic Church and attended the six o'clock evening vigil mass on Saturday, and it never failed that a thunderstorm would roll through while we were at mass. When we returned home, the first thing we did was check for leaks.

One evening as we returned from the six o'clock Saturday mass, we found a copperhead at our front gate. Although I hated to do it, I killed the snake with stones. There were children in the apartments above our home plus our dogs, and I had no way to keep the snake until someone could pick it up and move it. Snakes seemed to be part of our everyday summertime existence. One day Louise screamed out to me, "A black snake is eating the baby robins!" The nest was high in a pine tree at the back door. I climbed up and called down to Louise to get me the long pruners, then tried reaching out from the trunk to knock the snake off the branch. I finally succeeded, but it landed on a lower branch and started climbing right back up, wrapping its tail around the branches to help it climb. I knocked it down again, and this time it fell to the ground stunned. I picked it up and carried it over to Carter's Mountain, which was getting quite a population of black snakes from our yard.

On the morning of December 13, 1987, I awoke about six a.m. Jody, ourLab, was not on either of our beds. I went downstairs and found her lying under the kitchen table. About a month earlier she had had an operation for cancer in the upper part of one of her front legs. The medication she took afterward made her weak and groggy. I had stopped the medication to let her run free and enjoy her last few days. I picked her up from under the table and drove her to the vet. Jody died in my arms while the vet was examining her. I would later take her ashes to France and sprinkle them around our *caveau*. Jody was a very intelligent dog. When we had started out from Sag Harbor on our way to Virginia, we stopped at a hotel for the night. When I let Jody out in the deep snow for a walk, she started to walk away. I had to call her several times to get her back in. I guess she didn't want to leave. In Virginia, she never wanted to go down to the cellar even after I had cleaned it up. The owner had told us that her husband was buried on the property, but she wouldn't tell us where. I had a sneaking suspicion that Jody knew.

Once we had completed most of the renovations, we began to make use of our big new house. Louise's cousins George and Liliane visited from France that same December. We had a limousine pick them up at the airport in Richmond. The next morning we were having breakfast in the large kitchen, which had windows overlooking the entire front property. A light snow had fallen the night before, and we were enjoying the peaceful view. Suddenly two deer ran across our field of vision. George and Liliane were enchanted to see them; deer were unknown in southern France.

During the summer of 1988 we had beautiful weather when Arthur and Bobbie Baron came down from Bridgehampton to visit Louise. Louise prepared a wonderful dinner, and we ate out on the front porch. We took them up to visit Monticello. It was through the Barons that we met our neighbors Hanna and Robert Sabel, who had moved to Charlottesville from Bridgehampton before we moved from Sag Harbor. Louise knew them from Arthur Baron's antique store in Sag Harbor. They had invited us to dinner more than once when we were in Sag Harbor and again in Charlottesville.

The Sabels helped us get Coco, our Himalayan blue point. We purchased her from the mother of the Sabels' veterinarian, who bred Himalayans. Right after we brought Coco home, she developed a rare blood disease. She had to be fed and medicated intravenously for several days, but finally she pulled out of it. Coco had beautiful blue eyes, cream-colored fur, and splotchy beige paws. She and Kiki, our other cat, spent most days hanging out on one or the other of our ground-level screened-in porches or in her basket on the sunlit tiled kitchen floor. Kiki was a black domestic that had belonged to Louise's father. Louise had brought her back from France when her father died. Kiki ran the whole house, dogs and all. She liked olives, cheese, and everything a human ate.

I talked to Robert Sabel about my plan to build a gate at the entrance to our house, and he showed me two heavy old oak sections of a fence that would be perfect for the gate frame. He not only gave them to us but also delivered them. The gate turned into quite a project. I hack sawed two ten-foot pieces from a twenty-one-foot-long four-inch pipe, and then dug two deep holes between the two five-foot stone columns. I had to drill large holes for bolts that went through the strap hinges that supported the two sections. I tried to drill the holes myself, but the drill flew out of my hands. A mechanic from a nearby auto repair and gas station drilled them for me. I dug the holes about three feet deep and then ran into a stone that was about twelve inches long. I could grab it lying flat on my stomach, but to my surprise, I couldn't lift it. It was a surprise to find the limitation of my body. Louise had to help me wedge it high enough to lift it from a crawl position. Then I poured in a dry mixture of gravel and cement. I followed this with water, being careful to hold the pipes perpendicular. The final product was a beautiful two-section old-oak gate with large antique strap hinges. Louise planted clematis at the base of each stone post, and each spring and summer the plants were covered with beautiful pink flowers. Louise had a green thumb in addition to all her other talents.

Poco Coberly had helped dig the holes when he and his wife, Ruby, visited from West Virginia. Poco, whose real name was Herb got his nickname, the Spanish equivalent of our "Tiny," when he mistakenly parachuted into Spanish

Morocco. Although Herb was about a foot taller than the average Spaniard, the name stuck when he rejoined us in Italy. Poco played football in college in West Virginia and looked like a tall wide end receiver.

Those gates increased our security, but they cost me a good bit of money. One Sunday morning I was leaving in our slant-six Dodge Ram van and left the motor running while I got out to open the gates. I didn't think to apply the hand break. While my back was turned, the van popped out of park and into gear, and sped down about fifty yards down the incline and into the stream, where it wedged itself under the bridge. I chased after it, trying to stop it, but couldn't catch up. It took two tow trucks to pull it out. The repairs cost about three thousand dollars, and my insurance rate was increased, too. Once the key was put in the ignition the motor would start up by itself. I called in mechanics. They couldn't believe it. I took it to Dodge. They never saved me the defective part.

Once again, we could not seem to stay in one place. For some reason Louise decided that we should put the house up for sale. We asked two hundred sixty-five thousand dollars for it, but I'm sure the house was worth seven hundred fifty thousand dollars if it was worth a dime. We had put a lot of money and work into that beautiful house. In addition to the painting, new floors, and structural work, we had installed all new copper gutters and put in Douglas-fir fascia boards behind the copper gutters. That was hard and dangerous work. It took a very tall ladder to get at the gutters, and the young man who did the work removed bushels of bat guano.

Our Willow Lake Manor House, the home I had always wanted for Louise, sold in a couple of months at the bargain price we were asking for it. Louise wanted to get away, and quickly. Maybe she lacked confidence in the medical treatment she was getting in Virginia, or perhaps she did not want me to have to live in that enormous house alone after she died. I think she wanted to die in France. When we left Charlottesville, our goal was to move to France.

Toward the end of 1989, with Louise's condition getting worse, I had to have Mega, our Labrador retriever, put down. She was fourteen years old and incontinent, and I just couldn't handle the situation. She had been a brave and loving pet, and I was heartbroken to see her go. We were left with our little beagle, Fiston, and our two cats, Coco and Kiki.

After the house was sold, we had an auction to downsize our possessions. The auctioneer seemed very honest and likable, and he seemed to have planned the auction well. There was a large tent for the main auction and a smaller one for Louise's beautiful collection of dolls. To our disgust, we later discovered that the auctioneer, a woman, practically gave the dolls away. Louise was too sick to do anything about it when we found out, and we left so soon after the auction that there wasn't enough time to complain. Our library, mostly books in French, brought about ten thousand dollars. The book dealers complained after the auction that they couldn't buy any because the University of Virginia students bought them all.

The house was completely empty when we left. Only our antique chandelier over the stairway and the curtains that Louise had lovingly made herself remained. The house was beautiful even when it was empty. After all of the work we had done, the Willow Lake Manor House was now ready for the next century. It was destined to become a bed and breakfast. Frank and Darwin Pologruto told us later that there had been a chimney fire.

Chapter 13

Back in Maine

Our son rented a cottage for us up in Maine, and we started out with Fiston, Coco, and Kiki. We drove in our van, pulling a little U-Haul trailer, and had someone else drive our Ford Thunderbird. Louise was very, very ill—so ill she could hardly stand up—but she insisted on driving. She was groggy and in terrible pain, but she wanted to drive, so I let her. We drove until dark and then started looking for a place to stay. We were in Connecticut on the main highway, and when we stopped at a tollbooth, I told the toll taker that my wife was very sick and we wanted to get to a hotel. He gave us some complicated directions, and it took us quite a while to get there, but we finally found the hotel. After we checked in and went upstairs, though, I realized what kind of place this was. "This is a whorehouse, sissy" I told Louise. "Let's get the hell out of here." Apparently, the attendant at the tollbooth had thought that I wanted a place to shack up and sent us to this place. Anyway, we got back on the main road and easily found a Holiday Inn where we spent the night. The next morning we managed to drive only a few miles before we had a flat tire. We didn't have a cell phone, so I hung something white on the car and waited. It wasn't long before a Good Samaritan stopped and offered to help. He called U-Haul on his cell phone for us and took off. Shortly afterward, someone came and changed the tire and we continued on to Maine.

We arrived at the little cottage our son had rented for us in mid-September 1989. It was right by the water in East Harpswell, and two beautiful loons were poking around by the shore. There was one double bed plus a cot in the hallway. Louise was in terrible pain. She couldn't sleep on the bed at all, so she went out in the hall and tried to sleep on the cot, which was more rigid.

Our Virginia neighbors Hanna and Robert Sabel had recommended that Louise see Dr. Greenspan in New York, and he in turn arranged for her to see Dr. Dorsk, an oncologist at the Maine Center for Cancer Medicine (MCCM) in Portland. Unfortunately, Dr. Dorsk was on vacation, and Louise had to wait a couple of weeks before starting her chemotherapy. It was a frustrating and worrisome two weeks, but Dr. Dorsk finally returned, and Louise started chemotherapy on October 2, 1989. After less than three weeks she felt like a new person. The chemotherapy was working! I always took notes on the visits to Dr. Dorsk because of my short memory, and he would tease me about writing a story. At the time, it was the farthest thing from my mind.

Dr. Dorsk was the best—always positive—and Louise always felt better when we left after the chemotherapy. He became a friend as well as a doctor, even taking Louise out himself a couple of times—once to a wine tasting and once to a jewelry exhibit. He and Mrs. Dorsk invited us to dinner at their home, and during the conversation Dr. Dorsk commented that the quality of life was the most important for cancer patients. I responded with, "All I know is that every day that Louise lives is one day less I will live without her." Mrs. Dorsk added "Bravo" to that.

We rented a brand-new furnished home not far from the cottage in East Harpswell. The house, at One Howard's Hill Road in Gurnet Landing, was in the woods. We immediately set up bird-feeding stations and watched chickadees, crows, and other visitors from our large rear living room windows.

The basement was clean, dry, and accessible. We stored our belongings there and started indulging our love for antiques, purchasing old pieces from used furniture places. Life was quiet and uneventful in the house, and we had few outside interests. Every minute we spent together was precious. When there is a life-threatening illness in the family, one looks at everything from a different perspective. We loved each other; nothing could take that away from us, and we had the peace that comes only from God. We stayed there for a year.

We didn't expect Louise to live very long. The average life span once breast cancer metastasizes is seven months. Louise and I decided to take a trip to France so that she could have a final visit with all of her family. Our whole family went: Louise, me, Rich, his wife Barb, their children Vera and Ralph, and Barb's children from her previous marriage, Lana and Cosmo. And of course we took Fiston, Kiki, and Coco. We left for JFK on February 8, 1990, with return reservations for March 30, 1990.

Chapter 14

Visiting the Family in France

W e rented two apartments at the Marina Baie des Anges, three massive, curved, and modern structures on the shores of the Mediterranean just west of Nice. Louise and I rented a Dodge Espace van, and Rich and Barb rented what my son called the Renault Zipper because of its stripe around the middle. February is spring on the Riviera, and the mimosa trees were covered with clusters of fragrant yellow blooms.

Louise continued her weekly chemotherapy at Centre Antoine-Lacassagne, a large medical complex at the east end of Nice. Dr. Greenspan had recommended a doctor who was to coordinate with Dr. Dorsk, Louise's oncologist. The treatments didn't help, and we had to wait in a little room almost four hours each time before treatment. I paid in cash and don't recall even submitting claims for reimbursement.

We traveled extensively during that visit. Our first excursion was to Monte

Carlo with Louise's brother Henri, the builder; his wife, Maryse, a Cordon Bleu cook; Louise's brother Roger, an interior decorator; and his wife, Marionette, also an excellent cook. We took along Fiston but left Coco and Kiki back at the apartment. There was some walking after we parked and it was not easy for Louise, but she managed. Then it was to the beach at Juan les Pins with Louise's cousins George and Liliane, both retired from teaching and now working in real estate, and their two boys, Pierre and Oliver. We were godparents to Pierre. And, of course, there were all of our kids and Fiston (dogs are allowed on the beaches in France). It was a wonderful day; even Louise went in the water.

Our next excursion was the long ride into Italy, crossing Col de Tende and heading north to Cuneo, where Louise's stepmother, Marie, came from. Marie had given us a beautiful carved, fifteen-inch, eighteenth-century crucifix with a bronze corpus. A photograph of it, with the Divine Mercy St. Faustina crystal ruby rosary superimposed, adorns the cover of this book. We knew that the crucifix was from Indochina, but we never asked Marie who had given it to her. Louise's paratrooper brother Jeanot, who was mortally wounded at Dien Bien Phu and died in a hospital January 25, 1955 in Saigon, may have mailed it to her; or it may have been among his personal belongings. The Riviera had been warm and sunny, but it was winter in Cuneo. About four feet of snow blanketed the outskirts of the city.

On returning that night to the Marina Baie des Anges we found that our ground-floor apartment had been broken into. It was a very professional job. The thieves had cut a small hole through the thick plate glass just under the sliding door's lock and reached in to open it. Even firefighters have a tough time with this type of door. We had Fiston with us, and Coco had hidden inside the apartment, but Kiki escaped into the night. We called the family, and at least a dozen of them showed up almost immediately. Henri found Kiki in a backyard a hundred yards away. The next morning we drove to the nearest police station to report the incident. The response was a bored French version of "What else is new?" Fortunately, Louise had been wearing all of her jewelry, so the thieves got nothing.

On another day we visited our friends in Lantosque (forty-five kilometers of hairpin turns inland), one of the 509th's positions during the war, and stopped in to eat and visit at Paulin and Francine Maurel's very small restaurant, a favorite of ours through the years. By coincidence Johnny and Helen McDonald had stopped and eaten at Paulin's when visiting France many years after the war. Johnny, who had jumped with John De Vanie and others with the

Pathfinders in southern France, had written "509" on a piece of paper and handed it to Paulin. To Johnny's amazement, Paulin wrote Fisco alongside 509 and handed it back.

Then we went over to the Bar des Tilleuls, a bar and restaurant owned by Maria and her daughter, Didoun, in the center of Lantosque. Maria and her husband, Charles Audat, had run the bistro nearby and kept the men of the 509th supplied with pasta and wine during the war. Charles, a very big man, had suffered a heart attack when challenged to lift a keg. It was their one-year-old son, Paulin, for whom I had asked Doc Mullens to inject with penicillin. The morning after the injection Paulin was completely cured. Paulin is now in his mid-fifties.

On the sixteenth of February we were back in Nice for the big carnival that the city held every year, and we attended with the kids. Soon after that came the banquet at L'Aire Saint Michel Auberge de Cimiéz near Mont Chauve. About thirty-three family members were present, and everyone was smiling and happy, all trying to forget for the moment the purpose of the reunion. As the evening came to an end, everyone kissed Louise good-bye.

Louise's father and stepmother were buried in the small cemetery at Saint Antoine Ginestière, at the west end of Nice, and Henri took care of their *caveau* (gravesite). We visited, cleaned the monument, and Louise watered the flowers. I already knew that Louise wanted to be buried here when her time came. We used to attend Abbé Merlin's mass in the church nearby when we lived in the Villa on the Corniche Fleurie. Abbé Merlin's little dog was always present on the altar with him during mass.

One day we took a ride to the Baou de Saint Jeannet, enjoying as always the sight of the huge rock that towers behind the little village. The 509th bivouacked nearby for several weeks just before we were moved on December 29, 1944, up to an old castle in Villers-Cotterêts not far from Paris—the site where Louise dreamed I would be wounded in the left arm and my wedding ring would be changed to my right hand. Our unit left from there for the Battle of the Bulge, traveling all night through the snow in open trucks.

Eventually, March 30 arrived and we had to go back to the United States. The return trip from Nice to JFK went smoothly. Rich retrieved his van from the long-term parking area and dropped us off in East Harpswell, then returned to their rented home in Topsham, adjacent to Brunswick.

We thought that was to be Louise's last trip to France. Not so!

Chapter 15

A New Home in Maine

After our return from France, we resumed the weekly twenty-six-mile trips to Portland for Louise's chemotherapy. The trips were hard on Louise, and we began to think about moving to Portland to be nearer to her doctors. On one of our trips in the summer of 1990 we had lunch outside at DiMillo's, a boat restaurant in Portland on Commercial Street. We saw some very nice-looking apartments across the water on the adjacent pier and contacted a real estate agency on Commercial Street. The apartments, we were told, were the Chandler's Wharf condominiums, and a realtor showed us unit 5C on the ground floor. The condo came with two parking spots on the pier below. We signed a year's lease for about a thousand dollars a month. I asked the agent to put a clause in the contract that gave us right of first refusal to buy if the owner ever decided to sell and they did. Louise was very sick by then, and we were hoping to buy it and not have to move again. We moved into our beautiful apartment that same year. Our neighbors were mostly doctors, lawyers, and business people.

As the Lord would have it, about thirty of the apartments were put up for auction, and ours was one of them. Louise cautioned me not to go too high, but I was determined to buy it so that Louise wouldn't have to move again. When it came to unit 5C, the wife of the auctioneer was sitting beside me. The bidding reached one hundred sixteen thousand dollars and stopped. She asked me if I wanted it. I answered, "Yes." It was God's way of compensating us for our losses in Virginia. The condo had originally sold for about three hundred thousand dollars. I also had a feeling that something caused the other bidders to back off for me.

Toward the end of 1990 I called my younger brother, Joey. I talked about Louise, of course. She was always foremost in my mind, and I was so worried about her. He told me about a strange experience. He had been drinking in a bar when an old woman walked in, handed him a red rose, and asked for nothing. When he returned home, he found that an impossible miracle had happened. "Watch for the red rose!" he told me. Of course, the rose was from Saint Theresa of Lisieux, whose mother was said to have died of breast cancer. After hearing that, I prayed even harder for a miracle. If Joey had experienced one then why not Louise?

Anyway, our forty-sixth wedding anniversary, December 8, 1990, and Louise's birthday, December 10 (she was born in 1926), were very close. We celebrated both events at a dinner with Rich, Barb, young Vera, and Ralph in Topsham. Barb had ordered a cake for our anniversary, but it turned out to be an ordinary, and very stale, pound cake, so we decided to return it. The new cake was to be ready in two days. When Louise and I picked it up from the bakery, we saw that it was a large rectangular pastry like a cannoli. On top was a large red rose done in pastry, which we had not asked for.

Louise visited her gastroenterologist, Dr. Douglas A. Howell (the best) on November 30 and December 3, 1990, and we learned that Louise was in remission. All that remained of the six centimeter lesions in her liver was a tiny speck. I kissed Dr. Howell on both cheeks, and then we went home and celebrated. Ecstatic over Louise's reprieve, we left for another trip to France, leaving on December 9, 1990, and returning on January 17, 1991. As always, we took Fiston, the wise little old beagle, Kiki the black domestic cat, always in charge, and Coco the beautiful Himalayan Blue Point. They all traveled in the baggage compartment in separate kennels.

This time, Louise's cousins Liliane and George Feligioni had arranged for us to stay at the Motel Le Gazouillis at Ville Neuve Lubet. The rooms were like small apartments. The first week there we took a trip to Italy along with Henri and Roger, Louise's brothers, and their wives, Maryse and Marionette in a rented van. We wanted to find where Louise's mother was buried at the graveyard in Mentone, her hometown, where she was vacationing when she died.

We went to the graveyard, but no plaque or stone marked the gravesite we were looking for. Louise stood and cried. I looked where she stood and saw a round concrete stone beneath her feet covering an opening. I said to her, "Your mother is probably buried right under where you are standing." We lifted the cover and saw a pile of bones underneath ten feet below. I was right. A close cousin of Louise's mother who had been present when she died was still living. He had access to old village records and confirmed to Henri that their mother was buried in the community grave beneath where Louise had stood. Henri had a memorial plaque installed on the wall of the cemetery.

A second trip to Italy took us—including Fiston—to Anzio, where we visited the American cemetery in Nettuna where several 509ers were buried. Then we drove to Carano, where our front line had been located, and dropped in on Signor Spiragia, the owner of the house a hundred yards in from the Carano Road that had been our observation post. Rather than being glad to see me, though, he complained that we drank all his wine. He was wrong, I said; we didn't touch his wine, but we did eat some of his sausage and cheese, and we had fed some of the sausage to the two puppies he had left behind. He showed us a foxhole. It was a bit shallow, but was still recognizable. I asked him if any bodies had been found out where Joe Moffo and Ken Edney had been killed. He said, "No." Carano is still nothing but widely separated farmhouses. After that, we went to the shrine of Saint Francis of Assisi. The Franciscan priest just inside the main entrance would not let Fiston in, even when I said I would carry him, so I stayed outside with him and waited. There was an earthquake in later years. I always wonder if it was a wake up call since most people who visit Saint Francis are traveling and I wonder if they changed their rules.

On December 16, 1990, we had another farewell dinner with the immediate families at the Auberge Du Rayet, Chez Michel near Falicon and Mont Chauve. Henri and Roger and their wives, Maryse and Marionette, were there, and Marionette's daughter Nadine and her husband, Roger. Louise, at age sixty-four, is beautiful, healthy, and in full remission in the photo taken at that dinner. (Note: she made all her own clothing.) See color photo section.

Louise insisted that she was not returning to the States without a French toy poodle, so on December 21, 1990, we drove in our rented car to the Château de la Garoupe at Cap D'Antibes to have a look at five champion-bred mini poodles advertised in the local newspaper. The smallest of all went right up to Louise, and there was no question after that. We paid nine hundred dollars in French francs for the young male. His name had to be chosen, and it had to begin with the letter F because he had been born in 1990. Louise and Sabine, the breeder, wanted Fonzy, but I thought François was more appropriate. His actual name was entered on the record as Fonzy, but we always called him François. His champion father in France was Chocolate Boy. We took him to a vet for his shots, and then went back to the Gazouilles to introduce François to Fiston, Kiki, and Coco.

On December 27, Louise's cousin George drove us to Citibank in Monaco. From there, you could look up and see Tête de Chien, a formation at the top of the mountain that resembled the head of a dog. During the war, the Germans held out in a fort there, and the Navy had to shell them out. That was also the spot where I had looked down between the rocks and seen Monaco when I had scouted out the fort before our company advanced.

We spent New Year's Eve 1990 with Roger and Marionette at their beautiful apartment at Rue Valdilleta decorated by Roger himself. They had a little white Bichon Frise that they also named Fonzy. He was a little heavier than François and wasn't very friendly. Henri, Louise's other brother and Maryse were also there as well as Nadine, Marionette's daughter, and her husband Roger. There were delicacies, pastries, wine, and champagne galore.

A couple of days into 1991 we visited Biot, a little village west of Nice along the coast that is famous for its glass blowers. Fascinated, we watched them create works of art, and then selected a few whiskey and water glasses to take home with us.

On January 13 Henri and Maryse drove us in their Mercedes way up to Sospel to have dinner with Maryse's relatives Louisa and Fortune Gallis. The German army had retreated from southern France in World War II, but they held out in Sospel until the bitter end. The mountaintop was a fortress of tunnels and artillery built in conjunction with the Maginot Line in World War I. Fortune had the keys to let us in. It was an interesting spot.

On January 17 our "remission trip" came to an end. We left Nice with Fiston, Kiki, Coco, and François. All were in separate kennels except François, our puppy. He stayed with us on the plane in a little carrier and slept all the way home.

Louise holds François, our
mini puppy, in San Remo
with cousins George and
Liliane and her sister.

Louise in Monte Carlo. In
the background is Tête de
Chien, from where I
looked down into the
neutrality of Monte Carlo.

Sospel, France, at an underground fortress built as part of the Maginot Line. Here, the Germans held out 'til the very end.

Chapter 16

Louise's Final Illness

In the spring of 1991 the blood counts showed Louise's condition worsening. She was hospitalized quite a few times. I sneaked François in with me from time to time when I visited. The nurses condoned it, but since dogs weren't officially allowed in the hospital I had to get François by the security at the entrance desk. I would throw something over him, and he would be quiet even on the elevator until we got to Louise. Between my scouting expertise and François's intelligence, we always made it. In later years, my cardiologist, Dr. Minton, would ask me to visit the sick patients with François. I declined, knowing that he would be searching for Louise.

On July 24, 1991, I was sitting out on the balcony of our Chandler's Wharf apartment watching the lobstermen on the adjacent pier when I felt a heavy pressure in my chest. A visit to emergency at Maine Medical Center showed angina. I went in for angioplasty for a double blockage on July 25, 1991; Louise accompanied me. When the doctor visited me after the procedure, I asked him what he would do if he were in my shoes medically. He said that he would be a vegetarian, and so that is what I did. He also said my arteries were too small to perform a bypass. I guess that's why I was a long-distance runner and not a sprinter.

Henri and Maryse visited us in Portland from September 17 to October 4 in 1991. Henri, the French entrepreneur, was interested in everything. He would walk the lower parking level to the end of the pier and stroll out on the docks examining the footings. At the next condo association meeting I mentioned that Henri thought the pier was well built, and everyone applauded. Henri always spoke French at the supermarket, and somehow the cashiers always responded in French. I had been hoping that he would see what it was like to have to speak a foreign language.

It seemed that my entire little family was having one medical problem after the next. On May 3, 1992, my gall bladder was removed. When I woke up in the recovery room after the operation I had difficulty breathing. I called the nurse and told her I couldn't breath, that the doctor had sewed me up too tight. In fact, it was the first indication of the myasthenia gravis that would make itself known in 2000. A big French doctor told cousin Liliane later that he thought that Louise's breast cancer started in 1987 activated the M.G. While I was in the hospital, Fiston, who was by now very old, started toppling, and Louise had to pick him up and carry him around. He weighed over thirty pounds. After I returned from the hospital on May 7, we called a vet to come to the apartment and put Fiston down.

We had some early cold weather in the fall of 1992. We were still driving our slant-six Dodge Ram van, and it wasn't a good winter car. On descending the steep hill from Maine Medical in the van with Louise one day, I had trouble keeping the van from skidding. Several days later, Louise said, "Let's go trade in the van. I think I would like an Explorer." I went along with her wishes, knowing damn well she was worried about me after she died and that we were buying the four-wheel-drive Explorer for me, not herself.

We had to bring in private nurses to care for Louise at home until midnight. Arthur and Bobbie Baron called to see how we were doing, and several days later we received an envelope in the mail. There were two, ten thousand dollar checks inside—one from Arthur and the other from Bobbie—to pay for the nurses. I was worried because I didn't think the insurance would cover the night nurses. Eventually we were reimbursed for most of the expense, though.

One morning Louise was sitting at the breakfast table in our apartment at Chandler's Wharf. She turned to me and in a very weak voice said, "After I die, there are three things I would like for you to do. I would prefer to be buried in Nice, but the most important is that we be buried together. I would like for you to go on a cruise. And I would like for you to go and live with my family in France.

About the first day of November 1992, I was in my twin bed next to Louise's, an end table in between, keeping my endless vigil. It was daylight. Suddenly the beautiful eighteenth-century ebony crucifix from Indo-China left the wall, moved toward me, and then returned in a split second. It could have been my imagination, but I took it as a sign that the end was near.

A nurse, Anne Bersani, cared for Louise during the day; otherwise it was me. I watched her breathe through the night, counted her breaths, brushed her teeth, and gave her the medications. Anne and I didn't get along too well. She was not as tidy in the kitchen as I would have liked her to be. Somehow, her supervisor got wind of it—perhaps Anne told her—and South Portland Health Services decided to replace her. I said, "Don't you dare. The way Anne takes care of Louise has nothing to do with Anne and me." Louise was happy with her, and that's all that mattered. Anne and Louise played Scrabble, and Anne would take Louise in her wheelchair to the end of the pier. Anne knew how to turn Louise without hurting her.

Louise lived five years with her breast cancer, three of them after it had metastasized. When she began to get worse, they changed her doctor. She came in through the back door of MCCM for her chemotherapy because there was a ramp for her wheelchair. The nurses always commented how beautiful Louise looked. She dressed beautifully and she was beautiful.

I always kept charts and got copies of the hospital records while she was in the hospital. Her blood counts looked like she was responding to chemotherapy again. I told the new doctor that, but he paid no attention to me and decided to give her radiation. I called Dr. Greenspan in New York, and he said, "No way; it's too late for radiation. They should have done it in the beginning. Do not give her radiation now." Well, the new doctor went ahead and gave her the radiation, and she got worse. Once they gave her radiation she couldn't have chemotherapy for at least a month. It was downhill from there.

In the early morning hours of November 13, 1992, the feast day of Mother Frances Cabrini, Louise suffered severe pain. I gave her oral pain medication, but the pain continued. I called the ambulance and MCCM. The doctor at

MCCM who had insisted on the radiation answered my call. He said, "Okay, but if anything happens in the ambulance you are to let her go." I replied, "Okay."

An attendant called me at home the next morning to tell me that Louise was failing. I called my son in Topsham, fed the animals, and took François for a brief walk, then put him in the Explorer with me and drove to Maine Medical Center. Louise died at 9:05 a.m., just before I got there. Our son did get there in time to see his mother before she died. He told me that he had whispered in Louise's ear, "You can leave if you want. Don't worry about Dad. I will take care of him." Anne Bersani, the nurse who cared for Louise at home, was there, and had cared for Louise. I don't know how she knew. She had even washed Louise's feet. I gave her two hundred dollars.

On November 18, 1992, Henri and Maryse, Roger, and Cousin George arrived for Louise's funeral mass on November 20. Rich picked them up at Logan Airport in Boston. The mass was at the Cathedral of the Immaculate Conception in Portland, Maine. Father Plante celebrated the mass in French and English. After that, Louise's body was taken to Boston, to JFK then Delta to Nice, where Charlie Giraud, a postwar paratrooper in the French army and now the director of Roblot, the mortuary, picked it up.

In the following weeks, I consulted with five attorneys, seeking someone to represent me in a lawsuit against Louise's oncologist. Two of the women, who worked together, pondered for several days but ultimately also decided not to. I couldn't stand the stress. I was still in pain from the angina. As a practicing Catholic, I forgave the doctor. When Louise first got sick, I would ask God to heal Louise when I received communion at Sunday mass. Then I started saying, "Your will be done."

Louise's first wish, to be buried in Nice, took a lot of work; but with perseverance and my brother-in-law Henri doing the footwork, it was accomplished. There was no opening at the small cemetery up in Saint Antoine Ginestière where Louise had wanted to be buried, and the very large cemetery in Caucada, which Louise did not care for, was only for Nice's residents. We had lived in France three times. The last time was at the Villa les Gloriosa on the Corniche Fleurie in 1974. Good-hearted Mr. Verola, who was in charge of the cemetery and had cancer himself, accepted the address of the Villa from Henri and used it for residency. Mr. Verola died shortly thereafter.

A French gravesite, called a *caveau,* is a small concrete enclosure below the ground that is large enough for four French caskets or three of the smallest

American caskets. The caskets are lowered through a hole in the front of the caveau that is then covered by a round concrete slab. Louise's caveau cost fifteen thousand dollars. The monument combination over the grave and the head-stone cost another fifteen thousand dollars. I went to Nice with François from November 27 to December 13, 1992, to complete the arrangements.

Louise's closed casket was on display for the family at Athanee for several days. The funeral mass was at Saint Antoine Ginestière celebrated by Abbé Merlin. I sat in the front row on the right side of the aisle with François in my lap. He shook the whole time. Abbé Merlin's little dog lay on the altar throughout the mass.

Louise was temporarily interred in Ton Ton Alfred and Tantine Rose Feligioni's caveau on December 2, 1992. The security guard made me put François back in the car because animals were not permitted in the cemetary. A gentle rain was falling. It seemed that it always rained when we parted. Remember Rheims. I again returned to Nice with Kiki, Coco, and François on March 8, 1993, for Louise's final internment. François rode in the airplane cabin with me.

On Tuesday, Saint Amedee, March 30, at eight in the morning, Louise was transferred to our own caveau, number 115298, in Caucada. American Legion Riviera Post Five's commander, John H. Willms, with his wife, Raymond, read the prayers. I draped the French and American flags over the casket. Henri and Maryse, Roger and Marionette, George and Liliane, and Isabell Cecehetti, daughter of Henri were there. Abbé Merlin blessed Louise's body and our *caveau*.

On April 2, 1993, I returned to Chandler's Wharf in Portland and tried to get on with a life without Louise. I just couldn't believe that Louise, who was seven years younger than I, had died before me. Anyway, my faith was strong and I had my animals. I attended the daily 12:15 mass at the cathedral. In later years I decided that it was best that Louise had gone ahead of me. I would not have wanted her to go through my loneliness.

I took François everywhere I could with me. There were daily walks at the Eastern Promenade. In the winter he would manage the snow-and-ice-covered beach down to the water's edge and watch the Labs swim out in the cold water to fetch. Summers he wasn't afraid to walk through the shallow water. I doubt if I would have made it without François.

Chapter 17

Auld Lang Syne

Kiki, Coco, François, and I returned to Nice from November 26, 1994, to May 11, 1995. We stayed at 101 Avenue de la California; in a furnished apartment on the first floor (Americans would call it the second floor). It was a very convenient setup. There was a small market on the corner across the street, and my general practitioner's office was across the street, too. A nice card shop and a coffee and teashop were on the floor beneath my apartment. I walked François across and up the hill into residential Fabron during the day, and at first took him on a short ten p.m. walk on Rue de France at night. After someone in a passing car hurled an egg at me, hitting me in the left eye, I walked him on the Promenade des Anglais, across from the beach. There was always a pretty prostitute on the first corner. I would smile and say, "Bon nuit" in passing.

I would attend mass at Saint Helene's, about two hundred yards past the health food store where I bought my *pan de le cannet des maures*, country bread—a wheat mix. The pastor's name at Saint Helene's sounded like the French word for stairs (*l'escaliers*). It was a beautiful old church with stone floors, and the pastor had no objection to me bringing François in. I carried a little mat for him to lie on, and I would sit against the rear wall of the church with him at my feet. At communion time I would carry him in my right arm and the pastor would gently smile at me as if apologetic that our canine friend couldn't receive the host. At the end of the New Year's Day mass, everyone sang Auld Lang Syne. I was startled and tears came to my eyes. Louise wasn't with me, or was she?

From February 17-21st I was hospitalized in Nice at Tzanck for a left coronary spasm, which was probably caused by the nicergoline my doctor had given me to balance my blood pressure. My NYCFD Blue Cross covered the hospital bill, and my retired Mutual of New York Aetna insurance covered the doctor. Medicare covers nothing overseas.

Just before the fiftieth anniversary of VE Day, Bryant Gumbel of NBC evidently contacted the American counsel looking for an American paratrooper who had jumped in southern France on August 15, 1944. The counsel referred him to Commander John Willms, and John gave my name. The producers brought François and me the ninety miles to Saint-Tropez in a limo to be in the show. We had a brief impasse when Mr. Gumbel wouldn't let François come with me and I refused to go on without François. Mr. Gumbel eventually gave in, though, and several of my neighbors at Chandler's Wharf later told me that they had seen the program on TV and liked it.

The Hotel Les Fusains in Caucade became my home away from home in France. It was the only hotel in Nice that had studio apartments with kitchens, and it was only about three hundred yards from where Louise was buried. Louise and I had known the proprietors, Monsieur and Madame Druard, since 1970. They did everything themselves—reservations, breakfasts, housekeeping, grounds keeping, you name it. As busy as they must have been tending the five studio apartments up and five down, plus the rooms in front, they always had time to talk. They would even take care of my animals in an emergency. Eventually, in 2005, they put the hotel up for sale and took a much-deserved retirement. They never discussed the complicated transaction with me. They tried to sell the building to a private individual, but the city of Nice kept holding up the sale and eventually bought the building for seven hundred thousand euros instead of the nine hundred thousand euros the Druard's were asking. It now houses university students.

My life there became a satisfying routine. I would start each day with a bath. The short, deep tub had a hand-held shower for washing the hair. Then there would be exercises such as deep knee bends, toe raises on a block of wood, and upper and lower abdominal exercise using small weights; altogether they took about forty minutes.

A quick morning walk with François around the Plateau Sportifs, a hard-surfaced fenced-in track and athletic field used by the nearby university and casual soccer players, came next. Then came breakfast followed by a short walk to the Jardin Paul Scoffier, a small park where François got in his daily fetches; me being an old roadrunner, this was important. Then it was dinner followed by a one-kilometer walk up Napoleon III to the Avenue de la Lanterne. The five thirty p.m. daily mass in Saint Marc's Chapelle Sainte Bernadette was an important part of my day. I prayed before a small olivewood crucifix of our Lord that was hand carved to the contour of the branch and made our Lord look pitiful. One day I told our Lord, "me too," thinking that my suffering from my myasthenia gravis was similar to his. Later in this trip I regretted saying that.

After supper, before retiring, there was the short, dangerous ten p.m. walk. I kept close to the hotel, usually in the parking lot across the street, which was studded with small decorative pine trees. One night at the end of February, François was licking the branch from the root of one of these trees, and I looked up to Heaven and asked Louise if she saw what her little boy was doing. As I turned to cross Napoleon III to reenter the hotel from the rear entrance, I saw a larger than usual meteorite that streaked downward from southwest to northeast, descending toward Monaco or Ventimiglia at the Italian border. I called the observatory at Mount Vinaigrier the next morning to see if it had been recorded. There had not been anyone on duty, nor had there been any reports of what I had seen. I asked about it at the American Legion meeting on March 5. No one saw or heard of anyone having seen a meteorite.

In between my outings I did my daily chores. I hand-washed my clothing and hung the wet things on a clothes dryer on the balcony, cleaned the floors, and generally tidied up my apartment.

Caucade was a bustling *quartier* (neighborhood). On Saturday mornings the Bar-Tabac, which also sold newspapers, was jammed, as were the *boulangerie* and *patisserie* that sold bread and pastries. With François along, I would meet all my friends, stop for the papers, and then purchase some pastry to bring to my Sunday dinner at Henri and Maryse's. I would also pick up some salmon across the street in the Araucaria apartment development and a couple of small bottles of Baron de Lestac wine to take to Henri's. I would stop at Gerard's vegetable stand in the parking lot for a week's supply of juice oranges, string beans, carrots, tomatoes, etc., that they would carry up to the hotel for me. I bought flowers from Gerard's wife, who always offered to take them to Louise's grave.

My vet, Dr. Ruiz, was also conveniently located across the street in the Araucaria apartment development, which also housed the post office. There was a little newspaper and magazine shop where I could buy beautiful French greeting cards. When Dr. Ruiz had a prescription to be filled, the pharmacy was right next door.

I inserted a plastic screen in one of the windows so that Kiki and Coco could bask in the sun and watch the birds as they flew by. Madame Druard's small garden at the hotel had charming green tree frogs.

Louise's cousin George Feligioni and his wife, Liliane, were truly my own family in Nice besides my brother in-laws. They took care of me and bolstered my morale when I was down. They made my medical appointments and drove me to my doctors. George would stay outside and walk François while Liliane accompanied me inside. In later years, when my myasthenia gravis emerged, Liliane would hold my arm, fearful that I would fall. Liliane was beautiful—radiant and always overflowing with love, kindness, and cheerfulness. George was like a brother, even chiding me at times. They were both retired teachers now working in real estate selling properties on the Riviera to Italians. They were a solid, dedicated couple with two good, tall, strong sons, Olivier and Pierre.

Chapter 18

I Go It Alone with Kiki, Coco, and François

After Louise died, I went to Nice every winter with the animals, leaving in January and returning in May. On January 7, 1994, I returned to Nice with Kiki, Coco, and François. We spent most of that spring at the Hotel Les Fusains in Caucade.

I did many of the things I had always done in France. I attended American Legion Post Five's monthly meetings. At one of them, I gained a new cause. The discussion was about erecting a monument at the site of a recently discovered U.S. Air Force plane crash. I brought up my own unit's B Company, Captain Miller and his seventeen-man planeload that jumped in the sea off Saint-Tropez in the August 15, 1944, invasion of southern France. Certainly they deserved a memorial. The post commander, John Willms, agreed to investigate the possibility. Willms had been a paratroop officer in World War II and was one of the hardest-working post commanders I have ever known. The post was always represented on appropriate occasions. He even drove me to Saint-Tropez, ninety miles west of Nice, several times, once through a torrential rainstorm, to work on Capt. Miller's seveteen-man monument.

We met with Mayor Couve, Dr. Bourrier, 1st Deputy Mayor and Mr. Coppola (Deputy Mayor) and other local civic officials, who asked me what kind of monument the 509th would like to erect. I responded, "A monument by the sea with all seventeen names." I had been in touch with Charlie Doyle, president of the 509th Parachute Infantry Association, and the association had agreed to pay for it, but never had to.

While I was having dinner with Henri and Maryse on June 12, 1994, Charlie Giraud (formerly of the Marine Coloniale Dragon Parachutiste Regiment), who had not yet retired as director of Roblot, the undertakers who had buried Louise, telephoned. After examining the archives and making some telephone calls, he had determined that it was indeed Colomars that my seventeen-man combat patrol had liberated during the first two weeks of September 1944. Actually, the Germans had already left, but we helped them celebrate their liberation. Charlie had spoken to two Colomars officials, and at that very moment there was a banquet of *Anciens combattants* in progress at the hotel L'Auberge de Redier. We immediately jumped in Henri's car and drove to Colomars, but the banquet was over when we got there. Charlie was there with his daughter waiting for us. The eighty-seven-year-old president of the *Anciens combattants* kissed me on both cheeks, and the women who were present, concerned about me being a widower, offered to find me a good woman.

Henri returned me to the Hotel Les Fusains, where I continued packing for the departure the next morning. Traveling with three pets took a good bit of planning and preparation. Kiki's and Coco's kennels had to be prepared. As always, François would ride with me in the main cabin.

On September 23, 1994, I had another angioplasty to clear out two more right coronary blockages; one of the blockages was a repeat. During the procedure, Dr. Anderson's assistant noted a complete blockage and asked what to do. Dr. Anderson had replied, "Push right through." I was watching the screen and could see the blood start flowing again. That was interesting. More diet changes were in store for me. I had been on a vegetarian diet since 1991 but had continued to eat fish. There are probably safe and healthy ways to prepare fish, but frying isn't one of them, and I had been eating fried tuna steaks. I stopped eating fish and haven't had a pain since. My French Corsican cardiologist, Dr. Lodovici said it is okay if you cook it. Dr. Ornish who wrote *Reversing Heart Disease* cautions about fish.

About two-thirty one morning at Chandler's Wharf I bolted awake from a shocking chest pain that seemed to be centered in the area where my gall bladder used to be. Still groggy, I looked over my left shoulder and saw my guardian angel. He or she was wearing dark gray pajamas and was walking away, followed by his dog moseying along behind. I saw every detail of the dog. It was very tall, had black wavy hair, and its tail touched the floor, which told me that it must have come from Heaven. In Heaven they wouldn't shorten dogs' tails the way they do here on earth. It had a slim build and could have been an ungroomed royal poodle. I had to see the gastroenterologist, Dr. Howell, that day concerning the pain and also the cardiologist, Dr. Minton. I couldn't resist telling them about the guardian angel. Neither of them was surprised, and that surprised me. I asked Father Jim Nadeau if he thought the dog was François's guardian angel. "No," he said; "it's yours."

I had numerous experiences that told me I was being watched over from above. On New Year's Day 1999, for instance, Francois was attacked by a bull-mastiff in front of Parker Reidy's restaurant on Exchange Street in Portland. The bullmastiff came in for the kill from behind. I grabbed him by the collar as he went by, but he pulled me down on the ice and grabbed François. Lying face down, the leash taut, I screamed out to God, "He is going to kill my dog." The owner, a young man who had been walking his two large dogs off the leash because of the ice, came running over and took François out of his bullmastiff's mouth. François was motionless. "Give him to me," I said. François started to move. A passerby had flagged down a police car, and I asked the policeman to take me home. I took François to the emergency veterinary clinic on Warren Avenue. His back was chewed up a bit, but he survived; another miracle. The experience didn't discourage François; he fearlessly continued loving all other dogs regardless of size. François would not want to be anything but a dog even if he had the choice.

The winter of 1996-1997 at the Hotel Les Fusains in Nice turned out to be Kiki's last. Her kidneys continued to fail. At four in the morning on February 19, 1997, I called Dr. Ruiz. Kiki was howling from the pain. He came to the hotel and put her down. I asked him for her ashes, and when they came, I gave them to Henri to hold until I die and the *caveau* is opened for my burial. Then he will place her urn or sprinkle her ashes inside.

Erezee, France. The owner of this house, the French ambassador to the US, has invited all visiting 509ers to stay for free.

Clerheid

The 509 dug in here.

We attacked
in this direction
toward Sadzot

December 29, 1944. The 509 attacked from these hills to retake
Sadzot, Belgium.

This monument is erected in Erezee to the 509, the 87th Mortar
Battalion and an infantry regiment. To the far left is Michel Jacquet
Notare (its not me holding François).

A tiny restaraunt in Lantosque, owned by Paulin Maurel, in the middle. George, Louise's cousin, is on the right. Below, a German Tiger tank with the 88mm rifle.

The wall in Lantosque, where I was permitted to sit with Louise
pending trial. I was held prisoner in the garage below.

Chapter 19

Revisiting Old Haunts

The location in Sadzot where I was wounded in the left elbow.

Monument to Capt. Jesse Walls, C Company 509, for the taking of
Cap D'Ail on the Basse Corniche.

COMPAGNIE ``C`` DU 509ÈME
BATAILLON D INFANTERIE PARACHUTISTE (U.S. ARMY)
HOMMAGE AUX ANTI-FASCISTES ITALIENS
DU GROUPE M.O.I. (MAIN-D OEUVRE IMMIGRÉE)
A SES RÉSISTANTS A SES DÉPORTÉS EN ITALIE ET
EN ALLEMAGNE A SES INTERNÉS

LES TIRS DE LA ROYAL NAVY VENAIENT DE
L'EDGARD QUINET (ÉQUIPAGE ANGLAIS)

3 SEPTEMBRE 1984 40ÈME ANNIVERSAIRE

Details of the monument.

ICI
LE 3 SEPTEMBRE 1944
APRÈS 5 JOURS DE COMBATS
LES VOLONTAIRES DE LA BRIGADE ST JUST
< F-T-P-F- CIE CYRANO >
ET LES ÉLÉMENTS AVANCÉS AMÉRICAINS
DU CAPITAINE WALLS
SOUTENUS PAR LES TIRS DE LA ROYAL NAVY
ONT CONTRAINT LES FORCES ALLEMANDES
A LA RETRAITE ABANDONNANT
MORTS ET PRISONNIERS
LE 3 SEPTEMBRE 1945

Saint-Tropez, le 15 Février 1996

VILLE
DE
SAINT-TROPEZ
B.P. 161
83992 SAINT-TROPEZ CEDEX

Téléphone 94.55.90.00
Télécopie 94.55.90.10

N/RÉF. : JB/AD/96

Monsieur Richard D. FISCO
Hôtel "Les Fusains"
55 Avenue Sainte Marguerite
06200 NICE

Cher Monsieur,

J'ai bien reçu votre courrier du 8 Février 1996 avec les photos que vous avez eu l'amabilité de nous adresser.

Je vous remercie de cette sympathique attention.

Comme promis la municipalité de Saint-Tropez va ériger une stèle face à la mer pour glorifier les 17 parachutistes de la Compagnie B du 509ème Bataillon, disparus dans le Golfe de Saint-Tropez le 15 Août 1944.

Nous ferons une présentation "pour vous" le 8 mai 1996 et une Inauguration Officielle le 15 Août 1996.

Avec mes sentiments les plus cordiaux.

L'Adjoint Délégué,

Docteur Jacques BOURRIER.

A letter notifying me that St. Tropez consented to erect a monument for Captain Miller's seventeen-man planeload that jumped and drowned on August 15, 1944.

On my safari to Nice via Air France in the winter of 1999, I left Boston on January 14 with Coco and François. Coco traveled in a kennel equipped with food and water. I had, as usual, velcroed a four-inch covered plastic water bowl to the floor—with a hole cut in the cover to prevent splashing—and a nine-by-thirteen-inch plastic tray with a small amount of kitty litter. A small metal cup hanging on the inside of the door held Coco's dry food. There was additional food attached to the back of the kennel in case of emergency. A larger kennel and a little tip helped to promote the best care for my cat. Air France and Continental have air-, temperature-, and pressure-controlled compartments for animals, so I didn't worry too much about Coco. François traveled with me in the cabin in a collapsible carrier screened in on three sides.

One of the four suitcases I brought with me was entirely for gifts. There was a nice shirt for tall Pierre Feligioni, my godchild, whose twenty-sixth birthday would be on March 19. The suitcase also held seven pairs of Levis with updated sizes, three four-piece sets of Ralph Lauren towels, and three large boxes of Tylenol (which the French think are better than the ones they can buy in France). Now you know what kind of gifts to bring to France. I planned to fill the suitcase with gifts to carry home, as well. My son had made a forty two-by-ninety-inch dining room table, and I wanted to buy linens for that. When I arrived in Nice, Henri would bring to the motel six cartons of household items that I stored with him in between trips.

I quickly settled into the French part of my life. American Legion meetings were a big part of that, and I attended the meetings held on February 2nd, March

2nd, and May 4th. Commander John Willms was undergoing chemotherapy, so Tony DiPietro presided.

On February 20th, I went to tea with Dr. Christiane Abdelnour, a friend and fellow parishioner at Saint Marc's, and her mother. That same evening I suffered a recurrence of the transient amnesia that had resulted from a fall from a tree in 1972.

A large dinner in Lantosque, our stronghold in World War II, was a special evening. It was held at the Bar des Tilleuls bar and restaurant, owned by Maria Auda's daughter Didoun. George and Liliane drove Henri, Maryse, François, and me up through the hairpin turns. Along the way we crossed the small bridge at Saint Jean la Riviere that our jeep had crashed into during the war. Paulin Maurel and his wife, Francine, were invited, too. In addition to running his small restaurant Paulin was a volunteer firefighter and would respond to any emergency in the region.

I took photos on that trip, including one of the small garage in which Sgt. Bob Erickson had guarded me when I was being punished for having been AWOL because I overstayed by one day a two-day pass to Nice from Lieutenant Prichett. I also took a photo of the little wall in front of the garage where Bob had allowed me to talk to Louise when Monsieur Mignon drove her up to visit me. I remember that we reimbursed him with five gallons of gas so he wouldn't have to build a wood fire for his engine.

George and Liliane drove me to the May 8, 1999, VE (Victory in Europe) Day ceremonies in Saint-Tropez. After the mass for fallen comrades, there was the one-and-a-half-kilometer procession from the port of Saint-Tropez to the entrance to the Cimetière Marin, stopping at the monument to Captain Miller and his seventeen men that stood at the entrance to the cemetery.

The monument was saluted with dipped French flags on both sides. Mayor Couve accompanied François and me as we placed a beautiful wreath at the foot of the monument. The accompanying photos, taken with Mr. Cuppola, George, and Liliane, show the names of the lost men.

The procession returned to the port, where the main ceremony took place in front of the large monument. I was seated in front of the flags. The American, British, French, and Russian national anthems were played. Tears came to my eyes when I stood for the Star Spangled Banner, wishing some of my 509th buddies could be there with me.

On May 13, 1999, Coco, François, and I set out for the States. Our plane missed the connection in Brussels, and François and I were taken to a hotel, where we were treated very well. My four suitcases and Coco were left at the airport for the flight to Boston on the next day. I was extremely glad that I had followed my usual practice and provided Coco with food, water, and a litter box. Experience had taught me to expect such delays, and I never wanted to rely on others to take care of my pets.

ICI A L'AUBE DU 15 AOUT 1944 A BORD D UN DES
NOMBREUX C-47 , 17 PARACHUTISTES DE LA Cie B DU
509°BATAILLON ONT SAUTE DANS LES EAUX DU
GOLFE DE St TROPEZ POUR LIBERER LA FRANCE
AUCUN NE FUT RETROUVE.

CPT	MILLER Ralph R.JR	OH.
TEC-4	BECKNER Eugene C	MINN.
PVT	BUTLER Ira J.	ILL
PFC	CAMPOS Frank	CAL
SGT	CREVELLING Oscar F.	N.Y.
S.SGT	DAVID Robert B	FL.
T.5	DAWSON Albert T	IND
1ˢSGT	DORSA Anthony J.	TEX
PFC	FORD Jonnie C.	GA.
PVT	GARCIA Julius.	N.Y.
T-4	GILLMAN Marvin N.	MICH.
PFC	LYNCH George R.	N.Y.
PVT	PENNEBAKER Thomas W.	PHIL
PVT	PIPINO Alfred JR.	PHIL.
PFC	POTTER Leon V.	MO.
T-5	REID George W.	N.Y.
SGT	SUTHERLAND William A.	S.C.

Monument with the seventeen names of those who drowned in St.
Tropez on the jump in the invasion of Southern France August 15,
1944. The monument is located 1.5 kilometers from the port, in front
of the Cimetiére Marin.

Chapter 20

Life with François

From the time Louise and I got François in December 1990, he was an integral part of our family. After I lost Louise, he became my best friend. He went everywhere I went, church included, and once he was even on television with me. And of course he accompanied me to France. Coco came too, but she rode in the baggage compartment. François went in the cabin with me.

Foreign travel with animals requires a good deal of advance preparation. I had to give the dimensions of Coco's kennel and François's carrier to the airlines when I made my reservations. The animals had to have a health certificate signed by a USDA veterinarian before they could get on a plane to Europe—which meant a drive to the state capital in Augusta. Eventually I had my veterinarian in Nice, Dr. Ruiz, insert microchips for identification.

I had to do everything possible for my animals' comfort. Coco rode in her kennel with food, water, and a small litter box. François's carrier went under the seat in front of me. (Only animals that weigh 10 pounds or less were permitted in the cabin.) I could never anticipate how the flight crew would treat us. Some would bring water for François and allow him to lie outside his carrier. Others insisted that I keep him inside the carrier and even put the water inside, where it was bound to spill and make a mess. Ultimately, the best solution was to give him all the water he wanted and line the bottom of his carrier with absorbent material. François was a very good traveler. He would sleep unless he was thirsty or until my food tray was brought. He knew that I would give him most of it. I brought my own food on the plane—usually beans and brown rice, toast, egg whites, and fruit.

The winter trip to southern France in 2000 began in typical fashion. Our departure was scheduled for January 12. The three of us—Coco, François, and I— would fly Sabena Airlines from Boston to Brussels to Nice, arriving January 13 and staying, as usual, at the Hotel les Fusains. The return trip would be May 11.

I had already shipped two 40-pound packages of my health foods to the Hotel les Fusains. I don't know why, but American cereals on the supermarket shelves in France contained saturated fats. Henri would bring me large-grain oats (*gross flacons d'avoines*). Post shredded wheat—no fat and no salt, is also a good alternate but more difficult to swallow because of the myasthenia gravis.

The day after we arrived in Nice, Henri and George drove us in George's Mercedes to the Prefecture to renew my Carte de Sejours (ID card). George walked François outside while Henri accompanied me inside.

Several days later, I started showing flu symptoms. The timing indicated that it was something I had caught on the plane. Although later in the year, I would be diagnosed with myasthenia gravis, a rare disease of the immune system, affecting one in six million. Finally, after a week, the fever dropped and I began to feel better.

François kept me busy during my recovery. I had begun giving François his baths and haircuts myself soon after I got him. The groomers cut his topknot square; I liked it round. And they made the pom-pom on his tail look like a sausage, and I liked it round, too. The bath and blow dry took an hour. The haircut, clippers, fine trimmer, and scissors took another two hours. I enjoyed it, but he didn't. I always brushed his teeth at night before bedtime, too, and gave him a little treat.

When we were in Nice, I usually walked François in the Jardin Paul Scoffier, named after an early French pilot. I carried about nine racquetballs and had him fetch in an elevated area along a twenty-foot-wide corridor bounded by a wall on one side and a cypress barrier on the other. Walking François was often an adventure. I had to be on the alert every minute. He was a very masculine little dog, and he always wanted other male dogs to know that "he was the man." But almost every dog he encountered was larger and stronger, and I had to be ready to defend him. Once, while I was walking François on the hill at the Eastern Promenade in Portland, Maine, a large husky charged up the hill at us. I used my "zapper," a dog-training device, to try to call him off, but the dog paid no attention; he may not have heard it. I grabbed François in my arms and prepared for the attack, but fortunately the husky responded to his master's call. The French are much better at avoiding dangerous encounters. Anyone approaching with a large male dog will call out, "Male ou femelle?"

On Avenue Sainte-Marguerite opposite the hotel, though, a huge Rottweiler attacked from the rear and it was almost disaster. François dodged him and I grabbed the Rottweiler by the collar. I held on and François kept a leash distance away long enough for the dog's young master to come to the rescue. I never knew where my strength and courage came from, or why the other dog didn't turn on me.

The only things that frightened François were fireworks and flies. He couldn't sleep if there was a fly in the house. I had to run around with a fly swatter. François's allergies to cypress pollen and pollution were always a problem in the Riviera springtime, too. He was taking almost as much medication as I was. Eventually he was diagnosed with chronic bronchitis by Dr. Horgan in Brunswick, Maine.

My forty-pound food packages arrived at the hotel on January 30th and February 1st. I was glad to have my own food at last. It had been taking me fifteen minutes to extract the hard red grains from the brown rice I had been buying in France. I have always thought that some enterprising American exporter should sell U.S.-grown beans and rice to France. The quality would be much better.

Once a month, Henri would drive me downtown to American Express on the Promenade where I would cash two thousand dollars at an exchange rate of more than six francs to the dollar. If the rate was one dollar to 6.5087 francs, for example, I would get 13,017.4 or more francs, enough for rent and food for the month.

Sometimes I would make the trip into the old village (la vielle ville) in Nice. It was a long walk from the bus stop at Avenue de Verdun at Place Massena. François and I would attend noon mass at a beautiful old Dominican church where dogs were allowed. I purchased an *hachoir*, a wide, curved blade about twelve inches long with a wooden handle at both ends that made chopping

François's chicken easy. I always carried a backpack for purchases and for François's water, cup, treats, and a raincoat. François was always thirsty. I would place the cup on the floor in stores and put just a little water in it for him followed by a treat.

The 509th Parachute Infantry Association was still trying to find some trace of Captain Miller, and Bud Siegel (capt., ret) asked me to place an article in the newspaper asking if anyone had ever found anything belonging to Captain Miller or his seventeen men who were lost on August 15, 1944, when they jumped into the Gulf of Saint-Tropez. I wrote the letter on April 18th, and my friend Dr. Christiane Abdelnour translated it into French. Although I mailed it to *Var Matin*, the newspaper never published my letter or even contacted me, and I was never able to speak to anyone with any knowledge of the lost men. When I left for the United States on May 11th I still had heard nothing, and nothing arrived at the Hotel Les Fusains after I left.

Saturday night dinners with Henri and Maryse really spoiled me. She would make me whatever I wanted and top it off with an apple tart made using parchment paper to avoid the fat. I never had high cholesterol, but it has gone down (from 170 to 135) since I became a vegetarian. This is not to say that I didn't eat very well. Maryse's mother, Tata Toria, then Maryse herself after her mother died, would make me a huge board full of gnocci just like those Henri's mother used to make for me during the war with the flour that Nick DeGaeta dropped off to them.

Maryse's tomato sauce is also fantastic. I have tried but have never been able to duplicate it for taste or consistency. I think she gets rid of the skin, juice, and seeds, and cooks it down for a long time. I used to bring presents, but nothing I brought could compensate for the work involved in preparing those delicious meals. After dinner, Henri would drive me home with three-fourths of an apple tart and a quart of tomato sauce—enough for three suppers.

My neurological symptoms continued to worsen: choking on food, slurred speech, and legs weak, out of breath, tongue paralyzed, difficulty swallowing, and slurred speech. I had all of the symptoms of myasthenia gravis except one—the most important, the closing of the eyes or drooping eyelids—and that is why the doctors had trouble diagnosing the disease. I had double vision at an angle, but it didn't bother me. I have heard that Aristotle Onassis, who also had the disease, had to keep his eyelids taped open. I didn't know it at the time, but any antibiotics would have been dangerous. Fortunately, my general practitioner in Portland, Dr. Hotelling, had steered me away from antibiotics. He said that they weaken your immune system. He was so right.

VE Day, May 8th, was approaching, and Henri drove me to Saint-Tropez for the memorial ceremony, this time in a rented Mercedes because his own had broken down. I was seated in the seat of honor under the flags with François. Paratroopers formed the honor guard. I was given a huge wreath to place at the foot of the monument, but no one came up to help me carry it. I don't think anyone realized how much trouble I was having. Fortunately, someone came to my rescue as I neared the monument.

At twelve-twenty p.m. May 11, 2000, the three of us—François, Coco, and I—flew Sabena from Nice to Brussels to Boston, arriving the same day. My son was waiting in the no-parking zone to pick us up.

Chapter 21

Myasthenia Gravis

I had a May 15th appointment with a throat doctor in Portland for my difficulty swallowing. When he was no help, I went to see Dr. Hotelling about it on the 18th. Dr. Hotelling, in turn, sent me to a neurologist, Dr. Boothby, who sent me for tests at Mercy Hospital. When those turned up nothing, I saw a gastroenterologist, who recommended speech therapy. That was no help at all. Next I went to see a pathologist at Maine Medical Center. She went through the liquid and solid tests in a few minutes and concluded that my throat muscles were weak. Then it was an MRI. My medical expenses were skyrocketing, but nobody could diagnose what was wrong with me.

Through July, I continued having episodes of my mouth being paralyzed, slurred speech, and difficulty walking. Finally, Dr. Boothby sent me to Maine Med for blood tests. They drew two vials of blood on July 26th and sent them to the Mayo Clinic. The results came back positive for myasthenia gravis on

August 7th. Another test ordered by Dr. Boothby on August 10 came back positive on August 24th. The doctors were still skeptical because my eyes never closed. I could detect a little drooping of the lids, but the doctors couldn't.

My condition was so unstable at that point that I had to miss the 509th's reunion in Fayetteville, N.C., on September 15th. Not even myasthenia gravis could keep me away from France, though. Preparation for the trips had become a year-round activity. There were gifts to buy, reservations to make, and details to take care of. Everyone helped me. In early October, I called Sabena Airlines and made reservations to leave on January 11, 2001, returning on May 14, 2001. A call to Monsieur Druard at the Hotel les Fusains reserved a studio for me. In mid-November, I ordered a plaque with a durable finish that I could place on the monument over Louise's *caveau* in France. I wanted it to have the American and French flags, to represent both our nations, and was promised delivery on January 4, 2001, one week before my departure. I shipped sixty pounds of health foods to the hotel and made sure that the health certificates for Coco and François were updated and countersigned by the USDA vet.

At about this time, my living arrangements changed drastically. My health was precarious, and living alone was potentially dangerous, so when Rich called and asked me to come and live with them in Brunswick, I agreed. "I have to have my own place on the ground floor," I said, and he answered, "You'll have it." Rich did most of the remodeling work himself, and I paid his expenses. He walled off the back of his house, starting at the kitchen, and built me a separate apartment with everything except a washing machine. I had my own place to park in the courtyard. I sold my condo and began to pack. Then it was back to France.

Chapter 22

An Eventful 2001

Sportline Trophy brought the bronze plaque I had ordered for Louise's *caveau* early on the morning of January 11th, the day of my departure. I stuck it in a suitcase and headed off with Rich to Logan airport in my Ford Explorer, which has a truck chassis. It was a standard departure: I brought four, seventy-pound suitcases, Coco in her kennel, and François in his light carrier. We made the Sabena seven forty-five p.m. flight to Brussels. As usual, Coco went in with the baggage and François went with me in the cabin.

When we got to Nice, Henri applied acrylic to the plaque to preserve the finish, and I gave the plaque to M. Lucien Guirchoune of Pasando Monuments to install on the monument. Monsieur Guirchoune also had made a granite plaque made in Italy engraved with my U.S. Army discharge that will be placed on the *caveau*. The plaque shows the 509th's campaigns and "D" days from November 8, 1942, in North Africa to the Ardennes in 1945, after which, reduced to about twenty men, the 509th Parachute Infantry Battalion was disbanded. I have heard that although the *caveau* is perpetual, monuments that are not properly maintained are sometimes removed. Perhaps the 509th's Gingerbread Man patch emblem, the discharge plaque and the French and American flag plaque on the grave monument will persuade them to let us be.

I awakened one day during that trip with shocking chest pains. Henri took me to see my Corsican cardiologist, Dr. François Lodovici, that evening. Dr. Lodovici said my heart was fine. The chest pains were caused by the mestinon I was taking for my myasthenia gravis. My cardiologist and gastroenterologists back in Portland were unable to diagnose this when I had similar attacks there. Dr. Lodovici was the expert, though. During his medical studies he had been given an extra class of his choice on any one of the rare diseases, and he chose myasthenia gravis. He was probably far more familiar with the disease than the average neurologist. Dr. Lodovici told me I should continue taking the mestinon even if the pains continued. He always permitted me to bring François to my appointments. My appointment was his last of the evening, but he went out on house calls for another couple of hours after that. What a cardiologist! He liked Jack Daniels. Once in a while, Louise's cousin Lilien would give him a bottle from me. He always checked my heart with the Doppler, which traces the arteries.

Henri continued to bring me bread, eggs, wild rice, oats, protein etc. from the health food store. I don't know how he did everything for me and still worked full time as an assistant to a builder. Ultimately, the builder developed cancer, and Henri, a former builder himself, had to take over.

Although I was also dealing with double hernias by this time, I kept up all my walks and physical activities. A couple of times I went by bus to Place Massena. There was a statue there that Louise's brother, Jeanot had worked on before he joined the paratroopers. He was mortally wounded in Dien Bien Pfu and died in a hospital in Saigon on January 25, 1955. From Place Massena I walked to les Galeries Lafayette to shop for my return gifts. Bonnets for Barbara and Penelope, perfume for Mary, my niece, and Sister Theresa who is stricken with Alzheimer's and being cared for in a nursing home by Mary and her husband, Scott.

Before going home, though, I had to have the hernias taken care of. Dr. Betrand at Tzanck did the surgery. He said to me that he was honored to serve an American who fought to save his country. My friend Mme. Paulette Douchau had volunteered to care for Coco while I was in the hospital, and Madame Druard at the hotel had offered to help, too. Henri and Maryse took

François. They let him sleep in their bed with them, and he loved to ransack the bedclothes.

After that, we celebrated a cluster of birthdays—Maria Auda's and Monsieur Druard's on April 6th, mine on the seventh, and Madame Druard's on the ninth. I was a recognized member of the neighborhood in Caucade by then. I received *bises* (kisses on both cheeks) from almost everyone I met on my morning walks. Mme. Pierrette Du Puy and Mme. Paulette Duchau always got up from the bench in Jardin Paul Scoffier to kiss me when we met daily in the morning to walk our dogs. I really think they started kissing me on both cheeks so that the young French lads in the neighborhood would accept me. I think they also put out the word that I had been a paratrooper in World War II and had jumped in Saint-Tropez.

Then an alarming development occurred. I called Hélène Lery to thank her for another extra large wool scarf she had knitted for me for the Maine winter, but I couldn't speak. The same thing happened when I called Maryse. Dr. Durand upped my daily dose of Mestinon medications, and suddenly I began to respond. I was able to speak and swallow, and I could walk upright and without staggering. Nowadays I have to bend forward to walk. People think I have a bad back, but it's the myasthenia gravis. I can stand straight, but I topple over if I try to walk. I am able to walk normally for a few minutes now and then, when I experience remissions.

Before I attended the Saturday, April 14th, nine p.m. vigil mass for Easter Sunday at Saint Marc I had dinner with Henri and Maryse. I brought a large, dark decorated chocolate Easter egg, pastry, and two small bottles of "Baron de Lestac" Bordeaux wine, of which I could drink only a third of a glass. Any more and I would have been unable to speak or swallow because of the myasthenia gravis .

It was bad news on May 6th. John H. Willms, the best post commander ever, had died of colon cancer. Tony DiPietro was voted in and took over. On VE Day, May 8th, George and Liliane drove François and me to the ceremonies in Saint-Tropez, then to dinner at La Ponche.

On the day before our departure on May 14th, Coco started vomiting blood. Dr. Ruiz took care of her and she was OK. I think it was an attack by the devil. His protocol is to attack or harass anyone or anything you love just to hurt you. He can't get at you if you are in a state of grace.

Chapter 23

Living in Brunswick

The May 14, 2001 return flight went off without a hitch. Rich met us at the airport in Boston and drove us to the apartment he had made for me in his own house. The bathroom, kitchen appliances, and floor-to-ceiling bookshelves were all new. And I had my own parking place, a rarity in downtown Brunswick. I would be one block from the Morning Glory health food store and a half block from Mail Boxes Etc. I could take François to the Bowdoin campus fields to fetch and meet other dogs.

One of the first things I did after returning was to visit the Brighton Avenue Medical Center in Portland for shoulder x-rays. I had begun suffering intense pain in both shoulders right after my hernia operation in France. It was then that I began regretting my "me too" remark to our Lord in Saint Marc's Chapelle Ste. Bernadette while praying in front of the olive wood crucifix. Dr. Yung in Nice had treated me with cortisone injections, which seemed to help, but Dr. Durand the neurologist in France who treated my myasthenia gravis had ordered the injections stopped. My neurologist in Portland, Dr. John A. Boothby, referred me to Dr. Dennis Sullivan, an orthopedic surgeon, for my shoulder.

Dr. Sullivan diagnosed rotator cuff injuries and sent me to Larry Risigo for therapy. I had three appointments a week with light dumbbells and ultrasound cortisone massaging of my shoulders. They allowed me to bring François in with me. The treatments went on through October. Since the pain started when the pain medications were taken off after the double hernia surgery in Nice, my number one suspicion was that one of the stretcher-bearers dropped his end when they swung me over to the operating table.

In the meantime, I settled into my new home. The movers had delivered about eighty cartons of my personal belongings plus some furniture from Chandlers' Wharf in Portland just before my return from Nice. The cartons were stored on the floor over the little shop my son had rebuilt between the house and the barn. My grandson, Ralph, and my granddaughter, Vera, did the heavy unpacking for me in the evenings. During the unpacking we came across some beautiful fabrics of Louise's from China. I mailed them to Hélène Lery, who had retired from her art shop in Vence, sold her magnificent villa, and was now living in a villa she had purchased in Marseille. She called and asked me what she should do with them. I said, "Whatever you want to." Hélène was the only one I knew who could work with fabric like that.

In mid-July I had a brief remission from the ever-present fatigue of myasthenia gravis. It only lasted a short while, but it was great.

Artiste Trophy restored my Staten Island six-mile 1938 Tappen Post championship trophy. It was gold plated, hand engraved with three runners, one on each side of the cylinder and one on top. I can look at it now and remember how I used to love to run, and without feeling sorry for myself. Although the man who restored the trophy refused payment, I insisted on giving him sixty dollars.

During the first week of August, with temperatures in the nineties, I had a visit from Paul De Gaeta, Nick De Gaeta's nephew, and his nine-year-old son. Paul was a historian and secretary to the 509th Parachute Infantry Association. His other uncle, also named Paul, was a retired New York City fire chief. Paul's son walked around cradling Coco and she loved it. Paul left behind a recorder and tapes, knowing that someday I would write my story. I knew that it would have to come from me, especially after Bill Breuer's book, *Bloody Clash at Sadzot*, erred in saying that I punched a major when it was actually a mayor.

On September 11, 2001, Barb rushed in to my apartment and told me to turn on the TV. What a horrifying day that was. The Twin Towers destroyed by terrorists, the Pentagon badly damaged, and another flight lost over Pennsylvania. There must have been heroism on that plane! I called the Secret Service to remind them that England flew balloons to deter the Nazi bombings in World War II.

On the fourteenth of November 2001, the ninth anniversary of Louise's death, both Jim Nunn and Poco Coberly called me. I told Jim that I would go down swinging when I go.

François, who was eleven years old and feeling his age a bit, began to improve. He had been unable to jump up on my bed, and then suddenly he was able to. François always licked me on the mouth when I returned to the car after receiving communion at mass. He was my buddy. We held off many attacks together.

I paid for a typewriter at the end of 2005 that my friend Penelope Warren purchased and would come on Thursday evenings and Sunday afternoons, sit down at the typewriter, and say, "Speak!" She didn't want any compensation, but I paid her $25 per hour, so I had to say something. When she moved to Winston-Salem, North Carolina, I began to write it to her. My shaky handwriting (Parkinson's starting) was pretty bad, but somehow she managed to read it.

Rich located my other brother, Marty, through the Internet. I had not been in touch with him since the 1960s. Rich searched for his name and discovered that Marty was auctioning off paintings one of them sold for five million dollars. Rich and Marty emailed back and forth several times. Then there was a lull when we heard nothing. Finally we heard from a woman who had lived with him that he had died in his sleep. We didn't ask her, but I would like to have had my brother's violin for my grandson Ralph, who is a musician.

My days are always filled with little miracles. On August 30, 2002, for example, it was a hot day and I found the only shady spot in front of Macy's to park the Explorer so that François would keep cool while I was inside. A saleslady carried my two heavy bags of Ralph Lauren towels, gifts for France in 2003, all the way down and out to the car for me. I immediately said a prayer for her to myself. The same day I found my old prescription glasses in the grass at the Eastern Promenade while having François fetch. They had been missing since our last fetches three days earlier. The fourth miracle that day was an increase in V.A. disability benefits.

Poco Coberly had called with some good news. Boggs Collins, an old 509th gunfighter and a Poco's not-so-distant neighbor in West Virginia, told Poco to tell me that the word was out that World War II vets with purple hearts were eligible for increases in their disability payments and that I should apply for an increase in my thirty percent. Poco and Boggs got theirs over the phone. I had twenty percent disability for the gunshot wound in my left elbow, but a VA technician reduced it to ten percent. He told me he was a paratrooper; if he was, he probably flunked out. He decided that grenade shrapnel had made my wound, even though my discharge reads residuals of gunshot wound. I still have a deep seven-inch scar running through the length of the elbow, and it is deformed. When I was treated in England, the surgeon had wanted to send me home with eighty percent disability. I had refused because I wanted to get back to Louise and the 509th. What I didn't know was that General Ridgeway had disbanded the 509th in December 1944. I then saw a doctor the same day. He gave me the increase, for which I am grateful. I mailed Poco and Ruby a bottle of Veuve Clicquot champagne and Medoc wine to thank him for conveying Boggs Collins's message, unaware that shipping liquor across the state line is illegal. It arrived safely.

Another small miracle: On a fall day, as I was walking, bent over, my three hundred yards out and three hundred yards back at Bowdoin campus, I saw some shrubs at the base of a tree shimmered in the gentle breeze. The adjacent foliage did not. My scouting instincts told me, "Watch out!" Just as I turned back at three hundred yards, a large, shaggy white dog attacked from the rear, and I could tell that he wasn't coming to say hello. I grasped François in my arms and yelled, No!" at the dog, and he stopped.

In the winter of 2002 it was Swiss Air from Boston to Nice. Swiss Air refused to let Coco on the plane because she had no ID. François was okay since his left ear bore a tattoo. When I explained that I had a veterinarian in France, they let Coco go. After we reached Nice, Dr. Ruiz inserted microchips in both Coco and François to prevent such problems in the future.

That wasn't the only problem on this flight. Security in Boston took my mestinon out of my backpack without telling me. I didn't find out until an hour or so after takeoff. My four-month supply was in a suitcase with my other medications. I notified Logan airport security on my return in May 2003, but it was a waste of time. They never followed up on my complaint.

I purchased a 2003 Explorer when I got home at the end of May. The old 1992 Explorer went from me to Rich to Ralph, my grandson, who was sixteen years old. Ralph is a good boy who helps his father and me. I was glad that he got the car.

I had good medical attention the balance of 2003. When you are old, doctors only want you to come in with one complaint. If you need diet assistance, see a nutritionist if you can find one. Have good health insurance, and live a healthy life. Those things have been very important for me!

Chapter 24

To Nice

Winter of 2004 there were the usual preparations for departure with Coco and Francois. The departure would be January 21st from Boston and returning May 19th from Nice.

We settled in at the hotel Les Fusains.

I had been worried about Francois' eyes. I took him to our vet, Dr. Ruiz who recommended ophthalmologist up in Cimiez. If Francois had cataracts I was determined to have them corrected. George drove me there. Dr. Fabrice Thomazo, a certified graduate of studies Superieures d'Ophtalmologie after examining Francois's eyes with about a dozen different instruments came to the conclusion that Francois did not have the cataracts that had been suspected but degenerating retinas that would lead to blindness. He charged the equivalent of $35 for the visit. Back in Brunswick the only eye doctor would have had to come from Boston. Having seen all the specialized equipment used by

Dr. Thomazo I doubt that doctors driving from Boston could do their best.

Dr. Thomazo prescribed eye drops of Difraele and Chibro Cadron, which I discontinued. They caused Francois to keep his eyes closed except in the dark.

Dr. Christiane translated another letter for me that I could send to the Var Matin with the same success, nothing.

It was daisies to Louise.

There were no American Legion meetings. The Hotel Radisson was being renovated.

Masses were celebrated at St. John the Baptist church in Brunswick for Pvt, Ken Edny 509 the British paratrooper on March 23rd, my brother Marty on March 25th, Captain Charles Howland 509 on March 29th, and Cpl. Bobby Holcomb 509 on March 31st. George and Liliane invited me for my 84th birthday April 7th.

Penelope was taking care of my mail in Brunswick.

I happened to spot a camouflaged brilliant green tree frog in one of Mme Druard's flower boxes and photographed it. It was similar to the one that jumped into our motel room one night in Texas when the door was opened. It must have chased insects that hover outside the door.

George and Liliane drove me to the May 8th V.E. Day celebration. As usual I received all the hugs, kisses and thank you's for the 509, I finally promised, hopefully, but worriedly Mr. Coppola (retired deputy of several majors) that I would attend the August 15th 2004, "60th" anniversary of D Day "Dragoon" celebration in St. Tropez. I was worried about the heat. St. Tropez, in the Var River Valley is hotter than Nice and the traffic is bumper to bumper.

They wanted to take Francois and me by helicopter from Nice but I chose George and Liliane to drive us.

I called ahead to Rich and Barb. My return flight arrival was scheduled for the 19th of May 2004.

Chapter 25

The Assumption of the Blessed Virgin Mary and the 60th Anniversary of August 15, 1944

On July 13, 2004 at nine-thirty p.m. I was sitting up, fully dressed on my twin bed against four pillows making notes on all our medications. I raised my gleam over the record book that I supported against my knees and behold I saw the Blessed Mother Mary flash upward through my room as the Assumption.

Previously, when I was worried about going to France, she had let me know in some way on more than one occasion that it was ok. Once when we sang Don't Be Afraid at one of Father Jim Nadeau's twelve fifteen masses, I knew she was trying to tell me something. I went to my liturgical desk calendar and looked up August 15th since I was worried about going to the 60th anniversary ceremony of the 2nd D Day "Dragoon" in St. Tropez. We had jumped on the Assumption of the Blessed Virgin Mary, which I was never aware of.

Nor do I think that Major General Frederick in charge of the 1st airborne task force gave it a thought.

My first thought following the apparition was that it was ok to go, that the weather would be favorable.

I left Thursday August 12th with Francois; he went in the cabin with me. Coco was left behind. Karen Cheetham who is employed afternoons at Dr. Mat Horgan's veterinary clinic would take care of Coco in my apartment twice a day. She has three animals of her own.

Mr. Francois Coppola had arranged our stay at Major Noel's "Circle Navale De St. Tropez." It was a small hotel owned by the French navy and was opposite the beach on the shore road, D-98 (Ave Du 15 Aout 1944) in St. Tropez. George and Liliane would be with Francois and me in the Circle Navale.

Pierre and Laetizia drove up on their motorcycle and would stay at another hotel. Their four-year-old son, Batiste was brought to St. Tropez by Laetizia's parents. They would all stay at a hotel that had a swimming pool. Laetizia was able to take Batiste in the swimming pool with her.

Our plane arrived in Nice Friday the 13th at 8:55 a.m. George and Liliane were there waiting for us in their Mercedes to drive us to St. Tropez.

My large suitcase was missing. I had my Navy blue suit with campaign ribbons that Mr. Coppola had insisted on my wearing at the ceremonies.

When we arrived at the hotel, there was a problem. Mr. Coppola had not told Major Noel that we had a dog. Dogs were not permitted. George called on his cell phone and Mr. Francois Coppola came right over. There was a heated discussion with the Major. Mr. Coppola put the pressure on and an exception was made.

Liliane made several calls and Air France said they had the suitcase and would deliver it Saturday night late. The ceremonies would begin Sunday morning the 15th; hopefully I would be wearing my navy suit.

We all went to the beach, crossing heavy traffic on D-98. Liliane took Francois in the water with her. She was the only one wearing a swimsuit and loved the water. Francois was not afraid of the water. I took photos with my brand new canon digital camera. They had not told me that the new battery had to be charged. Liliane would take the photos thereafter with her camera.

These gigantic ceremonies only take place every ten years since our invasion of Southern France on August 15th 1944. The next one would be August 15th 2014.

Saturday the 14th we browsed around shopping, then to the supermarket. I never deviated from my strict, lacto-ovo vegetarian diet and needed some things for Francois and myself.

Then it was to Jacques Cadel's La Pesquiere calling itself, "Cuisine Traditionnell de Saint Tropez." It was the restaurant opposite and adjacent to La Ponche. I could have my ratatouille. I also asked for beans. They never had them at the other restaurants. Here they had them cooked in a pod, similar to our wax beans.

They didn't have separate tables, instead they were very long, possibly four or five, the length of the restaurant with hardwood benches on each side that you had to step over to be seated. There was enough space between the benches for the server.

The Tropezian Jacques Cadel's food was great.

Nine p.m. was the candle light procession and Vigil mass of the assumption of the Blessed Virgin Mary at the 17th century chapel of St. Anne, the mother of Mary, which was only open on three occasions during the entire year. The mass was celebrated by Le Cure Michel Hayle the pastor of Notre Dame De La Assumption in St. Tropez. That was the church where masses were always held at nine-thirty a.m. prior to ceremonies V.E. Day May 8th also August 15th Dragoon D Day invasion of southern France. Father Mike was British and from a country up near Scotland. The Ste. Anne hills are the area surrounding the St. Anne Chapel and where C and B Companies of the 509 PCT. INF. BN. jumped; five or six a.m., pre dawn hours of August 15th, 1944. It is a hilly rocky wooded area.

George and Liliane drove Francois and me to the ceremony. I sat on a rock, and then I was moved to a chair in the front row. There were hundreds present. Our candles were lit and the long procession around the chapel began with Father Michel in the lead. I remained seated with Francois lying down with his leash attached.

I was offered a light for my candle.

When the procession ended, the mass began. I was the subject of Father Mike's homily. All eyes turned towards me when he spoke of me as being an American paratrooper who had jumped in St. Tropez on the 15th of August 1944.

A huge miracle was unfolding. The invasion took place on the feast day of the assumption of the Blessed Virgin Mary. C & B Companies jumped in Saint Tropez on St. Anne's hills. We were supposed to jump in Le Muy about ten miles inland.

We jumped out of a C-47. The open door was in the back on the left hand side with its hinges taped so that our lines would not snag. I was Staff Sergeant and liked to stand in the door during flight looking down or sitting down in the door on the practice jumps before arriving at the DZ (drop zone).

However I could not see if we were flying in a southwesterly direction along the coast of France since my door was on the left side and we were in the dark for most of the flight. Remember, our planes going by awakened Louise in Nice and coming from Grosseto it was dark for most of the flight. Sergeant Ray Donovan said, "As B and C Companies approached the coast we suddenly turned back and out over the Mediterranean." (Taken from Charlie Doyle's book *Stand in the Door.*) I couldn't see through the window across on the right hand side since parachutists were sitting there shoulder to shoulder blocking the window.

Now we were in the sunlight, there were clouds below, the tops of which were white under the sun. Now and then I had seen water below whenever there was a small hole in the clouds. That's when we got the red light (stand in the door) then green light. (Go!) In response to Lieut. Ferris Knights question, "Sergeant Fisco, what do you think?" I responded," Let's get it," since I had not seen an opening in the clouds in several minutes. I believe I went out the door first. That would put me farthest from land. The second jumper may have hesitated which would bring him getting closer to land.

Our proper position going out the door is to turn left because of the prop blast, keep our heads down, arms folded over the reserve and legs together.

I had gotten ready for a water landing before reaching the top of the white clouds below. As I passed through and came out in the open I saw that I was over the water. Land was at about a fifteen-degree angle from the perpendicular in the distance.

I screamed out, "God please bring me to land!" Immediately the warm Sirocco wind from Africa blew at my back. So you see God even listens to soldiers. I pulled down on my two front risers and my chute spilled towards land. I am sure to this day that the Blessed Mother said to her son, "Get Richard to land!"

I had unbuckled my leg straps and gotten up into the seat of the harness ready to slip out on reaching the water. I was facing land. My chute must have made a one hundred eighty-degree turn on opening or I would have been facing out over the Mediterranean Sea. I could see green along the shoreline at a great distance. Trees were not distinct. The morning sun bathed the treetops.

Anyway, I swooped down over the water and landed on the steps of a Villa near the water. I sprained my left ankle, having been seated, my legs buckled under me on landing.

I think I may have landed at Cap Du Pinet. Sergeant Harvey S. Sutherland pointed out that I was in Bn. Plane number 29. He was in plane number 31 and landed in water up to his chest. I headed uphill through wooded terrain. It was still almost dark under the trees but light enough so that I could discern friend or foe. I saw this young man coming towards me carrying a bottle of wine. He was Francois Coppola, age fourteen. His mother had sent him out with a bottle of wine and told him to go find us and give us a drink. He would later work in a torpedo factory then become deputy to most of the mayors. I kept motionless in my Tommy gun crouch and let him approach. I became sure he was a French man but I refused the drink with words to the affect that I had to be ready to shoot. The refusal to the drink was what would identify me on our meeting in later years. Mr. Coppola later told me that our encounter was on the hill Potenze close to St. Anne.

Captain Miller's seventeen-man planeload as you know drowned at sea. Mr. Coppola said that all that was ever found were some pieces of camouflaged parachute floating with trapped air plus pieces of uniform, but none of the bodies.

I had asked Mr. Coppola if he could indicate the distances on a map of "La Ville De La Presq'ile." Tropezians don't call it a peninsula but "almost an island." He did so and indicated that there were only about three kilometers from the port of St. Tropez to the Plage De Pampelonne beach if our planes were flying in a southwesterly direction along the coast of France. I believe that B and C Company flew in from the east and Mr. Coppola also thinks that the planes flew inland from the east up the length of the peninsula dropping our boys over the St. Anne hills instead of crossing the peninsula southwest with only 3 kilometers or less. There is the miracle! Captain Miller's plane was probably crossing over land sporadically heading west along the eastern edge of the peninsula.

If you draw a straight line across the map from the St. Anne hills where most of the B and C Companies jumped using east to west as the perpendicular you cross the horseshoe, Baie Des Canebiers. That's the first likely place that Captain Millers planeload would have jumped and where the fog was. Thereafter they would have been over the Gulf of St. Tropez. Mr. Coppola disagrees with me. He does not think they jumped in the Baie Des Canebiers because of the numerous fishermen but that they jumped in the Gulf a little further west.

The southern France planeload manifests received from Charlie Doyle to Harvey Sutherland then to me were inaccurate. They show Captain Miller as a Lieutenant in the B Company and only five of the other 16 listed who died. He was in the B Company No. 1 plane also designated as Bn. Plane No. 25. I was in the B Company No. 5 plane, which was designated as Bn. Plane No. 29. Harvey Sutherland, who landed in water up to his chest, was in B Company plane No. 7 also designated as Bn. Plane No. 31.

Anyway, I thank God that the village of St. Tropez mayor, Dr. Jean Michel

Couve, Depute Maire de Saint Tropez, 1st Depute Dr. Jacques Bourrier and Depute Mayor, Francois Coppola approved mine and John Williams commander American Legion Riviera Post 5 request on behalf of Charlie Doyle, president 509 parachute infantry association. The plaque with the seventeen names was made and presented to John and myself May 8, 1996 since I would not be present for the official presentation August 15, 1996. I had asked for a monument to be placed by the sea since that is where my captain and the seventeen drowned and that's where the monument is today about one and a half kilometers from the port and about fifty meters in front of the Cimetiere Marin right by the water. On the anniversaries a little boat goes out and throws flowers. Captain Miller's monument will serve to bind France and the U.S. relations with the Normandy D Day invasion June 6th, 1944. Especially with France's new president Nicola Sarkozy.

After the St. Anne ceremonies, George drove us back to Major Noel's "Circle Navale de St. Tropez" hotel. The reason that we had eaten earlier was that George would have to stand vigil outside waiting for the delivery of my lost suitcase. He did and the suitcase arrived about midnight. I would be able to wear my navy suit with its campaign ribbons.

We had eaten supper in the hotel earlier. I ate some of what they had plus what I had in the room.

A young navy couple present with their three children complained about the presence of Francois, my fourteen-year-old mini poodle.

Sunday arrives, the 15th of August 2004; the 60th anniversary ceremonies of operation "Dragoon" the invasion of Southern France. The 509 had participated in the invasion as part of Major General Robert Frederick's 1st airborne task force.

Mr. Coppola got us to the port at 8 a.m. where we boarded the Balli de Suffren II, a rescue boat (sauvetage) named after a prominent Tropezian for whom a statue had been erected.

I was given the best seat up front with Francois behind the pilot. We were twelve aboard including three women. Mr. Coppola is along side Francois in the accompanied photo.

They headed easterly at first passing the citadel, then Cimetier Marin where Captain Miller's seventeen-man monument is located, then westerly around the Cap de St. Tropez, Cap Du Pinet where I may have landed. Then southerly along the Pampelonne beaches as far as the Cap Camarat and return.

On the way back, Captain Miller's monument was plainly in view. Since my digital camera was not working I asked for someone to take the photo. The photo was taken. I thought it would have been great for the 509 to have a photo of the seventeen-man monument taken from the water. I still have not received a copy. Next was the procession out to Captain Miller's monument in front of Cimetiere Marin where a pretty young lady was designated to accompany Francois and myself in the placement of a beautiful wreath at the base of the monument. Flag bearers lined both sides of us and dipped their flags in salute to our fallen comrades.

Local firefighters plus two fire officers were also in formation. They had been specially selected for me since I was a retired NYC fire Lieutenant. They were dressed in their fire fighter gear; metal helmets, boots, navy uniforms with wide white bands across the chest and shoulders and above the boots.

The next ceremony, the most important of the day took place at Place Des Lices in the middle of St. Tropez. There was a very large monument in tribute to all allied WWII forces. I was seated with Francois in front of French, American, British, and Russian flags, all four national anthems were played.

There Mayor Couve and 1st deputy mayor of St. Tropez, Dr. Bourrier, presented me with a one and a half inch gold medal and a certificate of honorary citizen of St. Tropez. A gentleman in the placement of a beautiful wreath escorted me with Francois.

I was asked to say a few words. I told them in what Louise called my Arab accented French that the 509 had jumped and fought in Africa, Italy, and France and then in the Ardennes (Battle of the Bulge). I also thanked them for loaning me Louise their Nicoise. Drinks and delicacies followed, plus the hugs, kisses and thank yous for our nation saving theirs or they would all be speaking German now.

Afterwards George drove me into the Var where Mr. Alain Spada, Pres. de Consiel General de Var the previous mayor of St. Tropez presented me with a three and a half inch bronze medal.

That afternoon there was a huge banquet at a very large restaurant in the outskirts.

George and Liliane were seated at another table. I was seated with French strangers. I had pasta with marinara sauce and ratatouille. I gave Francois some of my pasta under the table.

George and Liliane drove us all back to the hotel to rest.

The spectacular took place at about nine p.m. Sunday night of the 15th on the upper level of the Citadel (the old fort where the enemy held out) open to the stars in the sky.

Francois, myself, George and Liliane accompanied by Mr. Coppola ascended the passageways to the upper level. There were two thousand spectators who cheered us as we entered.

There were two massive separated screens on which film was projected above and behind a large stage.

The gingerbread patch of the 509 was displayed onto the right hand screen. Scenes before and after "D" Day were displayed on the left hand screen.

Actors on stage dressed in allied and German uniforms pantomimed the occurrences.

American and then British flags were raised one after the other on tall masts as the national anthems were played.

Fireworks went off to the tune of the Star Spangled Banner, as old glory was unfurled on high.

Francois was frightened at the deafening noise. I covered his eyes and ears whenever the fireworks went off busting over our heads.

There were long lines on leaving. Some stopped to hug, kiss me on both cheeks and thanking our nation for saving theirs.

We went straight to Jacques Cadel's "La Pesquiere" for supper.

There were six of us including Pierre and his wife, Lataezia, seated at the long wood tables and benches.

The food was the best ever. They even had beans for me cooked in the pod. George selected the wine, it was the table wine.

Monday George and Liliane drove us back to Nice to catch our plane. We were 15 minutes late. Mr. and Mme Druard at the Hotel Les Fusains, although closed, permitted Francois and me to stay over to the next day. I called Rich to let him know.

Chapter 26

I Receive a Mother Cabrini Class II Relic, I Lose My Two Closest War Buddies and The Devil Gets Physical

Francois' coughing continued in September '04. Dr. Horgan took X-rays and diagnosed him with chronic bronchitis from pollution. It was most likely the traffic in Nice. He was now age fourteen.

I called Poco in West Virginia.

I mailed a gold and pearl ring to Mary my niece. She and her husband, Scott were caring for my sister with Alzheimer's in a nursing home in Dallas.

I attended the mass for the anointing of the sick at St. Charles October 5th.

Rich, Barb, Vera and Ralph left for New Orleans in their old red Chevy van. They would visit my younger brother, Joey in Ocean Springs, Mississippi. I was now alone.

October 18th, 2004 our 509 gunfighter, Sgt. Boggs G. Collins died. He was about three or four years older than Poco and myself. Like all of us WWII Vets, he would be forgotten and uncared for. Boggs received the Medal of Honor and Distinguished Service Cross. Poco would no longer have to climb up and get Boggs down out of the trees.

October 18th I received a Class II Relic of Mother Cabrini from the St. Frances Cabrini Shrine in upper Manhattan. The same day I received a prayer card of St. Teresa of Lisieux from EWTN.

They are my two favorite saints. I believe Mother Cabrini's prayer brought my son home safely from Vietnam and I believe it was St. Teresa of Lisieux's prayer that got Louise her brief remission from breast cancer in 1990. I think St. Teresa's mother was supposed to have died of breast cancer.

Mother Cabrini was an immigrant saint and Louise was an immigrant.

At one a.m. October 19th, I had taken Francois out to the blue stone to p.p. On reentering I tripped and fell backward through the air on my left side off the second of the two stone steps onto the brick patio.

My left wounded elbow, left hip, left hand, left back of head; all involved. I lay there about twenty minutes. Finally I was able to get up still grasping Francois' leash. I made it to bed believing that I would be unable to move on awakening. Nine a.m. I awoke, put my feet on the floor, stood up and felt nothing.

I mailed a mass card for Boggs to Poco who would bring it to Bogg's family. The mass would be December 14th at the Cathedral of the Immaculate Conception in Portland. My old Diocese.

Dr. Horgan showed me how to use Francois' nebulizer and breathing equipment to be administered three times a day. He responded very well in about a week or so. I would eventually be able to reduce it to once a day. This however, would not be his downfall.

Frank and Darwin Pologruto, our neighbors in Charlottesville always kept in touch and I am sure prayed for me.

During the January winter of '05 we had seven inches of snow several times. Francois didn't like the nebulizer and kept trying to jerk his head out of the mask. I had to be firm.

I had been attending the weekday five p.m. mass at the chapel in the St. John Parish Center. Elderly Priscilla Pellitiere died on February 14th. She had always rung the bell at the consecration.

The next day Father Ed Sheehan celebrated the mass for Boggs Collins that I had requested.

Two weeks past and no one took Priscilla's place. I decided I would take Priscilla's place and ring the bell at the consecration.

My grandson Ralph replaced the VCR on my television. He used to carry in the groceries for me. Then he found a girlfriend. Poco called in March to tell me he received his V.A. disability over the phone, about time, we were both at age eighty-five.

Vera, my granddaughter cleaned for me every other week.

I kept touch with my sister, Theresa through Mary, my niece and Scott who cared for her in a nursing home.

The hotel Les Fusains was closed down pending its sale. I couldn't find a place in Caucade to stay for four months during the winter of 2005. Since I couldn't be near Louise's grave Liliane called Mr. Coppola in St. Tropez for me. His neighbors rented the ground floor of their villa a week at a time. I decided to go with Francois. Coco would stay back.

Penelope helped me tagging the luggage.

I left Logan May 3rd and returned May 10th. Rich drove me both ways. I stayed at Mr. et Mme Robert Kellinger's Villa plein soleil in Montee des Meuniers.

It was a beautiful villa in a hilly area of St. Tropez. They had a small apricot poodle so Francois had a friend. I was able to do my own cooking having brought my beans and rice, etc. with me plus Francois' diet food.

Mr. Coppola drove me to Cavalaire in his Land Rover. Cavalaire was one of the main assault landing sites. There were numerous monuments in memory of August 15th, 1944. He drove me along the beach and his Land Rover reactivated my back pains.

Francois and I were invited to dinner at Mr. Coppola's, "Villa coup de Soleil" about a hundred meters away. His wonderful German wife, Edith prepared everything.

I kept up with Francois' nebulizer three times a day during the one-week stay.

George and Liliane drove us back to Nice where we made our plane. Rich met us in Boston to take us back to Brunswick.

Because of my myasthenia gravis I try to stay off my feet and did my cooking, eating and dishes at the counter seated on a stool. I dozed off and fell off on the floor. Fortunately, I was able to take ibuprofen. This was not the end; I would break my ribs three times before I would make sleep a priority.

Then twice I experienced a reoccurrence of being awakened at night with violent chills and trembling. I am sure it is from having had malaria in Rome. Doctors always say it is not from the malaria but they don't know what it is from. I always wonder what that fever in Panama was from. It had shown negative for malaria.

The next reunion of the 509 parachute infantry battalion was arranged as usual by June Housman, President John De Vanie's daughter. It would be for four days at the Omni Royal Orleans Hotel in New Orleans July 5th to the 9th, 2005. The reunion was sandwiched in between two hurricanes. I liked it best of all of the reunions except for its heat and humidity. I could only walk Francois about one block. I had my beans and rice with Nick De Gaeta at the Old Orleans restaurant a few blocks away. We had to take a cab because of me. The gourmet vegetable dishes in the hotel were the finest. None of this lettuce and tomatoes. Ernest (Bud) Siegel (Captain A Co. Old 509) picked up the tab on one of these dinners.

Jimmy Nunn couldn't make it. His travel from St. Augustine would have been in the path of either of the two hurricanes.

I was able to reminisce with Johnny McDonald (Pathfinders Old 509) who, remember, helped me in finding Louise's wedding and engagement rings.

Many of the new active 509er's made their presence with Col. King at their head. They looked a lot snappier than we did. I don't doubt their capabilities in the least. Our Old 509 was kind of rough and ready and always in the field.

Nick De Gaeta and Bud Siegel put on their act reciting and singing the old 509 poems and songs.

The very first day on arrival I had trouble with Francois' nebulizer. The battery went dead. I had used it between plane rides on the flights down with stewardesses volunteering to help me.

I called Karen Cheetham at Dr. Horgan's vet clinic. She UPS'ed a fresh one to me from the Maine Street store. I received it in less than twenty-four hours.

Rich drove me back from Logan.

Francois developed a teeth infection in his right jaw and had to have three of them extracted. His weight dropped from twelve to nine pounds. He was on five medications per day, Rimadyl, Clindamycin, Batril, Hydrocodone, Albuterol with the nebulizer plus Adequan bone injection plus the old saw Palmetto that kept his prostate in check. It helped him but never me. I always brushed his teeth at night with just a plain brush.

I called my younger brother, Joey. He had been a paratrooper during Korea. He was in a rehab home in Mississippi recuperating from a stroke.

I was still dozing off with my head on the table giving me nosebleeds.

I purchased a beautiful ten-inch by twelve inch art work of the assumption from EWTN, had it blessed by Father Walter Goudreau and hung it on the wall by my twin bed where she had passed through.

I had masses said at St. John for Marty's wife, Shirley Galuskin, Louise and Lt. Jack Darden.

I seldom dream. I saw Shirley and Marty in an embrace in a dream.

On September 1st, 2005 at four a.m. I took Francois out to p.p., at four forty-five a.m. I had groomed Coco, at five thirty-four a.m. I had said my prayers and gone to bed. Ten minutes later the devil shook me awake on my right upper arm at the right shoulder. I had caught a glimpse of his claws. I usually sleep way over on my right side facing the wall. I can't sleep on my back because of the myasthenia gravis. It causes drooling into my lungs.

I saw Father Walter Gaudreau. He said, "No problem, just spray holy water before going to sleep!"

I went to the spigot on our beautiful old holy water font. It was faulty and leaked out through the button you pressed in addition to the spigot.

This indicated how infrequently our parish used the holy water.

Anyway, awakening me was the devils tactics. He just didn't want me to get any sleep. He tries harassing tactics to make me late for the five o'clock mass. Something happens or comes up as I go out the door but I always manage to get there on time.

Nicky always wakes me to take him out by tickling my feet. One night, I felt this tickling. I arose to tend to Nicky, but found him sleeping. My devil has a sense of humor. Nicky does not know the devil is there when the devil makes himself invisible. I am sure that the devil can imitate voices and cause the end of friendships.

I filled my little plastic cosmetic spray bottles with holy water. No problem since. The spigot was repaired thanks to the secretary, Elizabeth Bergeron's perseverance. I sleep with my trigger finger on the holy water spray bottle.

I mentioned the devil grabbing me to young Father John Granato later on. He said that he had had the same experience

Holy water is a sacramental blessed by a priest in the "rituale romanum." It is also used against spiritual enemies. It's good the devil didn't shake my left arm, that's where I have an exposed nerve at the elbow from the WWII gunshot wound.

September 30th I dozed off and fell from the stool at the kitchen counter and felt a rib snap. There followed ibuprofen and Tylenol codeine for a couple of weeks.

My urologist tried an Oxymtrol patch for my incontinence. That afternoon I could hardly get back to my '03 Explorer from my 600-yard walk with Francois at Bowdoin University. I jerked the patch off. It had an MG caution warning; this incontinence limits all your activities. If I ever get back to St. Marc in Caucade, Nice I will ask that elderly devout woman to put her hand on my shoulder again.

Mike, son of Herb (Poco) Coberly called to tell me his dad died November 9th. I called a florist in Elkins, West Virginia and asked for a red, white and blue wreath to be sent to the funeral home with an inscription about Poco's plane jumping in Spanish Morocco on the Africa jump and his having been interned in Spain with other 509er's where the Spanish people called him Poco because his six feet three inches was so much taller than them!

I also sent Mike a mass card.

Poco and Jim were my two closest war buddies. I notified John De Vanie, President of the 509 PCT. Inf. Assn., and Barry Simpson, Treas. I called Jim.

I had been taking proscar for the prostate since the early nineties. On November 14th, the same day of the year that Louise found a fatal lump on her breast in 1987 in Virginia; I found a lump on my right breast accompanied by pain. Dr, Gregory A. Kelly, oncologist at Mid Coast Hospital kept a monthly surveillance. The May 21st surgery scheduled was cancelled. He knew it was on its way out. The lump was still there but he knew it was over.

Mary Whitten, friend from daily mass at the Cathedral in Portland had called a couple of times concerned.

So you see I had three devout ladies praying for me, Penelope Warren, Mary Whitten, and Jackie Duval from the five p.m. daily mass in the St. John Baptist Chapel. Women have more compassion than men.

Then Nick De Gaeta called to tell me Jim died January 17, 2006. Evidently Jim's wife, Cynthia had called John De Vanie, Pres. 509, who must have called Nick.

I called Cynthia, she was crying terribly. She seemed to think that Jim's death was the end, that she would never see him again. I told Cynthia," I will know when I have died when I see my Guardian Angel coming for me with his large black dog." Cynthia said, "That's for me, anyone with that much faith."

In two months I had lost my two closest war buddies.

Chapter 27

The Ending

At the end of January 2006, Francois was having trouble getting started to walk. I began feeding him his chicken, chicken liver and KD diet food in a paper plate on the front seat of the explorer. He ate it all lying down.

Poco's mass was eight thirty a.m. February 5th at the Cathedral in Portland.

Coco was at the vet for not eating then eating on and off and Francois had problems with his teeth diagnosed as bacteria in the right jaw bone treated with Clavamax.

I started on my autobiography. Penelope would come Thursday evenings from her own work and Sunday afternoon. She would sit down at the new typewriter across from me and say "Speak." That's how it got started. She would then put it in the computer and send it to Melinda Louise Conner, the editor.

My niece Mary Hollock called to tell me my younger brother Joey died the day before. He was buried the 28th. The mass I asked for Joey would be April 21st at the Cathedral.

My grandson Ralph polished my '03 Explorer.

Cynthia, Jim's widow, had asked me to cancel her reservation to the 2006 509 Dayton reunion, she changed her mind.

Johnny McDonald drove himself from Las Vegas.

I had a good waitress, Kimberly Ford Peters, who helped me with most of my meals. She gave me the location of St. Joseph's for the Saturday Vigil mass. It was a small beautiful old church with a marble interior and statues. The pastor himself heard confessions before the mass. There were about twenty waiting in line compared to the one back at St. John's in Brunswick which was a much larger parish.

Rich drove Francois and me back and forth to Boston.

I mailed Cynthia the Devine Mercy rosary. Father Ridgeway at St. John had blessed it for me.

I started preparing for my own demise. Since Rich would own the caveau in Caucade Nice when I died, he would have to prove Louise and I were his parents. Although not usually shown on a birth certificate the parent's given middle names must show to coincide with caveau ownership

Louise's birth certificate from France took only a week with Henri helping although it had to be translated to English. My son and mine took four months from NYC. I then deposited a guaranteed amount through a local funeral director that will cover the cost of death including outside the state to return me to Brunswick and get me to Nice. There, Roblot will take over and there will be a separate fee. I deposited that amount with my brother in-law Henri who set up a separate account. Charlie Giraud who was a French paratrooper and former director of Roblot insists that he will personally take care of his American paratrooper buddy and will bury me with Louise in Caucade.

And of course this removes some of the burden from my son.

Bob Erickson visited me in June with his grandson. I opened up a bottle of Veuve Clicquot. Bob was the sergeant who guarded me in the garage in Lantosque while I awaited trial for a one day A.W.O.L.

June 12th Coco's weight was found to have dropped to six lbs. from eight and a half.

June 19th, Coco's nineteenth birthday, she wasn't eating. I took her to the Vet Clinic. Dr. Wood discovered a tumor the size of a silver dollar between the small and large intestine.

Cats have the most courage of all animals. They don't cost anything. When it is their time they go in a corner and die. Cat's courage compared to other animals is like comparing Saint Ignatius of Antioch to other saints. He wrote seven letters on his way to be eaten by lions. "Cool hand Luke."

Dr. Wood wanted a sonogram.

On June 21st I took Coco to Dr. Rossi on Warren Ave. in Portland. He said now is the time to operate, it hadn't spread.

June 28th, awaiting surgery, I went to Target in Topsham. They had the Pounces and Coco liked them so I purchased a half dozen cans.

On June 29th Coco was operated on by Dr. Wood to remove the two-inch tumor between her small and large intestine. I went to see her after the surgery. She was laying on her right side in a small cage with her little pink tongue hanging out. I returned home. At eight thirty a.m. I called and spoke with Dr. Horgan. He said lets wait two hours.

I asked God to let Coco hear me. I said to Coco, "Coco, this is Daddy, I love you, I'm sorry." Coco responded with a short weak "meow." eleven a.m. I called; Dr. Horgan said Coco had died.

I asked Karen Cheetham at the clinic to have Coco cremated. I found a small blue angel ceramic urn for her ashes. Karen sealed it. When I go to France I will give it to Henri and Maryse. They will place it with Kiki's. When I am buried and the caveau is opened up, the urns will be placed inside if possible if not, the ashes will be sprinkled around the caveau where the ashes of Jody, Mega, and Fiston had been sprinkled.

Back on the ibuprofen again. I dozed off and fell off a chair with a West Point Atlas on my chest. X-rays were negative, but the doctor believed there was a break.

I called Penelope. She is a wiz on the computer. I asked her if she could find me another Himalayan Blue Point. Within twenty-four hours she had found a one-year-old Seal Point in Auburn near where she lived. I gave her the green light.

July 13th, 2006 Penelope brought me Minou, that's what I named her, it means pussycat.

She came from a huge home that had a large Golden Retriever.

I took her to Dr. Horgan. She weighed less than five pounds. He thought we should hold off until she started eating and gained weight. In a couple of days she came out of hiding and ate her Solid Gold. She took a liking to Francois. She started gaining weight on July 24th she was spayed and declawed putting sentiments aside. Tammy, our cross-eyed alley cat back in the sixties ruined an eight hundred dollar two-piece sofa. We had learned our lesson. Tammy used to play red light green light, one, two, three!

Health wise, I experienced awakening with those frightening chills again.

Penelope kept coming on Thursday nights and Sunday afternoon. She would type as I dictated.

Francois was on all five medications and the nebulizer.

The '03 Explorer started with lemon problems. In September I traded it in for an '06, six cylinders, Eddie Bauer.

I kept up with Francois weekly Adequan injections for his bones.

On the evening of October 1st I was sitting at the table on a pine stool making notes in my record book. I fell asleep backward suspended in the horizontal position. I woke looking over the rims of my glasses and I screamed out to God to save me.

I had occasionally done upper and lower abdominal exercises. I was able through sheer strength to slowly raise myself up. If I had fallen, I think I would have been crippled for life.

One evening towards the end of November I couldn't sleep worrying about Francois. I thought I should put him down; he had so many things wrong. He was almost totally blind. Dr. Wood expected him to be completely blind by February '07. His right jaw was deformed from bone bacteria; he could only hear if I whistled I had to shred the chicken for him to be able to eat. He was on the nebulizer three times a day for chronic bronchitis from pollution. He lost most of the movement in his hind legs and I could hear a snap when they frequently dislocated. He could only lie down by keeping his hind legs stiff.

Besides the nebulizer he was on Batril and Clindamycin for the jaw, Rimadyl for pain, Hydrocodone should he cough.

I didn't have the courage to put him down. He was so brave and tried so hard to keep going.

This old man found a young friend, Reed Bartlett from walking Francois at Bowdoin University. He had a beautiful and extremely friendly and intelligent golden retriever named Chobe (we called him Tobey). Reed insisted on pushing the snow off the roof of my Explorer. I have frost bite in the fingertips on my right hand. He familiarized me with hand warmers and brought me some from L.L. Bean. He also gave me a pair of gloves from L.L. Bean. At twenty-three degrees Fahrenheit I could wear them without hand warmers. They kept my hands warmer than any of my other six pairs. They were nylon and padded with down but loose. They fit inside the grip of my twenty-six foot retractable leash and I was able to work the locking latch with my thumb while wearing gloves. These Mainer's who wear just t-shirts in the winter also know what keeps you warm. Dr. Horgan who played hockey said that Reed was a very good hockey player. Reed was a graduate of Bowdoin, He ran hard every day with Tobey for quite a distance. I mentioned to him that I thought he should jog and run hard only once a week. He still ran hard everyday probably to keep up with Tobey.

Francois couldn't hold himself up while eating. I began preparing his food just before leaving for Bowdoin. I would put his food in a paper plate then place the plate on the seat of the Explorer. He would lie on his right side and eat from that position. He would eat most of the eleven oz's of chicken, chicken liver and KD.

The kids invited me for Christmas dinner as usual. Barb baked me a full plate of those meringues that were pastries made with egg white. I refer to my son and daughter in-law as kids. My son was at age sixty.

'07 opened up with continued calls to Division of Vital Records, Dept. of Health at 125 Worth St. NYC, NY. Also the Dept. of Health and Mental Hygiene awaiting my son's birth certificate to show Louise and me as his parents with our given middle names so as to coincide with our ownership names on the caveau.

The French Embassy in Boston also required permission of the Mayor of Nice (Jacques Peyrat- French paratrooper Dien Bien Pfu) for me to be buried in my own caveau in Caucade, Nice. The latter was easily acquired through my friend, Charlie Giraud, French paratrooper that knew Mayor Peyrat well. Copies of the French Embassy's permission were received. We also received my son's accurate birth certificate.

I had two episodes in January of awakening with those horrible shivering shakes.

Francois was not putting his left rear down.

We had snow several times, then a blizzard in February.

I always made my own soup. The recipe was from Maryse my French sister in-law whose mother was a cordon bleu cook. I modified it and made enough to last three weeks. Four large broccoli crowns (organic where possible) about twenty brussel sprouts, two long leeks, two bunches of asparagus, two zucchinis, and two bunches of broccolini, one small egg plant and four shallots. Peel and chop everything removing the outer skin of the leeks. Fill two large pots. Press everything down tight and add filtered water to below two inches from the top. Cook for twenty minutes, drain, stir and save the juice, blend, adding the juice level to the top of the vegetables. Makes four large containers; freeze three. When defrosting remove from the refrigerator two days ahead—bon appetite.

We had a snowstorm March 3rd. When I applied the brake in parking, the snow on the roof slid down over the windshield and hood. I started pushing the snow off and developed chest pains.

I drove around the block back to the house. The pain was gone. I called Dr. Joshua Cutler. He asked, "What did you do after the pain left?" I said," things I normally do." He asked," And no pain?" I said, "No pain." He said," Then it's not your heart."

Francois continued his downhill trend. A urine test showed he was spilling protein into his urine. I carried him out to p.p. He toppled on the ice. I found him in the living room. He couldn't get back up on the rug.

I tried to put him down. I couldn't do it.

We had snow in April.

I called Cynthia, Jimmy's widow. She said if she found a sitter for her cat, Sugar, she would come to the 509 reunion, July in Reno. She later changed her mind.

I had been using Dr. Morgenstern at the Bowdoin Medical Group. I thought I should have a blood test since I had been a vegetarian and eating the exact same food for fifteen years without fish.

He permitted the blood test but I had to pay a hundred and twenty-five dollars out of my pocket. I complained to the women that handled the billing that I thought the Medical Group should pay the cost.

Dr. Morgenstern gave me a dismissal letter saying that I was too aggressive.

I immediately recalled having seen EWTN, the elderly widow arriving home to her children from work and saying," We are going to have a party!" The children asked," Why mother? Did you get a raise?" The mother said," No! I was fired; I am celebrating the new job that God will give me."

Sure enough I ended up with Dr. James Raker a superb general practitioner. With him I have learned so much about myself for example osteoporosis; I lost five inches in height from five feet, seven and a half inches. He put me on Fosamax +D.

Penelope moved from Auburn, Maine in September 2006 to Winston Salem, North Carolina. It was trial and error on how to keep the story going. My taping it didn't work out, the quality of my voice fluctuated because of the myasthenia gravis. Finally we settled in on my writing. My shaky handwriting caused back and forth corrections. At the same time Penelope continued working as an accountant, now working for Richard Childress Racing as an accountant. She does volunteer work for ARF in Winston Salem Tuesday's after work in the kitty section. She was indispensable knowing all the details, organizing the chapters, the chronologicalizing, detecting duplications, etc. She had her own Maine Coon cat pets. She already put down the aged Josh followed by Emily. She then adopted Morty an already huge Maine Coon cat kitten. She is saving room for my animals.

So now Michelle Sirois who works around the corner at UPS does the primary typing of my hand written script. Errors are weeded out before sending to Penelope who computerizes and sends to the editor, Melinda Conner, Jimmy Nunn's daughter. That's the inside scoop.

My late May day routine was the five o'clock mass, followed by Francois' second outing at Bowdoin, a stop for groceries at Hannaford, a ten or twenty minute stop at adoration in the Sacred Heart Chapel depending if I had time to say five decades of the rosary or the seven sorrows of the Blessed Virgin, then home.

The early afternoon of Friday May 25th, 2007 I went to Dr. Horgan's vet clinic for the third time to try to put Francois down.

I sat down with him then thought I would go out to the Explorer and think it over. I held him with both arms close to my chest grasping the railing with my left hand momentarily and descended the three wooden steps.

Just as I got to the bottom I was hit hard by an SUV backing out from my right. I was hit so hard on the right side I must have done a pin wheel to hit on top of my left shoulder clutching Francois close to me, I felt what must have been the rear bumper over me too frightened to open my eyes I screamed fearful the vehicle would continue to back up. Then I must have screamed six times to God, "Why? Why..."

I was moved back and away. I had such a grip on Francois sheltering him that they had to yell at me to turn him loose.

The Brunswick Fire Department Rescue Team was there tending to me. I started kidding saying, "It's a good thing I was an old paratrooper and knew how to roll." In response to their questions, I was hurting on the right side and on the left shoulder. They wanted to take me to the Emergency. I refused. I didn't feel anything broken and I didn't want to make a big deal over it. They wanted to drive me home. I refused.

Dr. Horgan had been there the whole time. They gave me back Francois and helped me up. I drove Francois home.

I recorded my pulse at one hundred seventy, applied a bandage to my left elbow, my left shoulder was in pain, my head hurt, my left hip hurt, my left knee was scraped, my right kidney hurt.

At one thirty-five p.m. Francois had eaten his plate of organic chicken breast and chicken livers. I had beans cooking. I heated and ate my wild rice with an Ugly Ripe tomato, tea with honey and toasted my frozen pan scuro. Then sliced three loaves of pan scuro into the freezer.

I attended the five o'clock mass, Father Ed Sheehan celebrating. Five thirty I went for a short walk in the woods at Bowdoin with Francois. He couldn't stand up, he kept falling. Six p.m. Francois ate two-thirds of his food on the front seat lying down. I called Dr. Horgan at home on my cell phone and made a seven thirty p.m. appointment at the clinic to put Francois down.

Disassociation, a gift from God had now come over me and I was sure I could go forward with it. In fact, to this day I don't remember what Francois looked like. Looking at a photo of him does not help.

I met Dr. Horgan at seven thirty, sat with Francois in my lap. I hugged and spoke to him. Dr. Horgan gave him the first tranquilizer injection. Remember, Francois was totally blind in his right eye and almost in his left. He looked up at me as if to say, "It's about time." I don't remember his eyes being opaque as he looked up at me. Dr. Horgan gave him the final injection (it was blue in color). Francois fell to eternal sleep at sixteen years and eight months.

Dogs I am sure, if they had a choice, would still want to be dogs running and frolicking with each other. We just help them to be happy in their own world and in return they just love us back.

That night I had my soup and frozen pan scuro from Black Crow toasted and went to sleep.

Saturday I decided to test my strength and courage. I would take the same walk that I always took with Francois at Bowdoin, three hundred yards out and three hundred yards back, bent over. I did and I made it. My injuries hardly bothered me.

I met the elderly woman with her mini apricot poodle, Bengy. Bengy always ran around with Francois. He came up to me but looked around for Francois.

Sunday I tried it again. I couldn't make it and turned back. The right kidney, left shoulder, everything hurt. I decided to go to Emergency at six thirty p.m. to Mid Coast Hospital. I was not bleeding (remember that wealthy Bobbie Baron whom I had taken to Maine Med was bleeding and had to wait) so I had to wait my turn. I was there until midnight. X-rays showed a separation in the left shoulder and they found a small amount of blood in the kidney. In the days that followed it was a CAT scan and cystology by Dr. Kinkead, exams by Dr. Boothby my neurologist, Dr. Holt my eye doctor and Dr. Raker my general practitioner.

The myasthenia gravis stepped in with what is called a crisis caused by the accident. I could barely walk the sixty yards to UPS to pick up my mail. A crisis could come on for almost any reason, a cold, the flu, surgery, anxiety, etc. It was not severe unless it affected the breathing.

I called Penelope in North Carolina. I said to her, "Francois kept me alive for fifteen years since Louise died, could you find me a champion bred toy poodle?" With her expertise she went on the Internet, called me back and gave me the telephone number of Kay Amen in Etoile, Texas. I called Kay; she had two male toys born May 11th, 2007. In response to her question, I told her that I would not breed him or alter him. He would cost twelve hundred dollars plus three hundred dollars for the shipping. I agreed and asked her to name him Nicky. I would receive him the first week of July.

Monday Rich and Barb returned from New Orleans. I told him about Nicky. He refused me permission to have another dog at my age.

I called Penelope to find me an apartment in Winston Salem, but not near her. I did not want to interfere with her career. Penelope said," No problem." In fact, she had one already picked out.

I wrote my son a letter but didn't give it to him that day. I told him about Francois keeping me alive since Mother died, that I was alone and didn't have a woman and that I would increase my rent.

As usual I went to the five p.m. mass at St. John celebrated by Father John Granato. I offered my communion for my son.

The next day my son walked in. He said he had talked it over with Barb. The Scientology minister then said," I was going at it the wrong way, you can have Nicky."

I handed him the letter I had written to him the day before but had not given to him.

In the meantime, Minou (which means pussy cat) was in a slump, hardly eating in the morning over having lost her friend, Francois. I replaced her vitality with Solid Gold, which she had had in the very beginning.

I went to Day's Antiques. They had a ceramic oriental ginger jar that I thought would be perfect for Francois' ashes.

Pains and weakness continued.

Rich drove me to the Saturday four p.m. mass. I cleaned the Explorer out and I removed Francois' pillows and things. I gave his nebulizer equipment back to the vet clinic for others.

Kay had sent me photos of Nicky. He was as big as her hand. She planned to ship him July 7th.

Jessica Reandeau's vocation was caring for animals. She was a friend of Rich and Barb. She would bring Nicky from Boston on his arrival. Cell phone and e-mails were exchanged between Kay, Penelope and Jessica. Penelope had maintained constant e-mail contact with Kay.

Minou was down to six pounds but had started eating the Solid Gold.

July 7th Nicky had arrived in Boston and at eight-thirty p.m. was on the way with Jessica (Jessica to Penelope, to me).

Ten forty-five p.m. Jessica arrived with Nicky. He ate two-thirds of an organic chicken liver. Kay had told me he weighed a little over one pound. Minou loved him and started eating half a cup a day of Solid Gold again.

I had planned to take Nicky with me to the 509 reunion in Reno July 18th to the 22nd.

His training was questionable so I cut out a piece of the inexpensive rug runner by the front door where he was in the habit of going when he couldn't make it. I took it to the Circus Circus Hotel and placed it on the floor between the two beds with a couple of sheets of Wee Wee Pads underneath.

Mary Hollock, my niece planned the flight schedule. It was American Airlines changing in Dallas, Fort Worth and Chicago, Ohara for the return.

Rich drove me back and forth to Boston. On arrival at Circus Circus nine p.m. the manager said," No pets." I told her June Housman who had arranged the reunion had gotten permission for Nicky. She called June, came back and said that there would be an extra three hundred and fifty dollar charge for any damage.

I took him out frequently especially after eating. It worked out as I had planned. I think he only did big numbers twice on the floor and it picked up easily plus a little cleaning.

Before departure on Sunday I had called the manager to inspect. She said it was not necessary. I am sure she had kept in touch with the two women who cleaned daily.

The reunion had been difficult for me. There were two buildings in Circus Circus. You had to take a tram that ran outside the buildings to get to the slot machines and restaurants. I ordered a dozen hard-boiled eggs. The chef had to charge me $40. He apologized and compensated for the ridiculous cost by giving me the tip to put vinegar in the boiling water.

I always took Nicky with me to the CP room. Everyone loved Nicky. In fact, John DeVanie (Pres.) almost bought Nicky's brother but decided to hold off.

It wasn't easy taking him out. He was distracted by so many people wanting to play with him.

We had a good reunion attendance, about 20 from the old 509 BN with their wives and about 50 of the new 509 regiment. Col. King was replaced by Col. Darron Wright.

I called the hotel desk for the location and the telephone number of the nearest Catholic Church. I called for the time of the Saturday Vigil mass. I took a cab with Nicky. He still weighed less than two pounds and I didn't anticipate any problem since I would carry him. The Cathedral was very old, small, beautiful and of wood construction. What it lacked on the outside was made up for on the inside, furnished with beautiful antique pieces.

The woman lector must have been a professional classical singer. She had a voice you would pay to listen to. On leaving I looked for the men's room and was directed to the exterior door on the side by a couple. They waited for us and asked us if they could help. They must have seen me at mass holding Nicky. The cab was supposed to be there but I was also supposed to call if it wasn't. I told the middle-aged couple that I was at the 509 reunion at Circus Circus but would like to have bought some yogurt for the return trip to Boston. They insisted on driving me to the supermarket where I purchased six yogurts. Four of those were taken away from me by security on the return trip. They then drove us back to Circus Circus. I told them I was writing an autobiography covering the depression, the war and the post war and told them the name. He gave me his business card and said he would like for me to send him a copy. His wife was considering writing about her dad. His business card showed him to be Matt James, General Manager of Kolo 8 News. It was unbelievable that anyone would go out of their way so far as to help strangers.

The Cathedral mass and their acquaintance made up for all my inconviences at Circus Circus.

All documents required, complete and correct pertaining to my burial were received by Bill Ouellette of Demers-Desmond Funeral Home in Brunswick that will care for my shipment to Nice where Roblot would take over.

I had a new will made up with Richard Lord, attorney leaving Nicky and Minou to Penelope.

Minou always waited at the door for our return. Nicky would lurch at Minou and be all over her, pulling her by the ears and tail. Minou loved it, but

I always pulled Nicky away yelling, "No!" Remember Minou was extremely intelligent and strong. I think she could really hurt Nicky if she wanted to without her front claws. In fact I heard him yelp once when he had been too rough. Minou drinks out of his water bowl and he lets her play with his toy. At Nicky's age he is free in the house and can be turned loose in the fields. When I blow the whistle he returns for his treats.

Nicky has his most fun with other dogs, big and small. I am careful since they could hurt him with their paws.

He goes muzzle to muzzle with St. Bernards, Newfoundland, shepherds, poodles and Labs.

Tina's Labrador, "Dudley" is one month younger than Nicky. Kim has a yellow Lab, named "Stella." Ricky's two adopted dogs, "Rusty" and "Nora" wouldn't hurt a fly though they always approach with a welcome bark.

Nicky is frightened though when the snow roars off the expansive roof of the nearby athletic buildings. He is also frightened in a snow squall.

Recall Reed Bartlett lost his brilliant golden retreiver, Chobe. He finally gave in; his pup's name is Lucy.

Later I met and became friends with a wonderful couple, Jim and Caroline Murphy PhD (ret.) and their toy poodle, Ginger. Nicky and Ginger are about the same size and age. They run for about an hour on weekday mornings on Bowdoine College Atheltic Field. They agreed to take Nicky and Minou when I kick the bucket. That's the end of my worries.

As for me, at age 90, it is full steam ahead with myasthenia gravis and Parkinson's.

Remember, "Spill the beans and forgive." Spouses should not reveal their sins to each other. I was sure when Father McDermot the Augustinian said, "Your lives will be beautiful," he knew that a beautiful life was not void of suffering. I thank almighty God, the Father, the Son and the Holy Spirit and the Blessed Mother for helping me to write this story from the beginning. May your lives be beautiful.

God Bless,

Dick Fisco, Minou and Nicky

A good wife is a white martyr. Sorry Dad, you can be a soldier of Christ.

Flight Manifests

North Africa - Headquarters Company Planes 1 - 7
Missing #3

Plane Number 1 - Headquarters Company

Personel Loading	S/N	Hometown	Wt. Fully Equipped
1. Lt. Col. Edsen D. Raff	O-19261	New York, New York	271
2. Cpl. Harold A. Bachman	35166933	Elkhart, Indiana	262
3. Pvt. Franklin W. Wolfe	35130651	Cincinnati, Ohio	266
24. Cpl. Clyde W. Scarborough	6921824	Anniston, Alabama	243
5. Capt. William J. Schloth	O-339137		284
6.			270
7. S/Sgt. Jack Pogue	885620	Moriarity, New Mexico	252
8. T/Sgt. Ellis L. Bishop	35165286	Ft. Wayne, Indiana	255
9. T-5 Aureliano S. Valdez		ElPaso, Texas	245
10. T-5 John Hayes	33075831	Perkiomemville, Pennsy.	257
11. S/Sgt. Cyrus C. Paks	35129768	Berea, Kentucky	275
12. Marshall R. Savell	34151596	Fisher Louisiana	255
13. S/Sgt. Alain Joseph		New York, New York	320
14. Maj. William P. Yarborough	O-20362		
		Total Weight	3725
		Equipment Bundle Weight	250
		Special Equipment	45
		Total Weight used for Tactical Mission	4020

Plane Number 2 - Headquarters Company

Personel Loading	S/N	Hometown	Wt. Fully Equipped
1. Capt. William A. Medlin	O-323684	Florence, S.C.	270
2. 1/Sgt. Jim Swain	6392329	Troy, Alabama	250
3. Pfc. Charles A. Audet	31025044	Fitchburg, Massachusetts	245
4. Sgt. John L. Billingsley	7080551	Athens, Alabama	255
5. Pvt. Albert A. Beauchesne	20112408	Webster, Massachusetts	250
6. Pvt. Leo W. Martin	31044945	Lewistiwn, Me.	250
7. Pvt. Ralph Marez	6897807	Philadelphia, Penna.	255
8. Pvt. Curtis C. Williams	34109464	Birmingham, Ala.	255
9. Pvt. Thomas L. Silas, Jr.	34052658	Jacksonville, Fla.	245
10. Cpl. Romaine W. Hutchings	35029219	Akron, Ohio	260
11. T-5 Ernest Boudoin	34079216	Kaplan, Louisiana	260
12. Cpl. William W. Sullivan	6918198	Galesburg, Illinois	260
13. Sgt. Janes W. Collins	15063705	Williamstown, Kentucky	260
14. Lt. John R. Martin	O-399024	Eagle Pass, Texas	250
		Total Weight	3565
		Equipment Bundle Weight	250
		Special Equipment	205
		Total Weight Used For Tactical Mission	4020

Plane Number 4 - Headquarters Company

Personel Loading	S/N	Hometown	Wt. Fully Equipped
1. Lt. C. E. Spires	O-380643	Hartville, Carolina	248
2. Pfc. George Voleta	36048603	Chicago, Illinois	255
3. Pvt. George J. Sheridan	33110740	Sharon, Pennsylvania	265
4. Pvt. Merse J. Process	20350108	Centerville, Pennsylvania	284
5. Cpl. Joseph W. Lee	35212348	Annapolis, Maryland	277
6. Cpl. Merle L. Shearer	34146066	Welisburg, West Virginia	272
7. Cpl. Leland R. Hottun	35108893	Memphis, Tennessee	288
8. Cpl. Elehm Puckett	33037842	Irvine, Kentucky	297
9. Pvt. William Cooper	35129930	Cross Creek, Pennsylvania	254
10. Pvt. Charles J. Lovday	35212885	Middlesboro, Kentucky	270
11. Pvt. William J. Holtz	35212714	Ironton, Ohio	236
12. Pvt. Robert L. Thomas	34087920	Pocha, West Virginia	255
13. Sgt. Clarence H. Thomas		Atlanta, Georgia	244
		Total Weight	3455
		Equipment Bundle No. 1	279
		Equipment Bundle No. 2	289
		Total Weight Used For Tactical Mission	4023

Plane Number 5 - Headquarters Company

Personel Loading	S/N	Hometown	Wt. Fully Equipped
1. Lt. John W. Teasley	O-422358	Columbus, Georgia	242
2. T-4 George Houston	35103811	Detroit, Michigan	286
3. Pvt. Adolph Fuessel	38034226	Buckholtz, Texas	304
4. Pvt. Stanley B. Gillman	35168247	Brookville, Indiana	261
5. Cpl. Wiley J. Flohr	35166067	Crestline, Ohio	256
6. Cpl. Charles O. Holmes	35168653	Bicknell, Indiana	288
7. Pvt. Vernon O. Walker	34056609	Lmmokalee, Florida	272
8. Pvt. Roland Weeks	34055873	Collier City, Florida	257
9. Pvt. Jack Alongi	36127657	Detroit, Michigan	218
10. Pvt. John T. Pierce	35168604	Walcottville, Indiana	240
11. Pvt. Charles J. Otzel	11019840	Bridgeport, Connecticut	228
12. Pvt. Haskel Hill	34146608	Knoxville, Tennessee	249
13. Pvt. George B. Chaffin	35035981	Springfield, Ohio	256
14. Sgt. Roderick Childs	32028873	Angelica, New York	255
		Total Weight	3612
		Equipment Bundle Weight	294
		Special Equipment	114
		Total Weight Used For Tactical Mission	4020

Plane Number 6 - Headquarters Company

Personel Loading	S/N	Hometown	Wt. Fully Equipped
1. Sgt. Edward Danish		Chicago, Illinois	294
2. Pvt. Robert Kealen	6918072	Quiney, Illinois	311
3. Pfc. Robert M. Barnthouse	35168853	Decatur, Indianna	272
4. Cpl. Martin L. Ullicny	36127619	Rochester, Pennsylvania	288
5. Pvt. Martin W. Crites	37082538	Kennett, Missouri	251
6. Pvt. Charles Cipy	33108388	Dundalk, Maryland	244
7. Pvt. John F. Robinson	35108558	Louisville, Kentucky	223
8. Pvt. Robert B. Waller	34087987	College Park, Georgia	240
9. Pvt. Russell P. Cook	35175159	Birdseye, Indiana	238
10. Pvt. Paul E. Legg	3516894	Vincennes, Indiana	260
11. Pfc. Harry Phillips	36022005	Moline, Illinois	232
12. Pvt. William Vandenberg	36159887	Grand Rapids, Michigan	261
13. Pvt. Clifford B. Faulkner	35212343	Power, West Virginia	286
14. Cpl. Paul Chorniak	35035688	Buchtel, Ohio	268
		Total Weight	3668
		Equipment Bundle Weight	280
		Special Equipment	72
		Total Weight Used For Tactical Mission	4020

Plane Number 7 - Headquarters Company

Personel Loading	S/N	Hometown	Wt. Fully Equipped
1. Lt. Seldon D. Harvey	O-337182	Portage, Wisconsin	263
2. Cpl. Henry R. Pardieck	35129995	Ann, Ohio	250
3. Cpl. Eugene Brewer	34145992	Collierville, Tennessee	262
4. Pfc. Jessee J. Luczyk	35028773	Cleveland, Ohio	279
5. Pfc. Walter Endlich	35028838	Stone Creek, Ohio	284
6. Pfc. George W. Michael	35028954	Mt. Overlook, Ohio	272
7. Pfc. Leonard Swatsenbarg	37139986	Senaca, Maryland	275
8. Pvt. Donald B. Ellis	35168555	Spencer, Indiana	268
9. Pvt. Gerald T. Hogan	36163675	Muir, Michigan	281
10. Pvt. Joseph Bauer	35166160	Evansville, Indiana	267
11. Cpl. Don W. Herrin	34024320	South Bay, Florida	259
12. Pfc. Francis L. Keane	32180425	Brooklyn, New york	249
13. Pfc. Johnny N. Boyce	35212472	Hammono, West Virginia	292
14. Sgt. Wesley Lee	37139895	Winston, Minnesota	247
		Total Weight	3748
		Equipment Bundle Weight	250
		Special Equipment	22
		Total Weight Used For Tactical Mission	4020

Plane Number 8 - Headquarters Company

Personel Loading	S/N	Hometown	Wt. Fully Equipped
1. Lt. Hugh G. Hogan	O-1283258	Owego, New York	253
2. Cpl. Edwin G. Wegner	36226687	Miami, Florida	297
3. Pvt. William Southerland	6392752	Gaffney, South Carolina	255
4. Pvt. James H. Ballentine	36127700	Hermitage, Tennessee	266
5. Pvt. Walter T. Borowiak	33111618	Hazelton, Pennsylvania	271
6. Pvt. Joseph W. Cernak	33118496	Johnstown, Pennsylvania	276
7. Pvt. Clare F. Granbit	37111394	Des Moines, Iowa	266
8. Cpl. John T. Martin	34087918	La Grange, Georgia	278
9. Sgt. Elwood Barnhardt	33100791	Philadelphia, Pennsylvania	288
10. Pfc. Fred R. Gerber	38068874	ElPaso, Texas	255
11. Pvt. Ross E. Bittinger	33067321	Essex, Maryland	282
12. Pfc. Guy W. Jeanes	38058524	San Augustine, Texas	274
13. Sgt. John F. Costello	33098475	Washington, D.C.	251
14. S/Sgt. William Campbell	34091991	Sheldon, South Carolina	225

Total Weight		3737
Equipment Bundle Weight		250
Special Equipment		33
Total Weight Used For Tactical Mission		4020

Plane Number 9 - Headquarters Company

Personel Loading	S/N	Hometown	Wt. Fully Equipped
1. Maj. Doyle R. Yardley	O-356190	Raymondsville, Texas	235
2. Lt. Stuart G. Cutler	O-394597	New York, New York	255
3. T-5 Jack A. Wagers	19099001	Brush, Colorado	270
4. Pvt. Arthur W. Von Essen	32120668	Woodhaven, New York	255
5. Pvt. Alphonse A. Zoucha	3816710	Cedar Rapids, Nebraska	287
6. Pvt. Walter A. Cherry	35166807	Eldorado, Arkansas	271
7. Pvt. Lincoln S. Sennett	31044632	Auburn, Me.	247
8. Pvt. Thomas S. Wimberly	34056778	Cochran, Georgia	284
9. Pvt. Robert H. Green	35108666	Cartland, Indiana	253
10. Pvt. Harold Seay	38010161	Roswell, New Mexico	282
11. Pvt. David R. Vail	34145373	Chattanooga, Tennessee	264
12. Pvt. Francis Tocci	6561311	Los Angeles, California	263
13. T-4 Leon C. Maenbout	35169598	Mishawaka, Indiana	235
14. Lt. Timothy			

Total Weight		3667
Equipment Bundle Weight		296
Special Equipment		57
Total Weight Used For Tactical Mission		4020

Plane Number 10 - Headquarters Company

Personel Loading	S/N	Hometown	Wt. Fully Equipped
1. Lt. Hugh C. DeLury	O-1283038	Corry, Pennsylvania	
2. Pvt. Herbert M. Coberly	33134321	Elkins, West Virginia	254
3. Pvt. Vernon L. Bass	20434753	Dupont, Georgia	264
4. Pvt. Robert T. Byrom	14079420	Huntsville, Alabama	254
5. Pvt. Daniel Brenner	33025780	Philadelphia, Pennsylvania	255
6. Pvt. Donald H. Kammer	34050279	Miami, Florida	246
7. Pvt. William T. Marshall	37053390	Drakesboro, Kentucky	241
8. Pvt. Joseph Barressi	11046075	Sanqus, Massachussits	229
9. Pvt. Leigh F. Fox	37053531	St. Louis, Missouri	249
10. Pvt. John L. Albert	34050284	Miami, Florida	231
11. Pvt. James E. McGrath	36010038	Prairie duChien, Wisconsin	254
12. Pvt. Clifford C. King	6287176	Waco, Texas	229
13. Sgt. James W. Clance	20434271	Port Orange, Florada	231
			236

Total Weight		3173
Equipment Bundle Weight		273
Special Equipment		273
Total Weight Used For Tactical Mission		4020

North Africa - Supply Planes 1 - 2

Supply Plane Number 1

Personel Loading	S/N	Hometown	Wt. Fully Equipped
1. Capt. Henry C. Tipton	O-376788	Horn Lake, Mississippi	270
2. S/Sgt. Maynard L. Carp	33661114	Baltimore, Maryland	290
3. T-5 John W. Ramsden	34105753	Dora, Alabama	270
4. S/Sgt. Allen W. Stafford	36159288	Hillsdale, Michigan	254
5. S/Sgt. Anthony J. Gorshe	36050397	Perkin, Illinois	270
6. S/Sgt. Silas A. Worley	6576218	Hillsboro, Texas	260
7. T-5 William D. Ates	34106238	Holt, Florida	250
8. T-5 Mifflin G. Glenn	6998604	Catonsville, Maryland	265

Total Weight		2109
Special Equipment		1911
Total Weight Used For Tactical Mission		4020

Supply Plane Number 2

Personel Loading	S/N	Hometown	Wt. Fully Equipped
1. S/Sgt. James C. Whittington	7096236	Oakdale, Louisiana	270
2. T-5 Chester A Thomas	37038517	Valentine, Nebraska	270
3. T-5 Robert B. Cakes	33067118	Capital Heights, Maryland	270
4. T-5 Joseph R. Rambin	34079149	Pelican, Louisiana	250
5. T-5 Harvey G. Peace	34049063	Laurel, Mississippi	240
6. T-5 Robert L. Jones	34106840	Flomanton, Alabama	240
7. T-5 Guadalupe Vasquez	6951835	Brownsville, Texas	250
8. Pvt. Lorenz C. Malberg	17018102	Cokato, Minnesota	270

Total Weight		2060
Special Equipment		1060
Total Weight Used For Tactical Mission		4020

North Africa - Company D Planes 1 - 6

Plane Number 1 - Company "D"

Personel Loading	S/N	Hometown	Wt. Fully Equipped
1. Capt. William J. Morrow	O-349971	Grand Folks, North Dakota	285
2. Pfc. George Matson	34106710	Sylacauga, Alabama	246
3. T-4 Thomas Crane	33082489	Corry, Pennsylvania	253
4. Sgt. Dwight Burns	37110017	Marshalltown, Iowa	254
5. Sgt. Alton Crocker	33082490	Union City, Pennsylvania	265
6. Cpl. Samuel M. Richards	33110658	Avalon, Pennsylvania	246
7. Pfc. Charles Boisvert	37139806	Osawatomie, Kansas	284
8. Pfc. Thadeous Czolgosz	36166550	Saginaw, Michigan	278
9. Pfc. Marvin E. White	35271526	Lima, Ohio	274
10. Pfc. Murphy Trahen	35164996	New Orleans, Louisiana	275
11. Sgt. William Bryson	33094557	Asheville, North Carolina	240
12. Pfc. Marion W. Shade	35127864	Miamisburg, Ohio	289
13. T-5 Elmer R. Maurer	33072099	Philadelphia, Pennsylvania	255

Total Weight 3457
Equipment Bundle Weight 250
Total Weight Used For Tactical Mission 3707

Plane Number 2 - Company "D"

Personel Loading	S/N	Hometown	Wt. Fully Equipped
1. Lt. Charles C. W. Howland	O-399875	Royersford, Pennsylvania	278
2. Pvt. Franklin Briedegan	33075868		242
3. Pvt. Thaddeus J. Dabrowski	31025288	Hopedale, Massachusetts	257
4. Pvt. Robert W. McHale	6660751	Clarksburg, West Virginia	253
5. Pfc. Harry E. Tracey	33084490	Pittsburgh, Pennsylvania	247
6. Pvt. John E. Pumphey	34054826	Apopka, Florida	247
7. Pvt. Paul B. Huff	34142155	Cleveland, Tennessee	254
8. Pvt. James W. Nunn	20418468	Jacksonville, Florida	268
9. Russell T. Neview	6910997	Saulte Ste. Marie, Michigan	249
10. Cpl. Richard LaForge	36125239	Au Sable, Michigan	254
11. Richard D. Fisco	6973808	Staten Island, New York	254
12. Sgt. Varna C. Shresbery	35209806	Rhodell, West Virginia	235
13. T-5 Tracey L. McCue	6928880	East Gaston, Alabama	240
14. T-5 Edgar F. Millisite	35026975	Canton, Ohio	260
15. Lt. John V. Jennings	O-1283113	Orange, New Jersey	

Total Weight 3750
Equipment Bundle Weight 250
Special Equipment 20
Total Weight Used For Tactical Mission 4020

Plane Number 3 - Company "D"

Personel Loading	S/N	Hometown	Wt. Fully Equipped
1. Lt. Robert W. Parker	O-425986	Crowley, Louisiana	225
2. Pfc. Kenneth DeWald	33110909	Williamsport, Pennsylvania	250
3. Pfc. Joseph J. Anslow	20203919	Troy, New York	261
4. S/Sgt. Lehman Lecompt	6928563	Elba, Alabama	240
5. Pfc. Ord E. Elmore	36262071	Walford, West Virginia	287
6. Pvt. Amos W. Wilder	14018975	Newman, Georgia	238
7. Pfc. Carey L. Tidwell	34084255	Atlanta, Georgia	239
8. Pfc. Edwin M. Stapleton	35209762	McComas, West Virginia	228
9. Pvt. Ray Carr	190655063	Hawarden, Iowa	265
10. Pvt. William B. Azline	36164138	Detroit, Michigan	230
11. Pvt. Houston C. Akins	14071587	Chattanooga, Tennessee	244
12. Pfc. Roy R. Barlow	34200089	Crestview, Florida	270
13. Sgt. Carl E. Bigham	36124594	Trenton, Michigan	242
14. Pvt. Carl R. Clegg	33033307	Pittsburg, Pennsylvania	261

Total Weight 3460
Equipment Bundle Weight 250
Special Equipment 290
Total Weight Used For Tactical Mission 4020

Plane Number 4 - Company "D"

Personel Loading	S/N	Hometown	Wt. Fully Equipped
1. 1/Sgt. Vernon T. Cartnay	6931114	Marion, South Dakota	254
2. Sgt. Michael Baranek	35026946	Akron, Ohio	249
3. Pfc. Everett J. Hall	31051063	Riverside, Rdode Island	243
4. Cpl. Leo E. Stambaugh	37087017	Big Horn, Wyoming	279
5. Sgt.Robert P. Akers	33048822	Roanoke, Virginia	276
6. Pvt. Milford L. Dugan	33082388	Muncy, Pennsylvania	265
7. Pvt. Edward H. Crowther	20109261	Providence, Rhode Island	270
8. Pfc. Lenwood R. Choquette	31039928	Northampton, Massachusetts	268
9. Pfc. Vincent J. Kleysteuber	36302910	Patoka, Kansas	262
10. Pfc. Percy R. Collins		Marthaville, Louisiana	283
11. Pvt. Daniel B. Reardon	20111604	Clinton, Massachusetts	248
12. Pvt. Augustine M. Digiovanni	33098797	Washington, D.C.	237
13. Pvt. Felix B. Marsh	34131349	Fentress, Mississippi	243
14. Pfc. Stanley T. Orzell	33022460	Scranton, Pennsylvania	217

Total Weight 3596
Equipment Bundle Weight 250
Special Equipment 274
Total Weight Used For Tactical Mission 4020

Plane Number 5 - Company "D"

Personel Loading	S/N	Hometown	Wt. Fully Equipped
1. Lt. Casper E. Curtis	O-372914	Norway, Maine	257
2. Pfc. Andrew J. Floyd	14022085	Stapleton, Alabama	292
3. Pfc. Lorenzo Boyd	34106184	Frisco City, Alabama	258
4. T-5 Frank Tilton	34082879	Savannah, Georgia	242
5. S/Sgt. Brad Chalkor (288 Radio)	6964534	Gibson, Georgia	275
6. Sgt. Soloman Weber (288 Radio)	32119797	Masbeth, Long Island, N.Y.	285
7. Pvt. Jack L. White	15010028	McConnelsville, Ohio	254
8. Sgt. Arthur R. Thompson	33063193	Kingston, Maryland	259
9. Pvt. John A. Bickle	37130976	St. Louis, Minnesota	263
10. Pvt. Robert L. Doyle	6946153	York, Pennsylvania	247
11. Pfc. Lester F. Barrett	39304963	Hubbard, Oregon	257
12. Pfc. Clyde S. Branthover	39304965	Astoria, Oregon	248
13. Pvt. Barney O. Debray	34087675	Leary, Georgia	261
14. Pfc. Edward K. McGaffick	6902251	Buffalo, New York	252

Total Weight 3650
Equipment Bundle Weight 250
Number 2 Bundle (288 Radio) 110
Special Equipment 10
Total Weight Used For Tactical Mission 4020

Plane Number 6 - Company "D"

Personel Loading	S/N	Hometown	Wt. Fully Equipped
1. Capt. Carlos C. Alden	O-381690	Buffalo, New York	251
2. Cpl. Odus M. Wardlow	34079020	Montgomery, Louisiana	240
3. Pvt. Curtis M. Whitehead	34079062	Lake Charles, Louisiana	270
4. 1/Sgt. Frank Jackson	7002491	Wilner, Alabama	245
5. Pfc. George F. Schaffer	37098022	Heron Lake, Minnesota	275
6. Pvt. Charles C. Yanush	33084786	Scranton, Pennsylvania	270
7. S/Sgt. William L. Hooker	14044608	Oak Park Station, Florida	254
8. Sgt. Lincoln Miller	34078849	LaFayette, Louisiana	266
9. Pvt. Roman L. Niewienglowski	36162477	Detroit, Michigan	239
10. Pvt. George J. Brodrick	32096557	Brooklyn, New York	264
11. Pfc. Wallace N. Eaker	6909874	Cleveland, Ohio	263
12. Pvt. Horace StringFellow	34055057	Miami, Florida	251
13. T-5 William R. Jameson	14043285	Greenville, South Carolina	257
14. S/Sgt. Douglas T. Robinson	33084023	Upper Darby, Pennsylvania	218

Total Weight 3521
Equipment Bundle Weight 250
Special Equipment 249
Total Weight Used For Tactical Mission 4020

North Africa - Company D Planes 8 - 9, missing #7

Plane Number 8 - Company "D"

Personel Loading	S/N	Hometown	Wt. Fully Equipped
1. Lt. William F. Threkheld	0-374478		272
2. Cpl. Elmer T. Cardwell	33095679	Alexandria, Virginia	245
3. Pfc. Raymond L. Brockman	35281711	Ft. Jennings, Ohio	285
4. Pfc. Stanley Beatham	31044588	Lincoln, Maine	235
5. Pvt. Woodrow Browder	6382355	Centurs, Florida	293
6. Pfc. Russell G. Harvey	7083955	Early Branch, South Carolina	236
7. Pvt. Pete Way	34092332	Pinewood, South Carolina	247
8. Pfc. John D. Egri	35040030	Lima, Ohio	266
9. Pfc. Bernard B. Schwarm	36045075	Chicago, Illinois	241
10. Pfc. Richard H. Coleman	37130567	Clarence, Missouri	249
11. Pfc. Walter Darrow	33088485	Elwood City, Pennsylvania	260
12. Sgt. Ernest R. Komula	37098117	Sebeka, Minn.	291
13. Pvt. Alcus Stokes	7080390	Laurel Hill, Florida	267
14. Sgt. Kelly C. Barth	14051683	Claxton, Georgia	256

Total Weight	3641
Equipment Bundle Weight	250
Special Equipment	129
Total Weight For Tactical Mission	4020

Plane Number 9 - Company "D"

Personel Loading	S/N	Hometown	Wt. Fully Equipped
1. Lt. Wilber B. McClintock	0-404855	Memphis, Tennessee	217
2. Pfc. John F. Eichhorn	35168863	Craigville, Indiana	239
3. Sgt. William H. King	6883529	Plainfield, New Jersey	225
4. Pvt. Charles W. Richards	32156809	Bridgeton, New Jersey	250
5. S/Sgt. Walter Rice	35210760	Catlettsburg, Kentucky	286
6. Pfc. John E. Campbell	34093870	Columbia, South Carolina	248
7. Pfc. Alphard L. Barnett	34107556	Red Bay, Mississippi	245
8. Pfc. Albert E. Brown	36163545	Croswell, Michigan	238
9. Pfc. John F. Alexander	37102834	Corning, Arkansas	267
10. Sgt. Ralph Thornton	34105456	Cropwell, Alabama	260
11. Pvt. Johnnie Graham	34093967	Little Rock, South Carolina	231
12. Pvt. Louis C. Burdsel	14053575	Greenville, South Carolina	234
13. Pfc. James M. Martin	32035577	Niagra Falls, New York	259
14. S/Sgt. Jack V. Greene	7001000	Chauncey, Georgia	261

Total Weight	3480
Equipment Bundle Weight	250
Special Equipment	290
Total Weight Used For Tactical Mission	4020

North Africa - Company E Planes 1 - 6

Plane Number 1 - Company "E"

Personel Loading	S/N	Hometown	Wt. Fully Equipped
1. Capt. John T. Berry	O-396199	Arkadelphia, Arkansas	296
2. T-4 Paul V. Wilson	52209705	Poca, West Virginia	241
3. Sgt. William E. Powell	35106249	West Baden, Indiana	270
4. Sgt. Edward T. Balcom	34054705	Tampa, Florida	266
5. Sgt. Ralph Maerz	6897807	Philadelphia, Pennsylvania	276
6. T-5 Charles R. Allen	31042205	Westport, Connecticut	300
7. Pfc. George Wetrisko	35281362	Elyria, Ohio	279
8. Pvt. Clarence G. Hawkins	34107483	Pisqan, Alabama	275
9. Pvt. Ira L. Brookins		Columbus, Georgia	255
10. Pvt. Arlie K. Graley	35210562	McCorkle, West Virginia	283
11. Cpl. Wilbert E. Sprenkle	33011736	Farm Grove, Pennsylvania	283
12. Lt. Albert V. Crosby	O-412160	Lochoven, Norfolk, Virginia	261
13. Pvt. John Westerlund		Bradford, Pennsylvania	257
14. Pvt. James L. Rodgers		Madison, Indiana	245
		Total Weight	3777
		Equipment Bundle Weight	250
		Special Equipment	0
		Total Weight Used For Tactical Mission	4027

Plane Number 2 - Company "E"

Personel Loading	S/N	Hometown	Wt. Fully Equipped
1. Lt. Dave C. Kunkle	O-422431	New York, N.Y.	251
2. T-5 James R. Boyle	6932565	St. Joseph, MO.	244
3. Sgt. Fred E. Harding	33099806	New Castle, Pa.	278
4. Cpl. Robert E. League	33060721	Baltimore, Md.	246
5. Cpl. Loran E. Chambers	36051037	Mt. Sterling, Illinois	279
6. Cpl. Eugene R. Hall	35212666	Bastion, Virginia	239
7. Pvt. Louis Homoki	35281377	Elyria, Ohio	262
8. Pfc. Charles L. Murdoch	34085021	Atlanta, Ga.	243
9. Pfc. Carl D. Miley	14059624	Moorville, Mississippi	247
10. Pvt. John Mackall	35281555	Westville, Ohio	272
11. Pvt. Laverne G. Shulion	36303140	Savannah, Illinois	273
12. Pvt. Andrew Panusko	36302969	Chicago, Illinois	254
13. Pvt. Arden O. Peterson	36303162	Rockford, Illinois	264
14. Pvt. Joseph M.Torpey	36034395	Chicago, Illinois	266
		Total Weight	3644
		Equipment Bundle Weight	250
		Special Equipment	126
		Total Weight Used For Tactical Mission	4020

Plane Number 3 - Company "E"

Personel Loading	S/N	Hometown	Wt. Fully Equipped
1. Lt. Charles W. Kurtz	O-430341	Tampa, Florida	244
2. Pfc. Herbert Ferguson	35127032	Elmanton, Kentucky	243
3. Pfc. William C. Price	13007471	Scranton, Pennsylvania	264
4. Pfc. Kalmer G. Thompson	37098075	Ulen, Minnesota	282
5. Pfc. Winfield Schadman	33077188	Emporium, Pennsylvania	246
6. Sgt. Robert B. David	34054782	Atlantic Beach, Florida	253
7. Pvt.William Simons	34054797	Sarasota, Florida	247
8. Pfc. Alvin L. Trumbull	31049833	Windsor, Connecticut	278
9. Cpl. Needham S. Smith	34084914	Eastman, Georgia	244
10. Pfc. Walter E. Graska	37097567	St. Cloud, Minnesota	256
11. Pvt. James C.Meachum	34114042	Burlington, North Carolina	263
12. Pvt. Albert Dager	33118235	Ambler, Pennsylvania	243
13. Sgt. Charlie B. Fuller	6969861	Warm Springs, Florida	287
14. Lt. Joseph J. Winsko	O-386568	Wilkes Barre, Pennsylvania	303
		Total Weight	3642
		Equipment Bundle Weight	250
		Special Equipment	116
		Total Weight Used For Tactical Mission	4020

Plane Number 4 - Company "E"

Personel Loading	S/N	Hometown	Wt. Fully Equipped
1. 1st Sgt. John j. Klish	6890139	New Castle, Pennsylvania	267
2. Sgt. Charles W. Hood	34084855	Atlanta, Georgia	280
3. T-5 Howard H. Herr, Jr.	33076970	Lancaster, Pennsylvania	280
4. T-5 James H. Nixon	33094099	Washington, D.C.	254
5. Sgt. Ralph R. Bourn	36043728	Jacksonville, Illinois	296
6. Pfc. Alexander W. Osmond	13004495	Taylor, Pennsylvania	297
7.			
8. Pfc. John H. Cross	34055040	Miami Beach, Florida	270
9. Pfc. William E. Paley	35281449	Youngstown, Ohio	258
10. Pfc. Richard J. Reusching	35027273	Jefferson, Ohio	275
11. Cpl. William E. Barker	34082808	Chickamauga, Georgia	273
12. Pfc. James W. Bates	34054726	Tampa, Florida	219
13. Pvt. Edward C. Holley	35214733	Hamlin, West Virginia	269
14. T-5 Howard E. Laudwig	36303072	St. Louis, Minnesota	256
		Total Weight	3752
		Equipment Bundle Weight	250
		Special Equipment	18
		Total Weight Used For Tactical Mission	4020

Plane Number 5 - Company "E"

Personel Loading	S/N	Hometown	Wt. Fully Equipped
1. Lt. Lloyd G. Wilson	O-412416	Micawber, Oklahoma	251
2. Pvt. Franklin J. Hall	31039846	Springfield, Massachusetts	252
3. Pvt. Henry Hamilton	6666603	Ary, Kentucky	272
4. Cpl. Harold D. Ramey	6292081	Los Angeles, California	259
5. Pfc.Lewis L. Jones	17010079	Nettleton, Arkansas	269
6. Pfc. Edward Burns	35168434	Indianapolis, Indiana	266
7. Cpl. George G. Fontanesi	33079760	Library, Pennsylvania	274
8. Pfc. Robert L. Johnson	15098837	Akron, Ohio	232
9. Pfc. Henry G. Cuethle	34054924	West Palm Beach, Florida	238
10. Pvt. James R. Prince, Jr.	34146207	Mt. Pleasant, Tennessee	279
11. Pvt. Earl M. Williamson	3529895	Sisterville, West Virginia	289
12. Pvt. George W. Caldwell	14019108	Manchester, Georgia	269
13. Pvt. Leonard S. Caruso	32134552	New York, New York	245
14. Pvt. Louis J. Catizone	32003189	New York, New York	250
		Total Weight	3629
		Equipment Bundle Weight	250
		Special Equipment	111
		Total Weight Used For Tactical Mission	4020

Plane Number 6 - Company "E"

Personel Loading	S/N	Hometown	Wt. Fully Equipped
1. S/Sgt. Paul E. McRill	36043789	Centralia, Illinois	276
2. Sgt. Wilbur D. Martin	32022345	Brooklyn, New York	276
3. Sgt. Charles M. Talbott	34054990	New Smyrna, Florida	256
4. Pvt. Jesse W. Bacon	34084577	Savannah, Georgia	274
5. Pvt. Richard G. Rhoads	34055080	Miami, Florida	263
6. Cpl. Robert V. Patsch	35281825	Sandusky, Ohio	247
7. Pvt. Woodruff F. Wilkerson	35127709	Cincinnati, Ohio	258
8. Pfc. John L. Betts	34054851	Frostproof, Florida	278
9. Pfc. Stanley D. Sjostrom	34055054	Miami, Florida	249
10. Pfc. Hilton E. Graham	34084826	Eastman, Georgia	242
11. Pfc. William B. Poole	34084610	Unadilla, Georgia	264
12. Cpl. Henry C. Faircloth	34084823	Summertown, Georgia	257
13. Pvt. Romas E. Holder	33119420	Dumbarton, Virginia	245
14. S/Sgt. Robert H. Paudert	6972398	Memphis, Tennessee	249
		Total Weight	3637
		Equipment Bundle Weight	250
		Special Equipment	133
		Total Weight Used For Tactical Mission	133

Plane Number 7 - Company "E"

Personel Loading	S/N	Hometown	Wt. Fully Equipped
1. Lt. Carl E. Dittman		Philadelphia, Pennsylvania	272
2. T-4 Claud H. Purvis	33095532	Washington, D.C.	264
3. Cpl. Elzie B. McCullough	34054816	Bonifay, Florida	238
4. Cpl. Chester Majchrzak	35166596	Gary, Indiana	232
5. Pfc. Carl R. Weaver	33094441	Washington, D.C.	239
6. Pvt. John V. Forni	31039874	Great Barrington, Massachusetts	240
7. Pvt. Harold L. Herbert	33098931	Washington, D.C.	241
8. Pfc. Marion W. Thomas	34054810	Milton, Florida	267
9. Pfc. Hugh D. Camp	34084489	Atlanta, Georgia	254
10. Pfc. Dixie C. Johnson	34054963	Jacksonville, Florida	235
11. Pvt. Lloyd G. Van Guilder	37097654	Fairbault, Minnesota	259
12. Pfc. Alfred R. Groom	20380015	Washington, D.C.	228
13. Pvt. Peter Carsetti	34079162	Seacaucus, New Jersey	281
14. S/Sgt. Uyless V. Haymes	34107117	Cullman, Alabama	
			3546
		Total Weight	250
		Equipment Bundle Weight	241
		Special Equipment	
		Total Weight Used	4020
		For Tactical Mission	

Plane Number 8 - Company "E"

Personel Loading	S/N	Hometown	Wt. Fully Equipped
1. Lt. Archie G. Birkner	O-416862	San Antonio, Texas	239
2. T-5 Howard N. Macleon	36124569	Port Huron, Michigan	225
3. Sgt. Artrur L. Kellar	6918151	E. Alton, Illinois	270
4. Cpl. Rodger B. Zeigler	34054965	St. Petersburg, Florida	266
5. Pvt. Hyman W. Anderson	14059628	Mt. Olive, Mississippi	271
6. Pfc. Wesley E. Gunderson	16023352	Aniwa, Wisconsin	249
7. Pvt. Charles B. Mask	34084242	Covington, Georgia	262
8. Sgt. Jackson T. Sapp	34107120	Hanceville, Alabama	263
9. Pfc. Clifford E. Fain	34107164	Selma, Alabama	274
10. Pfc. James C. Nesmith	34107194	Venemont, Alabama	264
11. Pfc. James E. Thomason	24106915	Florence, Alabama	262
12. Pfc. Avery Sellers	34084749	Graham, Georgia	260
13. Pvt. Otto Ekman	16023551	Winter, Wisconsin	262
14. Sgt. Robert T. Stier	14044586	Miami, Florida	238
		Total Weight	3647
		Equipment Bundle Weight	250
		Special Equipment	117
		Total Weight Used	
		For Tactical Mission	4020

Plane Number 9 - Company "E"

Personel Loading	S/N	Hometown	Wt. Fully Equipped
1. 1st. Sgt. James C. Anderson	6971875	Bowden, Georgia	253
2. Sgt. Dillard T. Winkler	6973622	Roswell, Georgia	280
3. Sgt. Andrew P. Omasta	6664028	Campbell, Ohio	257
4. Pvt. John E. Hendricks	33088812	Washington, D.C.	264
5. Pfc. Julius LeBlanc	34079229	Delcamube, Louisiana	254
6. Pfc. Clyde Thornton	34054835	Raiford, Florida	252
7. Pfc. Burl E. Bolesta	34054670	Tampa, Florida	263
8. Cpl. James B. Ray	34085048	Rome, Georgia	248
9. Pfc. William A. Soska	36309245	Chicago, Illinois	256
10. Pfc. John J. Perry	35281608	Ashtabula, Ohio	254
11. Sgt. William J. Herb	35166498	Coal Bluff, Indiana	264
12. Sgt. Clarence G. Callahen	34054873	Shamrock, Florida	260
13. Pvt. Warren F. Martin	13001329	Crellin, Maryland	245
14. Pvt. William J. Kerney	32172239	Brooklyn, New York	265
		Total Weight	3801
		Equipment Bundle Weight	250
		Special Equipment	153
		Total Weight Used	
		For Tactical Mission	4020

Plane Number 1 - Company "F"

Personel Loading	S/N	Hometown	Wt. Fully Equipped
1. Capt. Erven E. Boettner	O-379436	Roca, Nebraska	269
2. T-4 William Sherman	6143428	North Grovendane, Conn.	251
3. Pvt. William O. Wright	33047493		274
4. Pfc. Clifford E. Simonds	34078779	Kinder, Louisiana	280
5. S/Sgt. Joseph Viteritto, Jr.	32156950	Newark, New Jersey	274
6. Pvt. Leroy E. Ande	36159311	Detroit, Michigan	269
7. Pvt. Ocko F. Leonard	34114070	Lexington, N.C.	285
8. Sgt. William E. Moses	33081732	Altoona, Pennsylvania	249
9. Pfc. Archie O. Martin	35048877	Roanoke, Virginia	237
10. Pfc. Charlie A. Smith	33075780	Belle Fonte, Pennsylvania	225
11. Cpl. Samuel M. Flagler	34085397	Kingstree, South Carolina	261
12. Pfc. Leroy E. Dokey	36159299		231
13. T-5 Keith Argraves	39202734	Portland, Oregon	276
14. T/4 Joseph H. Moore	34084125	Sylvania, Georgia	239

Total Weight	3620
Equipment Bundle Weight	250
Special Equipment	150
Total Weight Used For Tactical Mission	4020

Plane Number 2 - Company "F"

Personel Loading	S/N	Hometown	Wt. Fully Equipped
1. Lt. Edmund J. Tomasik	O-373015	New Bedford, massachusetts	260
2. Pfc. William F. Withem	35034953	Glouster, Ohio	281
3. Pfc. Roger P. Derringer	35281777	DeFiance, Ohio	239
4. Pvt. Edwin C. Hicks	34084165	Rockmart, Georgia	254
5. T-5 Dorsey W. Moody	34054702	St. Petersburg, Florida	243
6. Pfc. Leroy Mills	35261846	Middletown, Ohio	257
7. Pfc. Demont S. Erland	34059447	Auburndale, Florida	243
8. Pfc. Robert G. Suarez	37109951	Vinton, Iowa	277
9. Pfc. Robert G. Suarez	34106597	Lillian, Alabama	246
10. Pvt. Joseph S. Moffo	33070015	Bristow, Pennsylvania	268
11. Pfc. James R. Hammonds	34085047	Rome, Georgia	228
12. Pfc. Floyd W. Calhoun	34107514	Gordon, Alabama	261
13. Sgt. Ortagus	14013763	Miami, Florida	245
14. Sgt. William H. Simmons	34106608	Fairhope, Alabama	277

Total Weight	3581
Equipment Bundle Weight	250
Special Equipment	189
Total Weght Used For Tactical Mission	4020

Plane Number 3 - Company "F"

Personel Loading	S/N	Hometown	Wt. Fully Equipped
1. Lt. Ralph R. Miller	O-1283116	Youngstown, Ohio	257
2. Pvt. Pete Mrvosh	33111127	Beaver Falls, Pennsylvania	260
3. Pvt. Roger W. Durant	35291735	Canton, Ohio	281
4. Sgt. Carl E. Salisbury	35164991	Frankfort, Indiana	264
5. Pvt. Harry F. Bailey	15060021	Louisville, Kentucky	261
6. Pvt. John F. Hendricks	20649027	Lake Butler, Florida	252
7. Pfc. Adolph Gennarelli	36044975	Chicago, Illinois	257
8. Pvt. J. J. O'Brien	31026494		219
9. Pfc. Marshall E. Mitchell	35212629	Norfolk, West Virginia	253
10. Pfc. Royden V. Vandervort	34055018	Tampa, Florida	229
11. Sgt. Roland Weeks	34056873	Collier City, Florida	281
12. Sgt. Walter L. McCook	6926143	Fitzgerald, Georgia	253
13. Cpl. William H. Leatherwood	34054885	Gainesville, Florida	250
14. T-5 Carroll C. Proctor	36043814	Salem, Illinois	260

Total Weight	3577
Equipment Bundle Weight	250
Special Equipment	193
Total Weight Used For Tactical Mission	4020

Plane Number 4 - Company "F"

Personel Loading	S/N	Hometown	Wt. Fully Equipped
1. S/Sgt. Tom W. Odom	6971808	Smithville, Georgia	247
2. Pvt. Bernard L. Roberts	34044772	Rockland, Maine	269
3. Pvt. John R. Patton	35212275	Ashland, Kentucky	256
4. Pvt. Earnest E. Nelson	34142154	Knoxville, Tennessee	288
5. Pvt. Henry G. Wilburn	16047429	Milwaukee, Wisconsin	274½
6. Pvt. Theodore J. Kotlowski	33082552	Cambridge Springs, Pennsylvania	278½
7. Sgt. Walter R. Patterson	34140111	Spring Cty, Tennessee	263
8. Pvt. Eugene J. Felippelli	32173166	Flushing, New York	235
9. Pvt. Robert D. Daves	34172325	Drexel, North Carolina	236½
10. Pvt. Harold T Caulfield	26045057	Chicago, Illinois	256
11. Pfc. Rosarie E. Cyr	31048024	Waterbury, Connecticut	233
12. Cpl. Leo C. Inglesby	33072277	Philadelphia, Pennsylvania	251
13. Sgt. Eugene R. Grafe	34052586	St. Petersburg, Florida	277
14. Sgt. Lloyd K. Bjelland	16006665	Taylor, Wisconsin	260

Total Weight	3614½
Equipment Bundle Weight	250
Special Equipment	155½
Total Weight Used For Tactical Mission	4020

Plane Number 5 - Company "F"

Personel Loading	S/N	Hometown	Wt. Fully Equipped
1. Lt. Fred E. Perry	O-395326	Dayton, Ohio	242
2. Pvt. Michael Sembrat	32135740	Syracuse, New York	243
3. Pvt. Lester L. Moore	35209893	New Martinsville, West Virginia	269½
4. T-4 Donald L. Sutton	36159286	North Adams, Michigan	242
5. Pfc. Harold H. Murren	37007994	St. Joseph, Missouri	261½
6. Pvt. Bert E. Dockins	34094078	Fair Play, South Carolina	273
7. Sgt. Frank Pflugler	33077758	Northhampton, Pennsylvania	221
8. Pvt. William D. Cross	34104803	Birmingham, Alabama	252
9. Pvt. Charles E. Parten	34107213	Selma, Alabama	250
10. Pvt. James M. Broadway	34142993	Pope, Tennessee	272
11. Pvt. William I. Eckroth	6945098	Harrisburg, Pennsylvania	239
12. Pvt. Carmine J. Manente	31048564	Hartford, Connecticut	229
13. Sgt. Harold O. Graff	34078495	New Orleans, Louisiana	240½
14. George Olesh, Jr.	33111596	Allentown, Pennsylvania	265

Total Weight	3499
Equipment Bundle Weight	250
Special Equipment	271
Total Weight Used For Tactical Mission	4020

Plane Number 6 - Company "F"

Personel Loading	S/N	Hometown	Wt. Fully Equipped
1. S/Sgt. Lowell W. Frank	12002260	Cuba, New York	243
2. Pfc. Steven Nowakowski	35019974	Toledo, Ohio	245
3. Sgt. Donald E. Davis	6965436	Whistler, Alabama	252
4. Pvt. George Russ	35045525	Canton, Ohio	257
5. Pvt. Kenneth M. Nolte	16047653	Onalaska, Wisconsin	245½
6. Sgt. Edward R. Miller	34054903	Lakeland, Florida	280
7. Pfc. Chester J. Witkowski	33077043	Erie, Pennsylvania	258
8. Pfc. Raymond J. Donovan	37110174	Bernard, Iowa	250
9. Pfc. Thomas F. Dunlavey	310333970	Lowell, Massachusetts	246½
10. Pvt. Russell C. Morris	35126953	Marmet, West Virginia	268
11. Sgt. Joseph L. Buchanan	14017112	Rayville, Louisiana	274
12. Pvt. Marcus Kukee	36231034	Milwaukee, Wisconsin	255
13. Pfc. Robert G. Williams	34114860	Durham, North Carolina	248
14. Sgt. Ray Cagle	39376053	Ellensburg, Washington	270

Total Weight	3591
Equipment Bundle Weight	250
Special Equipment	179
Total Weight Used For Tactical Mission	4020

North Africa - Company F Planes 7 - 9

Plane Number 7 - Company "F"

Personel Loading	S/N	Hometown	Wt. Fully Equipped
1. Lt. James H. Hardy	O-390713	Ecru, Mississippi	277
2. S/Sgt. Orval W. Webb	33093727	Washington, D.C.	297
3. Pvt. C. A. Schenk	35281731		270
4. Sgt. Tony J. Manzella	6660751	Bessemer, Alabama	230
5. Pfc. Kenneth Gridley	34054856	Peony, Florida	223
6. Pvt. William H. Davis	20342259	Cumberland, Maryland	233
7. Pfc. John F. Smith	30214281	Acpinwall, Pennsylvania	244
8. Sgt. Leverne S. Fox	34115127	Boone, North Carolina	237
9. Cpl. John W. McGee	35085021	Cabot, Pennsylvania	248
10. Pfc. Lloyd P. Bourn	36043741	Jackonsville, Illinois	265
11. Pfc. Robert H. Soden	39230111	Los Angeles, California	227
12. Pvt. Ivan A. Cooper	37015304	Lyons, Kansas	254
13. Pvt. Charles R. Coffell	34160317	Huntsville, Alabama	230
14. Cpl. James C. Hughes	34085020	Atlanta, Georgia	252½
		Total Weight	3475
		Equipment Bundle Weight	250
		Special Equipment	295
		Total Weight Used	
		For Tactical Mission	4020

Plane Number 8 - Company "F"

Personel Loading	S/N	Hometown	Wt. Fully Equipped
1. Lt. William M. Sherman	O-422279	Council Bluffs, Iowa	238½
2. Pfc. W. C. Collins	20417992	Jacksonville, Florida	287½
3. Pfc. Harold I. Shantle	32044872	Norfolk, New York	287
4. T-5 Ora A. Foster	36162028	Pontiac, Michigan	242
5. J. A. Bernado			268
6. Thomas F. Lustrtitz	35281755	Ravenna, Ohio	257
7. Sgt. Woodrow F. Dunlap	34085011	Rome, Georgia	241½
8. Pvt. Daniel H. Drumbeater	37098085	Gheon, Minnesota	250
9. Cpl. Burnett H. Fite	31527868	Mianesburg, Ohio	252
10. Pfc. Edward R. LeCarpentier	39230124	Washington, D.C.	252
11. Pfc. James W. Bussey	34093948	Modoc, South Carolina	226
12. Pfc. Adger S. Shirley	34093887	Hodges, South Carolina	233
13. Pvt. James S. Whitacre	35166060	Ft. Wayne, Indiana	258
14. Pvt. Charles C. Christensen	9631644	Chicago, Illinois	301
		Total Weight	3593
		Equipment Bundle Weight	250
		Special Equipment	177
		Total Weight Used	
		For Tactical Mission	4020

Plane Number 9 - Company "F"

Personel Loading	S/N	Hometown	Wt. Fully Equipped
1. T/Sgt. Lester C. McLaney	6966537	Hartford, Alabama	265
2. Sgt. Arthur E. Dickerson	14022595	Carriere, Mississippi	255
3. T-5 William D. Hubbard	31039938	New York, New York	260
4. T-5 Monroe E. Wills	14018863	Hartford, Alabama	260
5. Lt. Robert C. MacLane	O-403125	Chicago, Illinois	277
6. Pfc. Walter E. Mechowski	32135724	Syracuse, New york	273
7. Pfc. Leon P. Sporish	35157349	Newark, New Jersey	273½
8. Pfc. Ralph E. Colwell	33090495	Roanoke, Virginia	248
9. Pvt. Joseph W. Owens	33009860	Laurel, Maryland	273
10. Pvt. Harley Atkinson	6918127	Metropolis, Illinois	292
11. Pfc. Robert W. Miller	33110651	North Pittsburg, Pennsylvania	242
12. Pfc. C. L. Thomas	33109659		238
13. S/Sgt. Jesse A. Silva	31034086	Provincetown, Massachusetts	255
14. 1st Sgt. Mike O'Brien	6930541	Alden, Minnesota	268
		Total Weight	3593
		Equipment Bundle Weight	250
		Special Equipment	177
		Total Weight Used	
		For Tactical Mission	4020

I received the flight manifests from Harvey S. Sutherland, who had received them from Charlie Doyle, president of the 509 Association.

Bn. Plane # 10 — Hq. Co. — Staff Plane # 1

PARA-G-7   PART II

Operation:" LEDGER   Date:

Details of A/B Troops

A/C No (As per Para-G-5):

DROP ORDER	SERIAL NUMBER	RANK	NAME & INITIALS	UNIT Hq. Co. 509th Prcht Bn.
1	0-20362	Lt. Col	Yarborough, William P.	
2	0-461564	Lt.	Kelly, Alfred J.	
3	6918198	S/Sgt.	Sullivan, William W.	
4	0-2055819	Sgt.	Weber, Soloman A.	
5	35186548	Sgt.	Bishop, Ellis L.	
6	14124055	T/4	Dunlap, Amos H.	
7	35127657	T/5	Alongi, Jack	
8	39405966	T/5	Aleck, Johnie G.	
9	33110740	T/5	Sheridan, George J.	
10	33455725	Pvt.	Carson, Crote D.	
11	14045508	Pvt.	Batton, James W.	
12	32231874	Pvt.	Carnes, Joseph NMI	
13	18102851	Pvt.	Hamer, Fred G.	
14	37530283	Pvt.	Elliot, Richard F.	
15	33783706	Pvt.	Straccio, Arthur NMI	
16				
17				
18				
19				
20				
21				

CONTAINERS

Rack No.	Type	Contents (General)	Gross Weight	Parachute Color/Light
1	A-5	Signal Equipment	130	
2	A-5	Signal Equipment	130	
3	A-5	Signal Equipment	190	

Inspection Completed: Signed:

Bn. Plane # 11 — Hq. Co. — Staff Plane # 2

PARA-G-7   PART II

Operation:"   Date:

Details of A/B Troops

A/C No (As per Para-G-5):

DROP ORDER	SERIAL NUMBER	RANK	NAME & INITIALS	UNIT Hq. Co. 509th Prcht
1	0-301316	Maj.	Apperson, John H.	
2	0-399875	Capt.	Horland, Charles K.	
3	0-2053973	1st Lt.	Wess, La Verne P.	
4	32074714	Sgt.	Reiner, Abraham R.	
5	7001457	S/Sgt	Maddox, Charley L.	
6	32120658	S/Sgt	Von Essen, Arthur W.	
7	31044632	Sgt.	Sennett, Lincoln S.	
8	32357806	T/4	Fine, Theodore J.	
9	13042041	Col.	Grieder, John A.	
10	34165913	T/5	Foote, Walter C.	
11	32012593	Pvt.	Blass, Edward	
12	31026566	Pvt.	Chapin, Raymond A.	
13	32220746	Pvt.	Freeman, George F.	
14	12169743	Pvt.	Diebolt, John A.	
15	35231744	Pvt.	Easkow, Stanley	
16	20229796	Pvt.	Galuskin, Martin M.	
17				
18				
19				
20				
21				

CONTAINERS

Rack No.	Type	Contents (General)	Gross Weight	Parachute Color/Light
1	A-5	Comm. Equip.	150	Yellow
2	A-5	Comm. Equip.	150	Yellow
3	A-5	Comm. Equip.	150	Yellow
4	A-5	Comm. Equip.	150	Yellow
5	A-5	Comm. Equip.	150	Yellow
6	A-5	Comm. Equip.	150	Yellow
			1000 lbs	

Inspection Completed: Signed:

Bn. Plane # 12 — Hq Co. Plane #3

PARA-G-7   PART II

Operation:"   Date:

Details of A/B Troops

A/C No (As per Para-G-5):

DROP ORDER	SERIAL NUMBER	RANK	NAME & INITIALS	UNIT Hq. Co. 509th Prcht Bn.
1	0-399436	Capt	Alden, Carlos C.	
2	0-??	Lt.	Flenory, Herbert C Jr.	
3	35075970	T/4	Herr, Howard J.	
4	35270677	Pvt.	Baum, Charles O.	
5	13100308	Pvt.	Menikis, John G.	
6	38122011	Pvt.	Saiz, Anthony NMI	
7	37478751	Pvt.	McDonald, John E.	
8	32407273	Pvt.	DeVanis, John C.	
9	19062123	Pvt.	Pilcher, Edgar W.	
10	14123342	Pvt.	Echard, Lewis H.	
11	39179154	Pvt.	Mettlemeyer, Phenis C.	
12	6954560	Pvt.	McKnight, Jesse L.	
13	32187065	Pvt.	Trezkowski, Victor S.	
14	35723031	Pvt.	Karmas, Earl D.	
15	32787093	Pvt.	Sweetitz, Frank NMI	
16	34355824	Pvt.	McGee, Marion A.	
17	18016802	Pvt.	Justice, Stephen D.	
18	17060394	Pvt.	Barton, Ken NMI	
19	6284123	Pvt.	Bradley, Max L.	
20	35164905	T/4	Rundell, Ora Jr.	
21				

CONTAINERS

Rack No.	Type	Contents (General)	Gross Weight	Parachute Color/Light

Bn. Plane # 13 — Hq Co Plane # 4

PARA-G-7   PART II

Operation:" LEDGER   Date:

Details of A/B Troops

A/C No (As per Para-G-5):

DROP ORDER	SERIAL NUMBER	RANK	NAME & INITIALS	UNIT Hq. Co. 509th Prcht Bn.
1	0-1283335	1st Lt.	Siegfriedt, Alvin W.	
2	35168653	S/Sgt.	Holmes, Charles C.	
3	31025044	T/5.	Audet, Charles H.	
4	39528054	Pfc.	Buss, Royal L.	
5	38062496	Pfc.	Brown, Odus A.	
6	36201780	Pvt.	Bence, Allen H.	
7	11046075	Pvt.	Baressi, Joseph NMI	
8	33077136	Col.	Johnson, John J.	
9	19085996	Pfc.	Waters, Samuel NMI	
10	36560719	Pvt.	Fazlauskas, Alger P	
11	33084662	T/5.	Mulhalland, Francis H.	
12	39379463	Pvt.	Hendricks, Henry C. Jr.	
13	20318623	Pvt.	Brittain, Denzel G.	
14	38191535	Pvt.	Wells, Lloyd C.	
15	16144172	Pvt.	Tarbroski, Stephen G.	
16	0-1299154	Lt.	Shaw, Hugh P.	
17				
18				
19				
20				
21				

CONTAINERS

Rack No.	Type	Contents (General)	Gross Weight	Parachute Color/Light
1	A-5	Miscellaneous	60	
2	A-5	Miscellaneous	70	
3	A-5	Miscellaneous	80	
			210	

Bn. Plane # 14
Hq Co Plane # 5

U. S. CONFIDENTIAL
(Equals British Confidential)

PARA-G-7 PART II

Exercise/ Operation:" LEDGER Date:

Details of A/B Troops

A/G No (As per Para-G-5):

PERSONNEL

DROP ORDER	SERIAL NUMBER	RANK	NAME & INITIALS	UNIT Hq Co. 509th Prcht Bn.
1	O-1320057	Lt.	Lieber, Harry S.	
2	35106588	Pfc.	Robinson, John F.	
3	14079196	Cpl.	Platt, Edwin F.	
4	35122885	Cpl.	Holtz, William J.	
5	36458667	Pvt.	Frezon, Lawrence G.	
6	7083491	Pvt.	Pedigo, Dennis R.	
7	35676644	Pvt.	Laterra, Albert A.	
8	36295392	Pvt.	Martin, Joseph M.	
9	33017778	Pvt.	Stenger, John A.	
10	34050284	Pvt.	Albert, John A.	
11	34087897	Cpl.	Waller, Robert R.	
12	36804735	Pvt.	Barth, Otto H.	
13	39909563	Pvt.	Barry, Lawrence A.	
14	37469724	Pvt.	Garner, Paul G.	
15	20350080	Cpl.	Carroll, Henry W.	
16				
17				
18				
19				
20				
21				

CONTAINERS

Rack No.	Type	Contents (General)	Gross Weight	Parachute Color/Light
1	A-5	B.A.R.	75	

Inspection Completed: Signed:

U. S. CONFIDENTIAL
(Equals British Confidential)

Bn. Plane #2 / Co. "A" Plane #2

U. S. CONFIDENTIAL (Equals British Confidential)

PARA-G-7 PART II

~~PROTOCOL~~/ Operation:" LEDGER _____ Date:_____

Details of A/B Troops

A/C No (As per Para-G-5):_____

DROP ORDER	SERIAL NUMBER	RANK	NAME & INITIALS	UNIT Co. "A", 509th Prcht Inf Bn
1	0-519371	1st Lt	Darden, Jack M.	
2	36315585	Cpl	Wojcik, Edward F.	
3	36452011	Pvt	Smith, Merritt E.	
4	36192881	Sgt	Bluhm, John	
5	13167878	Pvt	Hart, Carl M.	
6	33430398	Pvt	Buzzard, James F.	
7	36690685	Pvt	Bethel, Jewell L. Jr.	
8	39316742	Pvt	Bennett, Joseph M.	
9	32093047	Pvt	Birdsall, Russell E.	
10	39034481	Pvt	Lugner, Joseph J.	
11	32774901	Pvt	Zawadzki, Joseph G.	
12	36549173	Pfc	Bruse, Thomas J.	
13	39383189	Pfc	Weldon, Charles J.	
14	35626804	Pvt	Carsey, Henry T.	
15	34531050	Pfc	Adams, Clayton C.	Medical Sect
16	35285413	Cpl	Hovaniak, Stanley F.	
17				
18				
19				
20				
21				

CONTAINERS

Rack No.	Type	Contents (General)	Gross Weight	Parachute Color/Light
1	A - 5	B.A.R. & Ammo	195	Red
2	A - 5	Camouflage nets	190	Red
3	A - 5	Bazooka & Ammo	200	Red
4	A - 5	1903 Rifle	165	Red

Inspection Completed:_____ Signed:_____

U. S. CONFIDENTIAL (Equals British Confidential)

Bn. Plane #3 / Co. "A" Plane #3

U. S. CONFIDENTIAL (Equals British Confidential)

PARA-G-7 PART II

~~XXXXXX~~/ Operation:" LEDGER Date:_____

Details of A/B Troops

A/C No (As per Para-G-5):_____

DROP ORDER	SERIAL NUMBER	RANK	NAME & INITIALS	UNIT Co. "A", 509th Prcht Inf
1	0-371088	1st Lt	Winship, Leslie D.	
2	20310415	Pvt	Broughton, John L.	
3	34397282	Sgt	Cannon, Jerome	
4	37130557	Pvt	Coleman, Richard H.	
5	34285374	Pvt	Houser, Charles H.	
6	35163341	Pvt	Bichel, Earl L.	
7	35546422	Pfc	Corfee, Harry F.	
8	34551614	Pvt	White, Prentiss	
9	34614612	Pvt	Bruce, Everette J.	
10	37601442	Pfc	Baker, Clyde D.	
11	20429255	Pvt	Sherpard, Robert E.	
12	39462468	Pvt	Gunderson, Theodore E.	
13	33584470	Pvt	Risky, Edwin F., Sr	
14	36857145	Pvt	Kalinowski, Edward	
15	36734224	Pfc	Boehmke, Warren F.	
16	14053575	Cpl	Burimal, Louis C.	
17	17077855	Sgt	McCaig, Milton R.	
18				
19				
20				
21				

CONTAINERS

Rack No.	Type	Contents (General)	Gross Weight	Parachute Color/Light
1	A - 5	B.A.R. & Ammo	195	RED
2	A - 5	Camouflage net	190	RED
3	A - 5	1903 Rifle	165	RED

Inspection Completed:_____ Signed:_____

U. S. CONFIDENTIAL (Equals British Confidential)

Bn. Plane #4 / Co. "A" Plane #4

U. S. CONFIDENTIAL (Equals British Confidential)

PARA-G-7 PART II

~~XXXXXXX~~/ Operation:" LEDGER Date:_____

Details of A/B Troops

A/C No (As per Para-G-5):_____

DROP ORDER	SERIAL NUMBER	RANK	NAME & INITIALS	UNIT Co. "A", 509th Prcht Inf Bn
1	0-1267506	1st Lt	Frazier, John W.	
2	39557230	Cpl	Casteneda, Salvador P.	
3	15140332	Pvt	Horacek, Theodore C.	
4	35547095	Pvt	Brown, Glenford	
5	35743953	Pfc	Jarvis, Charles R.	
6	12154083	Pvt	Kort, William A.	
7	35565292	Pvt	Gregory, Harry	
8	20101976	Pvt	Draper, Earl W.	
9	37674628	Pvt	Grover, Robert E.	
10	34722235	Pvt	Jolley, James B.	
11	34583968	Pvt	Jones, Barney C.	
12	37664467	Pvt	Leydens, Junior V.	
13	32853489	Pvt	DeFelice, Lorenzo F.	
14	32474441	Pvt	Abram, Teddy M.	
15	6883529	S/Sgt	King, William H.	
16				
17				
18				
19				
20				
21				

CONTAINERS

Rack No.	Type	Contents (General)	Gross Weight	Parachute Color/Light
1	A - 5	B.A.R. & Ammo	195	RED
2	A - 5	Camouflage net	190	RED
3	A - 5	1903 Rifle	165	RED

Bn. Plane #5 / Co. "A" Plane #5

U. S. CONFIDENTIAL (Equals British Confidential)

PARA-G-7 PART II

~~XXXXXXX~~/ Operation:" LEDGER Date:_____

Details of A/B Troops

A/C No (As per Para-G-5):_____

DROP ORDER	SERIAL NUMBER	RANK	NAME & INITIALS	UNIT Co. "A", 509th Prcht Inf
1	0-1293187	2d Lt	Berman, Bernard	
2	35678957	Pvt	Marcum, Walter	
3	33095579	Sgt	Cardwell, Elmer T.	
4	39123561	Pvt	Espinoza, Manual S.	
5	33572163	Pfc	Johnston, Thomas M.	
6	33257511	Pvt	Lunghofer, Robert L.	
7	6149141	Pvt	Kegy, Napoleon, Jr.	
8	35048859	Pvt	Mezzie, Donald C.	
9	32359812	Pvt	Johnson, William W.	
10	6893545	Pfc	Darrough, Theodore B.	
11	32642224	Pvt	Mangialomini, Joseph C.	
12	37526502	Pvt	Jordan, Eugene C.	
13	39700299	Pvt	Thompson, James W.	
14	13098414	Pvt	Dalessandro, Raymond P.	
15	36735555	Cpl	Lattanzi, Propersio P.	
16				
17				
18				
19				
20				
21				

CONTAINERS

Rack No.	Type	Contents (General)	Gross Weight	Parachute Color/Light
1	A - 5	B.A.R. & Ammo	195	RED
2	A - 5	Camouflage net	190	RED
3	A - 5	1903 rifle	170	RED

Bn. Plane #6 / Co. "A" Plane #6

U. S. C O N F I D E N T I A L
(Equals British Confidential)

PARA-G-7   PART II

IREEEEDEX/ Operation:" LEDGER   Date:_____

Details of A/B Troops

A/C No (As per Para-G-5):_____

PERSONNEL

DROP ORDER	SERIAL NUMBER	RANK	NAME & INITIALS	UNIT Co. "A", 509th Prcht Inf Bn
1	0-1303911	1st Lt	Livingston, Hoyt R.	
2	18150778	Pvt	Coupland, Leland C.	
3	35654651	Pvt	Evans, James	
4	34131349	Sgt	Marsh, Felix R.	
5	35658693	Pfc	Johnson, Arthur G.	
6	36375445	Pfc	Johnston, Leslie G.	
7	35650505	Pvt	Keaton, Noah, Jr.	
8	39336523	Pvt	Kohler, Harold A.	
9	33533600	Pvt	Jennings, Sherman L.	
10	35285049	Pvt	Eliszewski, Henry J.	
11	32653634	Pvt	Collazo, Charles M.	
12	34128576	Pfc	Polsen, Lee W.	Medical ?Sect
13				
14				
15				
16				
17				
18				
19				
20				
21				

CONTAINERS

Rack No.	Type	Contents (General)	Gross Weight	Parachute Color/Light
1	A-5	Mortar & Ammo	195	RED
2	A-5	Bazooka & Ammo	200	RED
3	A-5	Camouflage net	190	RED

Inspection Completed:_____   Signed:_____

U.S. C O N F I D E N T I A L
(Equals British Confidential)

Bn. Plane #7 / Co. "A" Plane #7

U. S. C O N F I D E N T I A L
(Equals British Confidential)

PARA-G-7   PART II

XXXXXXXX/ Operation:" LEDGER   Date:_____

Details of A/B Troops

A/C No (As per Para-G-5):_____

PERSONNEL

DROP ORDER	SERIAL NUMBER	RANK	NAME & INITIALS	UNIT Co. "A", 509th Prcht Inf
1	0-1303961	1st Lt	Shaker, Kenneth R.	
2	14075128	Cpl	Singleton, James F.	
3	31044588	Pvt	Beatham, Stanley, Jr.	
4	33500076	Pvt	Jones, Leslie K.	
5	39285554	Pfc	Walker, Albert J.	
6	38452126	Pfc	Eggratt, Elmer A.	
7	14416473	Pfc	Bryan, William J., Jr.	
8	34440820	Pfc	Meadows, Guy E.	
9	33776771	Pvt	McCauley, John B.	
10	11110897	Pvt	Bearse, Selwyn S.	
11	15394397	Pvt	Bloyd, David G.	
12	14133102	Pvt	Perlo, Hyman M.	
13	33183152	Pvt	Karnecheck, George F.	
14	35431647	Pvt	Austin, Harold B.	Medical S
15				
16				
17				
18				
19				
20				
21				

CONTAINERS

Rack No.	Type	Contents (General)	Gross Weight	Parachute Color/Lig
1	A-5	B.A.R. & Ammo	190	
2	A-5	Camouflage net	190	
3	A-5	1903 Rifle	130	
4	A-5	Bazooka & Ammo	190	

Inspection Completed:_____   Signed:_____

U.S. C O N F I D E N T I A L
(Equals British Confidential)

Bn. Plane #8 / Co. "A" Plane #8

U. S. C O N F I D E N T I A L
(Equals British Confidential)

PARA-G-7   PART II

IREEEEDEX/ Operation:"_____   Date:_____

Details of A/B Troops

A/C No (As per Para-G-5):_____

PERSONNEL

DROP ORDER	SERIAL NUMBER	RANK	NAME & INITIALS	UNIT Co. "A", 509th Prcht Inf Bn
1	0-384517	2d Lt	Pahl, William A.	
2	6509874	Cpl	Baker, Wallace H.	
3	13134759	Pfc	Bobb, Joseph A.	
4	37549178	Pvt	White, James E.	
5	14029725	Pfc	Watson, Billie	
6	39254226	Pvt	Grazza, Edward	
7	18231790	Pvt	Guerrero, Louis C.	
8	6904012	Pvt	Layman, LeRoy A.	
9	36678204	Pvt	Brown, Culver S.	
10	38479146	Pvt	Lester, R. Q.	
11	37673380	Pvt	Cooley, John C.	
12	20109068	Pfc	Cardell, Walter A.	
13				
14				
15				
16				
17				
18				
19				
20				
21				

CONTAINERS

Rack No.	Type	Contents (General)	Gross Weight	Parachute Color/Light
1	A-5	B.A.R. & Ammo	190	
2	A-5	Camouflage net	190	
3	A-5	1903 Rifle	145	

Bn. Plane #9 / Co. "A" Plane #9

U. S. C O N F I D E N T I A L
(Equals British Confidential)

PARA-G-7   PART II

IREEEEDEX/ Operation:" LEDGER   Date:_____

Details of A/B Troops

A/C No (As per Para-G-5):_____

PERSONNEL

DROP ORDER	SERIAL NUMBER	RANK	NAME & INITIALS	UNIT Co. "A", 509th Prcht Inf
1	7001000	1st Sgt	Greene, Jack V.	
2	20651122	Pvt	Hogge, William A.	
3	11062605	Pfc	Griffin, Maurice E.	
4	33565357	Pfc	Lynch, Earl C.	
5	38474678	Pvt	Ramsey, Ray F.	
6	15133365	Pvt	Doll, Ralph W.	
7	38193032	Pvt	McGervey, Raymond H.	
8	15377196	Pvt	McClung, French C.	
9	14047256	Pvt	Lindsay, Louis V.	
10	38452651	Pvt	Freman, James J.	
11	34440098	Pvt	Jones, Melvin E.	
12	16021254	Pvt	Griffin, Donald F.	
13	34142155	S/Sgt	Huff, Paul B.	
14				
15				
16				
17				
18				
19				
20				
21				

CONTAINERS

Rack No.	Type	Contents (General)	Gross Weight	Parachute Color/Lig
1	A-5	Mortar & Ammo	200	RED
2	A-5	Camouflage net	190	RED

Southern France - Company B Planes 1 - 4

Flight manifest of Battalion 25, Co. B, Plane 1 has been connected to include the 17 men who drowned with Capt. Miller.

Bn. Plane #25 — Co. "B" Plane #1

U. S. CONFIDENTIAL
(Equals British Confidential)

PARA-G-7   PART II

XXXXXXXX/ Operation:" LEDGER   Date:_____

Details of A/B Troops

A/C No (As per Para-G-5):_____   X = Name entered in error.

DROP ORDER	SERIAL NUMBER	RANK	NAME & INITIALS		UNIT Co. "B", 509th Prcht Inf Bn
1	37300492	T/4	Beckner, Eugene		
2	33094099	T/4	Nixon, James H.	X	
3	34055040	T/5	Cross, John R.	X	
4	32141270	Sgt	Crevelling, Oscar F.		
5	35571441	T/5	Dawson, Albert T.		
6	37608277	Pfc	Potter, Leon V.		
7	33397839	Pvt	Petty, Charles A.	X	
8	35732276	Pvt	Fennebaker, Thomas W.	X	X = Name entered in error.
9	32752166	Pvt	Moscatiello, Joseph	X	
10	33309229	Pvt	Steigner, Donald F.	X	
11	35546734	Pvt	Mullen, Clifton R.	X	
12	37292559	Pvt	Knapp, James J.	X	
13	36807777	Pvt	Powell, Robert R.	X	
14	35209270	Pfc	Osburn, Victor A.	X	Medical Sect.
15	0-1253116	Cpt	Miller, Ralph R. "Bing" Jr.		
16		Pvt	Butler, Ira		
17		Pfc	Campos, Frank		
18		S. Sgt	David, Robert B.		
19		M.Sgt	Dorsa, Anthony J.		
20		Pvt	Garcia, Julius		
21		T4	Gillman, Marvin N.		
		Pfc	Lynch, George R.		
		Pvt	Pipino, Alfred J.		
		T5	Reid, George W.		
		S.Sgt	Sutherland, William A.		

CONTAINERS

Rack No.	Type	Contents (General)	Gross Weight	Parachute Color/Light
1	A-5	Radio SCR 300	144	White
2	A-5	L.M.G.	130	WHITE
3	RR Bundle	Bazooka	190	YELLOW

Inspection Completed:_____   Signed:_____

Bn. Plane #26 — Co. "B" Plane #2

U. S. CONFIDENTIAL
(Equals British Confidential)

PARA-G-7   PART II

XXXXXXXX/ Operation:" LEDGER   Date:_____

Details of A/B Troops

A/C No (As per Para-G-5):_____

DROP ORDER	SERIAL NUMBER	RANK	NAME & INITIALS	UNIT Co. "B", 509th Prcht
1	0-493461	1st Lt.	Reuter, Edward R.	
2	16105218	Pvt	Gillman, Marvin N.	
3	12067554	Pfc	Reid, George W.	
4	35359614	Cpl	Helton, Clyde	
5	38468661	Pfc	Moore, Stanley W.	
6	12219417	Pvt	Marsullo, Albert S.	
7	39576986	Pvt	Mann, George H.	
8	35545753	Pvt	Fletcher, Robert L.	
9	35601772	Pfc	Kambrick, William J.	
10	33108212	Pvt	Knopp, James R.	
11	37616930	Pvt	Nachefski, Phillip K.	
12	15335588	Pvt	File, James W.	
13	35790180	Pvt	Patrick, Justus T.	
14	34214516	Pvt	Powell, William J.	
15	34054816	S/Sgt	McCullough, Elsie B.	
16				
17				
18				
19				
20				
21				

CONTAINERS

Rack No.	Type	Contents (General)	Gross Weight	Parachute Color/
1	A-5	B.A.R. & 103	145	WHITE
2	A-5	Mortar	150	WHITE

Inspection Completed:_____   Signed:_____

Bn. Plane #27 — Co. "B" Plane #3

U. S. CONFIDENTIAL
(Equals British Confidential)

PARA-G-7   PART II

XXXXXXXX/ Operation:" LEDGER   Date:_____

Details of A/B Troops

A/C No (As per Para-G-5):_____

DROP ORDER	SERIAL NUMBER	RANK	NAME & INITIALS	UNIT Co. "B", 509th Prcht Inf Bn
1	0-1319523	2d Lt	Martinez, Nick M.	
2	38432785	Pvt	Neill, Bernah E.	
3	33137792	Cpl	Nagurne, Nicholas	
4	36418003	Pfc	Stewart, Walter R.	
5	39678250	Pvt	Newman, Wesley O.	
6	36510196	Pfc	Larson, Anton	
7	36676805	Pvt	Hisinski, Walter	
8	38219760	Pvt	Succte, L. J.	
9	36538503	Pvt	Robertson, J. G.	
10	37570276	Pvt	Ofethun, H. O.	
11	35044715	Pfc	Haynes, Homer	
12	36758503	Pvt	Pabish, L. E.	
13	36642738	Pvt	Steele, E. M.	
14	20226417	Pfc	Fuhrer, C.	
15	31252893	Pfc	Maxwell, H. J.	Medical Sect.
16	34084489	Pfc	Camp, H. D.	
17				
18				
19				
20				
21				

CONTAINERS

Rack No.	Type	Contents (General)	Gross Weight	Parachute Color/Light
1	A-5	B.A.R.	145	WHITE
2	A-5	Mortar	150	WHITE

Bn. Plane #28 — Co. "B" Plane #4

U. S. CONFIDENTIAL
(Equals British Confidential)

PARA-G-7   PART II

XXXXXXXX/ Operation:" LEDGER   Date:_____

Details of A/B Troops

A/C No (As per Para-G-5):_____

DROP ORDER	SERIAL NUMBER	RANK	NAME & INITIALS	UNIT Co. "B", 509th Prcht
1	34054782	S/Sgt	Dorsa, A. J.	
2	20111390	Pvt	Feck, Milo P.	
3	36812547	Pvt	Matuszewski, J. R.	
4	33025780	Sgt	Brenner, D. J.	
5	6879269	Pfc	Fitzgerald, J. J.	
6	34050279	Pfc	Kammer, D. J.	
7	39847905	Pvt	Hirsles, R. V.	
8	31316951	Pvt	Lancaster, Y. E.	
9	15075931	Pvt	Kortes, N. J.	
10	16144173	Pfc	Smith, J. F.	Medical
11	33097721	Pvt	Langley, R. E.	
12	33820858	Pvt	Kaplar, J.	
13	36867079	Pvt	Kosidlo, J. M.	
14	36402694	Cpl	Knapp, Burl J.	
15				
16				
17				
18				
19				
20				
21				

CONTAINERS

Rack No.	Type	Contents (General)	Gross Weight	Parachute Color/
1	A-5	B.A.R.	145	WHITE

PARA-G-7   PART II

XXXXXXX/ Operation:" LEDGER   Date:_____

Details of A/B Troops

A/C No (As per Para-G-5):_____

DROP ORDER	SERIAL NUMBER	RANK	NAME & INITIALS	UNIT Co. "B", 509th Prcht Inf Bn
1	O-499498	2d Lt	Sorrells, J. H.	
2	33077738	Cpl	Pflugler, F.	
3	31224416	Pfc	Glynn, H. J.	
4	32931782	Pvt	Lundquist, A. E.	
5	38554324	Pvt	Lozano, H. J.	
6	32380354	Pfc	Kubic, J.	
7	34824777	Pvt	Lastinger, A. T.	
8	14005804	Pfc	Rizer, J. L.	
9	38381661	Pfc	Lirette, N. J.	
10	39700032	Pvt	Rich, L. L.	
11	33601731	Pvt	Luszczek, C. J.	
12	36605076	Pvt	Lindner, H. O.	
13	36464634	Pvt	Robertson, W. R.	
14	35765154	Pvt	LaFlem, G. L.	
15	6973808	Sgt	Fisco, R. D.	
16				
17				
18				
19				
20				
21				

CONTAINERS

Rack No.	Type	Contents (General)	Gross Weight	Parachute Color/Light

Inspection Completed:_____ Signed:_____

PARA-G-7   PART II

XXXXXXX/ Operation:" LEDGER   Date:_____

Details of A/B Troops

A/C No (As per Para-G-5):_____

DROP ORDER	SERIAL NUMBER	RANK	NAME & INITIALS	UNIT Co. "B", 509t
1	O-1287967	1st Lt	Turner, J. F.	
2	36447757	Pfc	Lewis, R. H.	
3	38518283	Pvt	Madden, G. S.	
4	39504888	Pfc	Green, L. E.	
5	37175525	Pvt	Gould, J. R.	
6	39619047	Pvt	Resser, C. A.	
7	33674408	Pvt	Relling, E. H.	
8	32469702	Pfc	Mangen, J. V.	
9	32981213	Pvt	Lynch, G. B.	
10	37480362	Pvt	Pearce, D. D.	
11	37097654	Sgt	Van Guilder, L.	
12				
13				
14				
15				
16				
17				
18				
19				
20				
21				

CONTAINERS

Rack No.	Type	Contents (General)	Gross Weight	Parachut
1	A - 5	Mortar	150	WHITE

Inspection Completed:_____ Signed:_____

PARA-G-7   PART II

XXXXXXX/ Operation:" LEDGER   Date:_____

Details of A/B Troops

A/C No (As per Para-G-5):_____

DROP ORDER	SERIAL NUMBER	RANK	NAME & INITIALS	UNIT Co. "B", 509th Prcht Inf Bn
1	O-1295730	1st Lt	Knupp, G.	
2	10726224	Pfc	Hemsworth, G. P.	
3	35251718	Sgt	Bensley, R. R.	
4	20802074	Pfc	Flores, N. N.	
5	12012551	Pfc	Masten, E. J.	
6	36451373	Pvt	Seymour, J.	
7	20210150	Pvt	Borrelli, J. J.	
8	31364556	Pvt	Burns, F. M.	
9	33565339	Pfc	Bryant, W. E.	
10	15140320	Pvt	Butt, Charles S.	
11	6716813	Pvt	Dusenbury, W. W.	
12	37476134	Pvt	Osmen, H. W.	
13	31357888	Pvt	Sutherland, H. W.	
14	6963923	Cpl	Crabb, W. E.	
15				
16				
17				
18				
19				
20				
21				

CONTAINERS

Rack No.	Type	Contents (General)	Gross Weight	Parachute Color/Light

PARA-G-7   PART II

XXXXXXX/ Operation:" LEDGER   Date:_____

Details of A/B Troops

A/C No (As per Para-G-5):_____

DROP ORDER	SERIAL NUMBER	RANK	NAME & INITIALS	UNIT Co. "B", 509th
1	O-1016711	2d Lt	Stewart, R. W.	
2	16126583	Pvt	Dyer, H. F.	
3	12048883	Sgt	Britton, C. T.	
4	19081556	Pfc	Chow, On	
5	19083538	Pfc	Dalrymple, H. F.	
6	34499871	Pvt	Duncan, J. E.	
7	35611767	Pvt	Erickson, G. E.	
8	39461974	Pvt	Critchfield, R.	
9	35648145	Pvt	McClurg, W. D.	
10	38407313	Pvt	Estes, J. S.	
11	17143768	Pvt	Goldstein, F. H.	
12	35532458	Pvt	Smith, R. D.	
13	35870174	Pvt	Ender, G. E.	
14	39258965	Cpl	Spoeneman, H. R.	
15				
16				
17				
18				
19				
20				
21				

CONTAINERS

Rack No.	Type	Contents (General)	Gross Weight	Parachut
1	A - 5	B.A.R.	145	WHITE

Bn. Plane #33
Co. "B" Plane #9

U. S. C O N F I D E N T I A L
(Equals British Confidential)

PARA-G-7

PART II

XXXXXXXX/ Operations: LEDGER   Date: _____

Details of A/B Troops

A/C No (As per Para-G-5): _____

PERSONNEL

DROP ORDER	SERIAL NUMBER	RANK	NAME & INITIALS	UNIT Co. "B", 509th Prcht Inf Bn
1	0-1316080	1st Lt	Oldham, A. W.	
2	20310254	T/5	Grant, S. U.	
3	14065823	Pfc	Ford, J. C.	
4	39410050	Pfc	Campos, F.	
5	32953299	Pvt	Gracia, J.	
6	36060609	Pvt	Butler, I. J.	
7	37617693	Pvt	Roediger, J. B.	
8	36678431	Pvt	Eolseth, E. L.	
9	36557440	Pvt	Solak, E. W.	Medical Sect
10	34054782	S/Sgt	David, R. B.	
11				
12				
13				
14				
15				
16				
17				
18				
19				
20				
21				

CONTAINERS

Rack No.	Type	Contents (General)	Gross Weight	Parachute Color/Light
1	A - 5	Mortar	150	WHITE
2	A - 5	Camouflage nets	175	WHITE

Inspection Completed: _____   Signed: _____

U. S. C O N F I D E N T I A L
(Equals British Confidential)

Bn Plane # 34 — "C" Co Plane # 1

U. S. CONFIDENTIAL
(Equals British Confidential)

PARA-G-7 PART II

Recovery/ Operation:" LEDGER ____ Date:____

Details of A/B Troops

A/C No (As per Para-G-5): ____

PERSONNEL

DROP ORDER	SERIAL NUMBER	RANK	NAME & INITIALS	UNIT Co C 509th Prcht Bn.
1	0-379436	Capt.	Boettner, E.E.	
2	36162028	T/4	Foster, O.S.	
3	31033970	T/4	Dunlavey, T.P.	
4	34078779	Sgt.	Simonds, C.E.	
5	36273918	Pvt.	Canfield, D.R.	
6	33673105	Pvt.-	Ross, B.L.	
7	32372299	Pvt.	Piechnak, S.J.	
8	31254924	Pvt.	Pietras, J.A.	
9	34736973	Pvt.	Burrell, R.L.	
10	33081732	Sgt.	Moses, W.E.	
11	32578770	Pfc.	Vandergaag, J.	
12	12216615	Pfc.	Kaim, E.J.	
13	33186150	Pvt.	Falstitch, P.B.	
14	16162441	Pvt.	Dellaca, T.J.	
15		Pvt.	Wilson, P.	
16				
17				
18				
19				
20				
21				

CONTAINERS

Rack No.	Type	Contents (General)	Gross Weight	Parachute Color/Light
1	A-5	Mortar and Ammo	137	Blue
2	A-5	300 Radio	123	Blue

Inspection Completed:____ Signed:____

U. S. CONFIDENTIAL
(Equals British Confidential)

Bn Plane # 35 — "C" Co Plane # 2

U. S. CONFIDENTIAL
(Equals British Confidential)

PARA-G-7 PART II

Recovery/ Operation:" LEDGER ____ Date:____

Details of A/B Troops

A/C No (As per Para-G-5): ____

PERSONNEL

DROP ORDER	SERIAL NUMBER	RANK	NAME & INITIALS	UNIT Co C 509th Prch
1	0-1301545	1st Lt.	Rose, H.	
2	37472277	Pfc.	Crawford, B.M.	
3	20225693	Pfc.	Bacon, M.E.	
4	38389522	Pvt.	Miller, T.	
5	14140033	Pvt.	Dillard, E.C.	
6	36578912	Pvt.	Brethen, R.E.	
7	6585037	Cpl.	Spess, W.E.	
8	31346805	Pvt.	Chevalier, J.A.	
9	32591408	Pvt.	Demling, J.	
10	39110593	Pvt.	White, V.C.	
11	35787032	Pvt.	Stacy, A.L.	
12	37557834	Pvt.	Pearson, J.R.	
13	32517102	Pvt.	Lutkaus, S.J.	
14	34084165	Sgt.	Hicks, S.C.	
15				
16				
17				
18				
19				
20				
21				

CONTAINERS

Rack No.	Type	Contents (General)	Gross Weight	Parachute Color
1	A-5	BAR, US Rifle, Ammo	108	Blue

Inspection Completed:____ Signed:____

U. S. CONFIDENTIAL
(Equals British Confidential)

Bn Plane # 36 — "C" Co Plane # 3

U. S. CONFIDENTIAL
(Equals British Confidential)

PARA-G-7 PART II

Recovery/ Operation:" LEDGER ____ Date:____

Details of A/B Troops

A/C No (As per Para-G-5): ____

PERSONNEL

DROP ORDER	SERIAL NUMBER	RANK	NAME & INITIALS	UNIT Co C 509th Prcht Bn.
1	0-443400	2nd Lt.	Reichers, W.H.	
2	35346498	Pfc.	Amstutz, D.	
3	34490071	Pfc.	Bergeron, O.E.	
4	14180769	Pvt.	McGee, E.H.	
5	35790946	Pvt.	Culley, J.P.	
6	37117331	Pfc.	Johnson, L.E.	
7	35367931	Cpl.	Crumley, W.L.	
8	31266315	Pvt.	Peters, A.G.	
9	32710122	Pvt.	Pius, A.	
10	18122646	Pvt.	Gallegos, M.G.	
11	33550462	Pvt.	Campbell, J.C.	
12	36458577	Pvt.	Flach, W.H.	
13	35275416	Sgt.	Collins, B.G.	
14	37110174	Sgt.	Donovan, R.J.	
15				
16				
17				
18				
19				
20				
21				

CONTAINERS

Rack No.	Type	Contents (General)	Gross Weight	Parachute Color/Light
1	A-5	BAR, US; Ammo.	108	Blue

Bn Plane # 37 — "C" Co Plane # 4

U. S. CONFIDENTIAL
(Equals British Confidential)

PARA-G-7 PART II

Recovery/ Operation:" LEDGER ____ Date:____

Details of A/B Troops

A/C No (As per Para-G-5): ____

PERSONNEL

DROP ORDER	SERIAL NUMBER	RANK	NAME & INITIALS	UNIT Co C 509th Prcht B
1	32156950	1st Sgt.	Viteritto, J.	
2	35209893	Sgt.	Moore, L.L.	
3	37070099	Pfc.	Graber, L.E.	
4	33266692	Pfc.	Vuckan, M.	
5	38588104	Pvt.	Boyd, C.G.	
6	39909541	Pvt.	Lunsford, W.K.	
7	17055898	Pvt.	Chavex, B.A.	
8	16046563	Pfc.	Nolte, K.M.	
9	35049860	Pvt.	Posticil, G.A.	
10	33517473	Pvt.	Shemo, J.	
11	35135724	T/5	Seabrat, M.	
12	35221777	T/5	Derringer, R.P.	
13	35653653	Pvt.-	Coutts, A.S.	
14	34095029	Sgt.	Hughes, J.C.	
15				
16				
17				
18				
19				
20				
21				

CONTAINERS

Rack No.	Type	Contents (General)	Gross Weight	Parachute Color
1	A-5	Mortar & Ammo	137	Blue

Bn Plane # 38 — "C" Co Plane # 5

U. S. CONFIDENTIAL
(Equals British Confidential)

PARA-G-7   PART II

Exercise/ Operation:" LEDGER   Date:_____

Details of A/B Troops

A/C No (As per Para-G-5):_____

DROP ORDER	SERIAL NUMBER	RANK	NAME & INITIALS	UNIT Co C 509th Prcht Bn.
1	0-1313177	1st Lt.	Sammons, R.L.	
2	32513709	Pfc.	Monk, W.H.	
3	35345686	Pfc.	Speer, F.M.	
4	32043926	Pfc.	White, M.D.	
5	32370033	Pvt.	Swidergal, M.	
6	39260045	Pvt.	Bryant, W.A.	
7	20350094	Cpl.	Aponte, V.D.	
8	33444292	Pvt.	Pearson, V.R.	
9	34082215	Pfc.	Robinson, C.E.	
10	14139492	Pvt.	Chambless, B.L.	
11	31292325	Pvt.	Rondeau, G.E.	
12	35648543	Pvt.	Bonham, V. E.	
13	16122353	Pfc.	Bledsoe, M.O.	
14	33472745	Pvt.	Pierce, F.B.	
15	35164966	Sgt.	Tilney, G.K.	
16				
17				
18				
19				
20				
21				

Rack No.	Type	Contents (General)	Gross Weight	Parachute Color/Light
1	A-5	BAR, 03 Rifle, Ammo	108	Blue

Inspection Completed:_____   Signed:_____

U. S. CONFIDENTIAL
(Equals British Confidential)

Bn Plane # 39 — "C" Co Plane # 6

U. S. CONFIDENTIAL
(Equals British Confidential)

PARA-G-7   PART II

Exercise/ Operation:" LEDGER   Date:_____

Details of A/B Troops

A/C No (As per Para-G-5):_____

DROP ORDER	SERIAL NUMBER	RANK	NAME & INITIALS	UNIT
1	0-1703049	2nd Lt.	O'Brien, W.	
2	11072895	Pvt.	Botti, R.I.	
3	20222880	Pfc.	Ayres, D.W.	
4	19005580	Pfc.	Moody, F.L.	
5	36477866	Pfc.	Burcham, J. C.	
6	35767628	Pvt.	Bumgarner, B.L.	
7	13003117	Cpl.	Zadlo, J.L.	
8	31254804	Pvt.	Roy, E.H	
9	6344974	Pfc.	Cawley, T.J.	
10	32209238	Pvt.	Laidlaw, W.J.	
11	31293341	Pvt.	Iedevaia, L.	
12	31309197	Pvt.	Dodge, G.A.	
13	32531143	Pvt.	Jones, U.L.	
14	19115681	Sgt.	David, R.T.	
15	14017112	S/Sgt	Buchanan, J.L.	
16				
17				
18				
19				
20				
21				

Rack No.	Type	Contents (General)	Gross Weight	Parachute Color
1	A-5	BAR, 03, Ammo	108	Blue

Inspection Completed:_____   Signed:_____

U. S. CONFIDENTIAL
(Equals British Confidential)

Bn Plane # 40 — "C" Co Plane # 7

U. S. CONFIDENTIAL
(Equals British Confidential)

PARA-G-7   PART II

Exercise/ Operation:" LEDGER   Date:_____

Details of A/B Troops

A/C No (As per Para-G-5):_____

DROP ORDER	SERIAL NUMBER	RANK	NAME & INITIALS	UNIT Co C 509th Prcht Bn.
1	0-1284042	1st Lt.	Rodrigues, L.L.	
2	20342259	Sgt.	Davis, M.H.	
3	36733746	Pfc.	Darrell, L.E.	
4	32215490	Pvt.	Coddington, H.S.	
5	39272655	Pvt.	Stevenson, B.E.	
6	20365878	Pvt.	Maitland, D.	
7	33439107	Pvt.	Derasmo, L.	
8	33254110	Pfc.	Verage, C.M.	
9	35602312	Pvt.	DiGenova, J.	
10	34739492	Pvt.	Hawraker, W.H.	
11	17012095	Pfc.	Adams, E.	
12	11050793	Cpl.	Colbert, J.M.	
13	33513160	Pvt.	Houghton, T.R.	
14				
15				
16				
17				
18				
19				
20				
21				

Rack No.	Type	Contents (General)	Gross Weight	Parachute Color/Light
1	A-5	Mortar and Ammo	137	Blue

Bn Plane # 41 — "C" Co Plane # 8

U. S. CONFIDENTIAL
(Equals British Confidential)

PARA-G-7   PART II

Exercise/ Operation:" LEDGER   Date:_____

Details of A/B Troops

A/C No (As per Para-G-5):_____

DROP ORDER	SERIAL NUMBER	RANK	NAME & INITIALS	UNIT Co C 509th Prcht Bn.
1	0-1294881	1st Lt.	McCarthy, J.T.	
2	19062804	Pfc.	Bernardes, J.	
3	37604754	Pvt.	Franklin, W.A.	
4	4203633	Pvt.	Galicki, B.M.	
5	34824503	Pvt.	Furr, E.M.	
6	11045716	Cpl.	Metzger, H.D.	
7	15314487	Pfc.	Gerk, S.V.	
8	11055366	Pfc.	Kaills, R.J.	
9	36867504	Pvt.	Gallagher, H.A.	
10	35462543	Pfc.	Koran, R.S.	
11	39246161	Pfc.	Provost, L.E.	
12	35034610	Pvt.	Simpson, R.N.	
13	36737188	Pfc.	Krysnowski, F.	
14	19176501	Pvt.	Pearson, R.A.	
15	6364812	Sgt.	Smith, E.J.	
16				
17				
18				
19				
20				
21				

Rack No.	Type	Contents (General)	Gross Weight	Parachute Color/Light
1	A-5	BAR, 03 Rifle, Ammo	108	Blue

C O

Bn. Plane #42
Co. "C" Plane #9

U. S. C O N F I D E N T I A L
(Equals British Confidential)

PARA-G-7   PART II

XXXXXX/ Operation:" LEDGER   Date:_____

Details of A/B Troops

A/C No (As per Para-G-5):_____

DROP ORDER	SERIAL NUMBER	RANK	PERSONNEL NAME & INITIALS	UNIT Co. "C", 509th Prcht Inf Ba
1	O-1321725	2d Lt	O'Brien, J. W.	
2	39212177	Pvt	Potest, J. C.	
3	17077506	Pvt	Haemes, D. M	
4	34105790	Pvt	Hall, F. B.	
5	37542568	Pfc	Schwartz, L. F.	
6	34160372	Cpl	Coffell, C. R.	
7	15051541	Pvt	Silvers, A. D.	
8	39300480	Pvt	Robinson, E. L.	
9	35500579	Pvt	Sikora, J. A.	
10	35228457	Pvt	Sinien, E. A.	
11	35750995	Pvt	Haller, L. R.	
12	35350712	Pfc	Lohrig, W. W.	
13	6912546	Pvt	Murphy, L.	
14	6148870	Pvt	Cavanaugh, G. F.	
15	35127868	Sgt	Bussey, J. W.	
16	30493948	S/Sgt	Fite, B. H.	
17				
18				
19				
20				
21				

Rack No.	Type	Contents (General)	Gross Weight	Parachute Color/Light
1	A - 5	BAR, '03 & Ammo	180	BLUE

Inspection Completed:_____ ; Signed:_____

U. S. C O N F I D E N T I A L
(Equals British Confidential)

Index

About the Author

Richard "Dick" Fisco is a World War Two veteran, who served in the 14th Infantry Jungleers and as a staff sergeant for the 509th Parachute Infantry Battalion. Mr. Fisco is a devout Catholic and received a Class II Relic of Mother Cabrini from the St. Frances Cabrini Shrine in Manhattan. He is currently a retired New York City fire lieutenant living in Brunswick, Maine.